Managerial Economics

Managerial Economics

SECOND EDITION

YOGESH MAHESHWARI

Associate Professor
Faculty of Management Studies
National Law University, Jodhpur

Prentice-Hall of India Private Limited

New Delhi - 110001

2005

Rs. 195.00

MANAGERIAL ECONOMICS, 2nd Ed.
Yogesh Maheshwari

ISBN-

The export rights of this book are vested solely with the publisher.

Fifth Printing (Second Edition)   ...   ...   **November, 2005**

Published by Asoke K. Ghosh, Prentice-Hall of India Private Limited, M-97, Connaught Circus, New Delhi-110001 and Printed by Meenakshi Art Printers, Delhi-110006.

Contents

Chapter Eight   COST ANALYSIS

Chapter Nine   PRICING

Preface

'LUCID AND YET PRECISE'. This is what the majority of reader's feedback has been for the first edition of this book. The ability of this book to explain the most complicated topics in a very simple and user-friendly manner, with the explanation of a concept closely followed by numerical illustrations exposing the reader to its managerial application has been the factor in motivating the author to bring out the second edition of this book.

This book continues to stick to the principles that have guided it through the first edition. It is a sincere attempt to add more to the areas, which were found to be wanting more in the first edition. The major difference comes in the Chapter 11 on Introductory Macroeconomics. While the existing topics have been explained in more detail, new ones have been added. The chapter now stands extensive. But even while adding text, efforts have been made to focus on conceptual learning and avoid bulky and unnecessary coverage where the reader is at a loss to find out how much is of use.

Case studies helps immensely in grasping the theoretical concepts, more so when the cases are based on real life situations of the Indian economy. Realizing this, case studies have been added to this second edition at the end of each chapter. Another feature that has been maintained in the second edition is that management is an area of study that requires interdisciplinary excellence. It has its learners from various backgrounds such as science, arts, commerce and engineering. Every concept has been explained in the simplest manner possible, such that even a layperson is able to appreciate the meaning. Some complicated figures in the book have been simplified further so that the reader can find learning easier.

Although there is no formal partition, the book has been informally designed into three portions. The first portion consists of introduction to the basic concepts, theories and methodologies of economics and mathematics to familiarise the readers with basic principles and defintion of economics and the knowledge of basic applied mathematics. The concepts of function, slope and differential calculus and its applications, which are central to many discussions in managerial economics, are reviewed.

The second portion of the book covers all the important subject areas of managerial economics, namely, demand, production, cost and pricing. This part consists of chapters on introduction to managerial economics where the nature, scope and relationship of managerial economics is discussed along with the basic underlying concepts, demand analysis and estimation of future demand, production analysis and its application in the short and long run, analyzing cost and its relationship with the changes in output and the most important decision area of pricing through the explanation of the different market structures. There is a separate chapter on linear programming that will help the reader to understand the process of solving the linear programming problems through both, graphical as well as algebraic methods.

Macroeconomics forms the third portion of the book, which deals with the aggregates of income, growth and employment, thus need to be known to the student of managerial economics. The last chapter of this book introduces the macroeconomic concepts of income, growth and employment of the nation as a whole.

In each of the three portions as described above, every chapter has been scheduled in a manner so as to enable the reader to appreciate the contents easily. Each chapter begins with the learning objectives so that the reader knows as to what he is required to learn from the chapter. The text is supported by a good number of figures, wherever necessary, with a view to assist the reader in developing a clearer understanding of the topic. Solved illustrations and end-of-the-chapter questions further help in forming a self-feedback on ascertaining the extent of learning. An extensive glossary and index at the end of the book will be of good help to the reader in having a faster and better learning.

The text is designed to provide an accessible introduction to the techniques and business applications of managerial economics. The author strives to ensure that learning becomes a fun and not a burden. The book will be useful to the students of management, commerce and economics. Although the book is based completely on the UGC model curriculum for the MBA course, even the BBA students will be able to comprehend. The author welcomes any constructive suggestions towards the improvement of the book.

YOGESH MAHESHWARI

Preface to the First Edition

Management is an area of study that requires interdisciplinary approach. It has its learners from varying backgrounds such as science, arts, commerce, and engineering. An essential prerequisite to comprehend the subject of managerial economics is some exposure to the topics of economics. This book therefore provides students, first, with a strong introduction to the concepts of economics.

The knowledge of basic applied mathematics is also a *must* to understand the models and theories of economics and the underlying ideas. Chapter 2 attempts to do just that by reviewing the elementary concepts of calculus and its applications which are central to many discussions in managerial economics. Managerial decision-making involves maximizing or minimizing a function, under a given set of constraints. The chapter strives to explain the concepts of maxima and minima in the most lucid manner. Concepts of total, average and marginal, and their mathematical basis, are also illustrated in this chapter.

Chapter 3 discusses the concepts, nature, and scope of managerial economics. Managerial economics is related to a number of subjects as it prescribes solutions to practical problems of business. This relationship is explored in this chapter. The quest for maximizing profits is always the objective of business organizations. The chapter suggests a model which generates the necessary and sufficient conditions for profit maximization. It closes with explanations of opportunity cost, marginal analysis, and discounting.

Demand analysis, which forms the core of all major decisions of a firm, is the mainstay of Chapter 4. It tries to explain consumer behaviour through two prominent views on understanding utility, namely cardinal and ordinal, which is essential to analyzing consumer demand.

Chapter 5 is a sequel to the previous chapter. Indeed, it goes a step further to work out the responsiveness of demand to the changes in the factors determining it. After introducing the concept of elasticity, the chapter focuses on different elasticities of demand and their importance in the managerial decision-making.

A number of techniques are available for forecasting the expected levels of demand of a good. While some of them are qualitative, others are quantitative in nature. Chapter 6 presents an analysis of the merits and demerits of these techniques. Qualitative methods such as expert opinion and survey techniques, and quantitative ones like trend method and regression analysis, have been discussed in detail. Besides, the chapter exemplifies also the use of least square method in trend and regression analysis.

After the demand side of the story, the book deals with the supply side. Chapters 7 and 8 meet this requirement. Chapter 7 explains the concepts of production function and isoquants. After establishing that there can be more than one combination of inputs for producing any given output, the graphical and algebraic techniques for determining the combination that costs least are described. Also elucidated are the short- and long-run concepts of production in the form of factor productivities and returns to scale. Output elasticity further explains the responsiveness of output to the changes in inputs.

Chapter 8 analyzes cost. It deals with the basic concepts and factors determining cost. Identifying output as the most important determinant, the chapter develops a relationship between cost and output in the short- and long-run. It ends with the estimation of the cost-output relationship after discussing the factors causing economies and diseconomies of scale.

Price theory is the major concern of microeconomics. It relates costs to the revenue. Chapter 9 highlights the characteristics of some important market structures, namely perfect competition, monopolistic competition, oligopoly and monopoly and discusses the pricing of products under these structures. The chapter also describes the mechanism of price discrimination and other pricing methods in vogue.

The penultimate chapter is on linear programming. It establishes the importance of this mathematical technique for finding out optimal solutions to business situations.

The decisions of a firm always affect and are affected by the environment in which the firm operates. Macroeconomics, which deals with the aggregates of income, growth and employment, thus needs to be thoroughly understood by those who want to know managerial economics. The last chapter of the book introduces the macroeconomic concepts of income, growth and employment of the nation as a whole, and further enumerates the related parameters and the regulatory mechanisms concerned with it, so as to provide a holistic coverage of the subject.

The text is designed to provide an accessible introduction to the techniques and business applications of managerial economics. The author has endeavoured to make the subject easy to understand and interesting for students with limited mathematical background and skills. The book will be useful to students of management, commerce and economics. The author will welcome any constructive criticism for improvement of the book.

YOGESH MAHESHWARI

Acknowledgements

Life is a journey to excellence. Every milestone that one reaches, during this eternal journey, is marked by the guidance, help and support of the near and dear ones. And this endeavour of mine is no exception.

A teacher is a guide to life. The persons mentioned below have been a source of immense motivation to me all through this time. While some of them have given me keen insights into some topics covered herein, others have supported the cause by motivating me to achieve progressively higher standards. I take this opportunity to express my deep sense of gratitude to my teachers and guides as under:

Prof. B.P. Bhatnagar, Former Vice Chancellor, Rajasthan Vidyapeeth, Udaipur.

Prof. A.K. Singh, Former Vice Chancellor, Mohanlal Sukhadia University, Udaipur.

Prof. L.K. Maheshwari, Director, Birla Institute of Technology and Science, Pilani.

Prof. O.P. Chawla, Former Director, National Institute of Bank Management, Pune.

Prof. S.L. Bapna, Indian Institute of Management, Ahmedabad.

Prof. Shyam Lodha, Southern Connecticut State University, USA.

Prof. J.D. Agarwal, Chairman and Director, Indian Institute of Finance, New Delhi.

Prof. C.P. Shrimali, Management Development Institute, Gurgaon.

Prof. Bharat Bhalla, Fairfield University, Connecticut, USA.

Prof. Azhar Kazmi, International Islamic University, Kuala Lumpur, Malaysia.

Prof. D.K. Banwet, Indian Institute of Technology, Delhi.

Prof. Uday Salunkhe, L.N. Welingkar Institute of Management Development and Research, Mumbai.

Prof. A.K. Dasbiswas, S.P. Jain Institute of Management and Research, Mumbai.

Prof. H.K. Bedi, Dean, Faculty of Management Studies, National Law University, Jodhpur.

But without the perseverance and motivation of my beloved parents, Shri Naresh Maheshwari and Smt. Shanta Maheshwari, sister Sunita and other relatives and friends, the book would not have witnessed such a successful completion. I am glad that they bear with me for all this time. I thank my colleagues at BITS Pilani and NLU Jodhpur for the related discussions and my students Stuti and Akash for helping me with one of the case studies each. My thanks are due also to Mr. Alok Jain for taking good care of the manuscript typing and composing work.

I am highly thankful to the publishers, Prentice Hall of India, New Delhi for transforming this dream into a reality.

YOGESH MAHESHWARI

CHAPTER | ONE

Introducing Economics

Economics is the science of choice in the face of unlimited ends and scarce resources that have alternative uses. Since resources are scarce and the uses to which they can be put to are unlimited, one is required to choose the best amongst the available alternatives. Of all the subjects, economics is the one most closely associated with everyday life, at all levels. Individuals, firms, societies, industries and nations, all use economics. The span of economics is almost all pervasive. The concepts and theories of economics help us to economize i.e. to achieve the maximum output by using the minimum input.

Several thinkers have given different definitions of economics. Here we will outline the most commonly accepted views.

According to Alfred Marshall, economics is the study of man's actions in the ordinary business of life, it enquires as to how he gets his income and how he utilizes it. Thus, on the one hand it is the study of wealth, on the other it is the study of man.

Marshall's definition treats economics as the science of wealth. This is in keeping with the earliest view on economics. But he added so much emphasis on the study of wealth that the *purpose of studying wealth* became more important than the *study of wealth*. The primary objective became the study of man, his actions, his material welfare and how he utilized his income. Wealth was studied only to the extent it affected human welfare.

Material welfare is that welfare which can be measured in money terms and is very different from general welfare which being abstract is difficult to be measured in some units. Because of its focus on welfare, this particular branch of economics is also known as *Welfare Economics*.

1

Another important definition of economics was given by Lionel Robbins. According to him, economics studies human behaviour as a relationship between unlimited ends and scarce means, which have alternative uses. Thus, economics can help a man to choose how to make use of his scarce means for the maximum satisfaction of his unlimited ends. Economics was thus looked upon as a *science of choice*.

Yet, this definition could not highlight the complete scope of economics. It remained limited to the study of man and his behaviour. It was J.M. Keynes who pointed out that economics also dealt with issues concerning the nation as a whole. Keynes defined economics as the study of administration of scarce resources and of the determinants of employment, income and growth.

CONTENTS OF ECONOMICS

There are two views about the subject matter of economics—*the traditional view* and *the modern view*. According to the traditional view, there are four aspects of economics: consumption, production, exchange and distribution. *Consumption* relates to the study of the consumer, the nature of human wants, their satisfaction and the nature of demand. In *production*, the factor inputs are converted into outputs. Land, labour, capital and management are the four agents of production. Different combinations of these agents yield different outputs. *Exchange* refers to transactions between producers and consumers. It examines the price and output decisions under various market conditions. *Distribution* studies the respective shares, i.e. rent, wages, interest and profit that go to the four agents of production.

According to the modern view, economics is composed of *price theory, income* and *employment theory* and *growth theory*. The price theory, and the income and growth theory are better known as microeconomics and macroeconomics respectively. **Microeconomics** is concerned with the determination of price, which is a function of demand and supply. All the four aspects of the traditional view are covered in microeconomics. Micro, meaning small, studies the small parts of the economy, be it individuals or firms. On the other hand, **macroeconomics** is concerned with the economic system as a whole. It analyses the total income, expenditure, employment and growth of the entire economy.

THE STAGES OF ECONOMIC EVOLUTION

The economies of today are very different and much more developed than what they were earlier. All this has not happened in a single go. Economies have passed through several stages to reach the stage they are in today. The most common such stages are those involving hunting and fishing, pastoral, agricultural, handicraft and industrial activities.

In hunting and fishing, which form the most primitive stage, man lived a nomadic life. He had no permanent residence. Instead, he used to move from one place to another in search of food and shelter. Slowly he began to train the animals he was eating earlier. The concept of private property took birth as man began to own cattle. This happened in the pastoral stage. In the agricultural stage, man started settling down.

Thus, land also became private property and man began cultivation. As the economy developed, society came into being. Social needs became the basis for man to make some goods by hand, using simple processes. The needs then were relatively simple and hence could be satisfied by handmade goods. This was the handicraft era. People organized themselves into small groups having similar value systems and expertise. The society started differentiating between those who produced and those who got them produced. Thus the economy witnessed the emergence of machines, factories, large-scale production and expanding markets, i.e. the industrial stage, with monetary system replacing the barter system.

ECONOMY

Economy refers to the conditions under which goods are produced in a country and the manner in which the people are gainfully employed. There are different ways of classifying economies: rich or poor; socialist, capitalist or mixed; developed, underdeveloped or developing; agricultural or industrial; planned or unplanned and so on.

An economy in which people are very well employed and thus have high standards of living and high per capita income, is known as a *rich economy*. An economy where people are not well employed and where per capita income is low, is a *poor economy*. An economy where the state is the owner of the means of production and people are employed as per the government's prescriptions is a *socialist economy*. An economy where production and employment are controlled by private entrepreneurs is a *capitalist economy*. In other words, in such an economy there are no public sector undertakings, only private sector enterprises. While profit maximization forms the basis of a capitalist economy, a socialist economy is characterized by social welfare. An economy which is a mix of socialist and capitalist economies, is called a *mixed economy*. In such economies, the state retains the ownership and control over important basic industries, which are essential for the survival and growth of the economy. The rest of the industries are open to the private sector under the overall governance of the industrial and trade policies of the state. Thus, in mixed economies, the private and public sectors exist side by side so that a win-win situation emerges wherein the plus points of both kinds add up while the disadvantages are neutralized.

Another way of classifying economies is to call them developed, underdeveloped or developing. *Developed economies* are characterized by high productivity and standards of living. The level of technological development is very high and consequently inputs are converted into outputs in the most efficient and economical manner. Generally, these economies have a low or moderate population leading to a high per capita income. On the other hand, economies that do not have a balance between agriculture and industrial productivity and predominantly rely on agriculture for sustenance are known as *under-developed economies*. Such economies have low standards of living, productivity and low per capita income. Economies that are in a stage of transition from the under-developed to developed stage are termed *developing economies*. Economies where the majority of people earn their livelihood by engaging in agricultural activities are *agricultural economies*, while those where industrial activities predominate are known as *industrial economies*.

Still another way of classifying economies is on the basis of the conduct of economic decisions. When the major economic decisions are taken by a central body and are governed by the plans and policies laid down by this central body, the economy is said to be a *planned economy*. The regulatory authority works out a detailed plan for controlling the major economic activities such as investment, production and consumption. While individual units may have their individual objectives, it is essential for them to fit in with the overall plan. All economic activities are ultimately directed towards achieving optimal utilization of resources and the growth of the nation as a whole. However, when economic decisions are guided solely by the market with no central plans or regulations of any kind, the economy is an *unplanned economy*. In other words, there is complete economic democracy. While production decisions will be taken by individual entrepreneurs, it will be the consumers who will guide consumption. Profit is the guiding factor of all economic decisions in an unplanned economy. There is complete freedom of enterprise. Unlike in a planned economy where there are price controls, in an unplanned economy, the prices of goods, which form the basis of exchange and allocation of resources within the economy, are determined by the market supply-demand equations.

ESSENTIAL PROCESSES OF AN ECONOMY

Regardless of the type of economy, there are some activities that are essential for the functioning of every economy. These are known as the *essential processes of an economy*. Normally, there are three such processes:

1. Production: Any economic activity directed towards the satisfaction of human wants is known as production. The production of goods and services is necessary for the existence of an economy. The level of production in any economy is the best measure of its performance, living standards of its people and the extent of technological development and growth. The broad definition of production, as given above, includes both the manufacturing of material goods as well as the provision of services. Thus, the retail of scooters by an automobile dealer is as much a production activity as is the manufacture of scooters by Bajaj Auto Limited. Likewise, the work of teachers, doctors, lawyers, etc. are all production in the economic sense.

2. Consumption: The act of satisfying one's wants is called consumption. Goods and services are produced only because human wants need to be satisfied. No one will produce if there is no consumption. The quality and quantity of consumption reflect the levels of income and employment in an economy.

3. Investment: Investment is the addition made to the total stock of capital. This addition can be only made out of the remains of production. Such remains are the excess of production over consumption and are known as *savings*. An economy cannot grow if it consumes all that it produces. Because then it will continue to produce and consume at the same levels for all times to come. If it desires to increase its productivity, it must consume less than what it produces or produce more than what it consumes. An economy can grow only if it saves something from its present production and invests it again in the production process. Thus, investment is essential for the growth and development of an economy. It adds to the productive capacity of an economy.

FUNDAMENTAL PROBLEMS OF AN ECONOMY

All economies are characterized by two basic facts: the wants for goods and services are unlimited while the resources used to produce these are scarce. These facts force an economy to think and decide on an ongoing basis how to best use the available resources for the maximum possible satisfaction of its members. This necessitates finding the solutions to the three fundamental problems of an economy. We shall now discuss these problems.

What to Produce

The problem of *what to produce* calls for deciding which goods to produce and in what quantities. The problem arises because of the scarcity of resources. Had resources been unlimited, this question would not have arisen because then, the economy could have produced whatever the consumers would have demanded and in the desired quantity. But since this is not the case, one good can be produced in greater quantity only at the cost of another.

For example, take the case of Bata India Limited. Since the resources (leather, capital labour, etc.) are scarce, the company has to decide whether it has to produce shoes, sandals or *chappals* or a combination of these and also what quantities of the selected goods should be produced. Given the fixed quantity of resources and the quest to achieve optimum utilization of available resources, the economy has to constantly solve the problem of what to produce.

Likewise, economies also have to choose between the production of consumer goods and producer goods i.e. between current and future consumption. *Consumer goods* are those goods that are directly utilized by consumers to satisfy their wants. On the other hand, *producer goods* are those that are used to produce further goods. Thus, while bread, butter, shoes, biscuits, cigarettes, etc. are consumer goods; machines, tools, etc. are producer goods. However, depending on its use, a good can be both. For example, if a piece of cloth is purchased by a consumer from a retail cloth store, it is a consumer good. If it is purchased by a garment manufacturer from a cloth producer, for making shirts and trousers for selling to the consumer, it is a producer good.

How to Produce

The second central problem of any economy is how to produce, i.e. what combination of resources and technology should be used for producing the goods which have been decided on in response to the first problem. This question arises because any given good can be produced through various alternative methods.

Take the case of shoes. Shoes can either be hand produced by cobblers or produced by machines. Different technologies require different combinations of resources. The making of shoes by hand, for instance, would require more of skilled labour and less of capital. Machine produced shoes would require less labour and more capital. Thus, the shoe manufacturer would have to choose between labour-intensive and capital-intensive methods of production. Such decision-making would require an analysis of the prices of various resources and their availability. The labour-intensive process will be chosen by a poor economy which has a low capital base and an abundance of human resource. On the other hand, a rich economy will choose a capital-intensive method of production.

For Whom to Produce

After goods and services are produced, the question of distributing them among the various members of the economy arises. In other words, the economy has to decide who should get how much of the total amount of goods and services produced. Essentially, this is a problem of sharing the national product and deciding the criteria for its distribution.

BASIC TERMS AND CONCEPTS

Before moving on to a discussion on managerial economics, it would be worthwhile to know the meanings of some commonly used terms and concepts of economics. This will help us build a strong base for further study.

Goods

Anything that can satisfy human wants is called *a good* in economics. While services also satisfy human wants, the difference is that goods are tangible but services are not. Goods can be of various types. They can be free or economic, consumer or producer, material or non-material, transferable or non-transferable, private or public and so on.

Some goods are available in plenty and can be had free of cost. Such *free goods* include air, sunshine, etc. Some goods are scarce and require payments. Such goods are *economic goods*. In economics, we are concerned only with economic goods. The distinction between free and economic goods is a function of time and place. For example, at places near rivers or lakes, water may be a free good. However, in a desert, water would be available only for a price and hence would be an economic good. Producer's and consumer's goods have been discussed earlier. *Material goods* are tangibles like pens, scooters, etc. Services are *non-material* goods. Goods that can change ownership are *transferable* as are almost all the material goods. Things such as intelligence, skills, etc. are *non-transferable*. *Private goods* are the property of private individuals, for example an exclusively owned car, house, etc. Goods common to all and collectively owned are *public goods*. For example, colleges, hospitals, etc.

Utility

The want satisfying quality of a good is known as *utility*. Utility is subjective, since it does not lie in the good but is a function of the consumer's mind. Though seemingly similar, utility is different from usefulness or pleasure. A good may satisfy human want but it may not be useful or may not give pleasure. For instance, cigarettes may be injurious while medicines like Crocin give no pleasure when consumed, but they definitely possess utility.

Also, utility of a good changes with the change in conditions and circumstances. Accordingly, there are three main forms of utility—*form utility, place utility* and *time utility*. Water best exemplifies these three forms of utility. It has different utility when used for drinking/bathing, in a desert/fertile land and in winter/summer.

Value

The value of a good denotes the goods/services that we can have in exchange for it. Although to a layman, value may have the same meaning as utility, in economics the two are quite different. For a good to have value, besides possessing utility, it should also be scarce and transferable. Unless all these three attributes are present in a good, it cannot have value. For example, air has utility but since it is not scarce or transferable, it has no value. Since rotten eggs are scarce and transferable but possess no utility, they also don't have value. A car, since it possesses utility and is scarce as well as transferable, has value.

Price

Value when expressed in terms of money is called price. In the early stages of economic evolution, when the barter system was prevalent, price was the same as value. Now, since goods are exchanged for money, the price of a good is its *money value*. However, it should be noted that value is relative since it is expressed in exchange. There can be a general rise or fall in prices but not in value.

Wealth

Anything that has value is called wealth. In economics, wealth does not only refer to money, but to all goods that have value. Since wealth is likened to value, all the three attributes of value are also applicable to wealth.

Income

The amount of money which wealth yields is known as income. Thus, wealth is a fund while income is a flow. Take the case of a man who owns a car and runs it as a taxi. The car is worth Rs. 4 lakh and the man earns Rs. 10,000 per month from the taxi operations. Here Rs. 4 lakh is the wealth and Rs. 10,000 per month is the income.

Equilibrium

Equilibrium refers to a state of balance. It is an ideal situation when the forces acting on an object in opposing directions are exactly equal. In such a case, the object does not have any motive for change. An equilibrium may be stable, unstable or neutral depending on the reaction of the object to the disturbing forces. If the object comes back to it original position it is said to be in *stable equilibrium*, failing which it is a case of *unstable equilibrium*. In *neutral equilibrium*, it stays where it is. Economic analysis most commonly uses stable equilibrium.

QUESTIONS

1. Define the terms *economics*. Give the views of different thinkers on the nature of the subject.

2. 'Economics is the science of choice when faced with unlimited ends and scarce resources having alternative uses.' Comment.

3. Describe the different stages of economic evolution.

4. There can be several ways of classifying an economy. Discuss these in detail.

5. Whatever may be the type of economy, there are always some essential processes for its functioning. Elucidate.

6. Explain the fundamental problems of an economy.

7. State which of the following statements are *true* and which are *false*:

    (a) According to Marshall, economics is primarily concerned with the study of wealth.

    (b) The modern view holds economics as being composed of price, income, employment and growth theories.

    (c) The agricultural stage is followed by a pastoral stage in economic evolution.

    (d) The act of satisfying one's wants called production.

    (e) A capitalist economy is one where production and employment are controlled by private entrepreneurs.

    (f) Investment is essential for the growth of an economy.

    (g) Utility, usefulness and pleasure mean the same.

    (h) There can be a general rise or fall in price but not in value.

CHAPTER TWO

Basic Applied Mathematics

LEARNING OBJECTIVES

- ❋ *the concept of derivatives*
- ❋ *derivatives of different types of functions*
- ❋ *different types of equations*
- ❋ *the concept of slope*
- ❋ *the mathematical basis of total, average and marginal revenue and cost*

 ELEMENTARY DIFFERENTIAL CALCULUS

Of all the branches of mathematics, the one that is most frequently used in managerial decision-making is differential calculus. The concept of *marginal*, which is central to all discussions in managerial economics, is nothing but an application of differential calculus.

Differential calculus involves finding the derivative of a function. A *derivative* is a mathematical concept for finding out the change in one variable due to a very small change in some related variable. For differentiating a variable, with respect to another, it is essential that both of them are related in some manner. Here it is necessary to introduce the concept of function.

Function

A *function* is a mathematical relationship between two variables wherein one of the variables depends on the other. A typical form of a function is

$$y = f(x)$$

9

This represents that 'y is a function of x'. Here x is the independent variable while y is the dependent variable. The derivative of this function, obtained by differentiating y with respect to x is given by

$$\frac{dy}{dx}$$

This in other words is an indication of the change in y due to a very small change in x.

A *variable* is something whose magnitude can vary. Selling price, profit, cost, demand, etc. are some prominent examples of variables used in managerial economics. All these can assume various values. In contrast to variables, there are *constants* whose value remains fixed under a given situation. The value of π is always 3.14. This is an example of a constant. Decision-making involves planning for the future using the past as a guiding source. Planning for a desired future outcome involves the study of the concerned variable by establishing a relationship between that variable and the variables on which it depends. The dependent variable is studied as a function of the independent variables on which it depends. For example, total cost is a function of quantity. That is,

$$TC = f(Q)$$

This form of function is a general relationship between cost and quantity. It merely tells us that cost depends on quantity. Managerial decision-making, however, requires a specific and explicit relationship between variables. Thus, if

$$C = 3Q^2 + 5Q - 12$$

where C is the cost and Q is the quantity then for any given value of Q, the corresponding value of C can be found out precisely. Thus, when

$$Q = 2$$

Then,

$$C = 3 \times 2^2 + 5 \times 2 - 12$$
$$= 10$$

Types of Functions

Linear function. A function in which the power of the independent variable is 1, is known as a linear function. It is represented in the following manner:

$$y = f(x) = ax + b$$

where, y is the dependent variable, x is the independent variable, and a and b are constants.

Quadratic function. A function where the power of the independent variable is 2, is called a quadratic function.

$$y = ax^2 + bx + c$$

Cubic function. When the power of the independent variable of a function is 3, it is a cubic function.

$$y = ax^3 + bx^2 + cx + d$$

Logarithmic function. A function where the dependent variable is a logarithmic value of the independent variable is known as a logarithmic function. It is represented by

$$y = \log_a x$$

where a is the base.

The two most widely used bases for logarithms are 10 and $e \approx 2.7182$. While the logarithm of any number to the base 10 is called *common logarithm*, that to base e is called *natural logarithm*. The logarithmic function is an inverse of the exponential function. That is, if

$$y = \log_e x$$

Then,

$$x = a^y$$

Thus, an *exponential function*, is a function where the independent variable appears as the exponent of any constant.

The linear and quadratic functions are the most commonly used forms of relationships in managerial economics. Any function of a higher degree needs computerized treatment as it is almost impossible to solve it manually. Such functions are therefore not discussed at this level. Instead, we will discuss the solutions of linear and quadratic equations.

Linear equation

The root of a linear equation,

$$y = ax + b$$

is given as

$$x = -\frac{b}{a}$$

This is obtained by equating the function to zero.

Quadratic equation

For a quadratic equation,

$$y = ax^2 + bx + c$$

the roots are given as

$$x = \frac{-b \pm \sqrt{b^2 - 4ac}}{2a}$$

It may be noted that the roots of a given function are always equal to the highest power of the independent variable.

ILLUSTRATION 2.1 Find out the roots of the quadratic equation $x^2 - 6x + 5 = 0$.

Solution We know that a quadratic equation has two roots. The roots of quadratic equation $ax^2 + bx + c = 0$ are given as

$$x = \frac{-b \pm \sqrt{b^2 - 4ac}}{2a}$$

Thus, the roots of the given equation are

$$x = \frac{-(-6) \pm \sqrt{(-6)^2 - 4 \times 1 \times 5}}{2 \times 1}$$

Here,

$$a = 1, \ b = -6 \text{ and } c = 5$$

$$x = \frac{6 \pm \sqrt{36 - 20}}{2}$$

$$= \frac{6 \pm \sqrt{16}}{2} = \frac{6 \pm 4}{2}$$

$$= \frac{6 + 4}{2} \text{ and } \frac{6 - 4}{2}$$

$$= 5 \text{ and } 1$$

 CONCEPT OF DERIVATIVE

The following figure illustrates the concept of derivative.

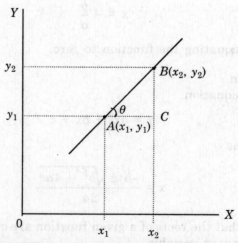

FIGURE 2.1 Concept of Derivative

Consider two points A and B on the given line as in Figure 2.1. Let the coordinates of these points be (x_1, y_1) and (x_2, y_2) respectively. The change in a variable is symbolized by d. Accordingly, the change in x and y are represented by dx and dy respectively. A change in the independent variable, causes a given change in the dependent variable. Thus, dx change in x, causes dy change in y.

∴ 1 unit change in x, causes dy/dx change in y.

This dy/dx change in the dependent variable y due to a unit change in the independent variable x is called the *derivative* of y with respect to x.

Rules for Differentiation

The derivative of a constant is always zero. For a given function,

$$y = a$$

where a is a constant,

$$\frac{dy}{dx} = 0$$

This is because y always remains constant and does not change with the change in x.

Power Function

The derivative of a power function is equal to the exponent multiplied by the variable raised to the power of the exponent minus one. Thus for a function,

$$y = x^n$$

$$\frac{dy}{dx} = nx^{n-1}$$

where n is a constant.

ILLUSTRATION 2.2 Find out the derivative of a function $y = x^3$.

Solution

$$y = x^3$$

$$\frac{dy}{dx} = 3x^{3-1}$$

$$= 3x^2$$

It may be noted that a constant function is a special case of power function with the exponent as zero. That is,

$$y = 2$$

$$= 2 \cdot x^0$$

$$\frac{dy}{dx} = 2 \cdot 0 \cdot x^{0-1} = 0$$

Logarithmic Function

The derivative of a logarithmic function $y = \log x$ is given as

$$\frac{dy}{dx} = \frac{1}{x}$$

The derivative of logarithmic function is thus the inverse of the variable concerned.

Sum of Two Functions

The derivative of a sum of two functions is equal to the sum of the derivatives of the individual functions. That is, if

$$U = f_1(x) \quad \text{and} \quad V = f_2(x)$$

$$y = U + V$$

Then,

$$\frac{dy}{dx} = \frac{dU}{dx} + \frac{dV}{dx}$$

Difference of Two Functions

Similarly for the difference of two functions, if

$$y = U - V$$

Then,

$$\frac{dy}{dx} = \frac{dU}{dx} - \frac{dV}{dx}$$

Product of Two Functions

The derivative of the product of two functions is equal to the sum of the product of the first term and the derivative of the second term and that of the second term and the derivative of the first term. That is, if

$$y = U \cdot V$$

Then,

$$\frac{dy}{dx} = U \cdot \frac{dV}{dx} + V \cdot \frac{dU}{dx}$$

Quotient of Two Functions

The derivative of the quotient of two functions is equal to the denominator multiplied by the derivative of the numerator, minus the numerator multiplied by the derivative of the denominator and the entire expression divided by the square of the denominator. That is, if

$$y = \frac{U}{V}$$

$$\frac{dy}{dx} = \frac{V \cdot \frac{dU}{dx} - U \cdot \frac{dV}{dx}}{V^2}$$

A practical illustration will help to understand these derivatives better.

ILLUSTRATION 2.3 Given the two functions $U = 5x^2$ and $V = 2x^3$. Find out the derivatives of the

  (a) sum of these two functions
  (b) difference of these two functions
  (c) product of these two functions
  (d) quotient of these two functions.

Solution Here we have

$$U = 5x^2 \quad \text{and} \quad V = 2x^3$$

(a) Sum of these functions

$$Y = U + V$$
$$= 5x^2 + 2x^3$$

the derivative of the sum of functions is

$$\frac{dy}{dx} = \frac{dU}{dx} + \frac{dV}{dx}$$

$$= \frac{d}{dx}(5x^2) + \frac{d}{dx}(2x^3)$$

$$= 5 \cdot 2 \cdot x^{2-1} + 2 \cdot 3 \cdot x^{3-1}$$

$$= 10x + 6x^2$$

(b) Difference of these functions

$$Y = U - V$$

$$= 5x^2 - 2x^3$$

the derivative of the difference of these functions is

$$\frac{dy}{dx} = \frac{dU}{dx} - \frac{dV}{dx}$$

$$= \frac{d}{dx}(5x^2) - \frac{d}{dx}(2x^3)$$

$$= 5 \cdot 2 \cdot x^{2-1} - 2 \cdot 3 \cdot x^{3-1}$$

$$= 10x - 6x^2$$

(c) Product of these functions

$$Y = U \cdot V$$

Then the derivative of the product of two functions is given as

$$\frac{dy}{dx} = U \cdot \frac{dV}{dx} + V \cdot \frac{dU}{dx}$$

$$= 5x^2 \cdot 6x^2 + 2x^3 \cdot 10x$$

$$= 30x^4 + 20x^4$$

$$= 50x^4$$

(d) Quotient of these functions
The derivative of the quotient of two functions, which is represented by

$$y = \frac{U}{V}$$

is given as

$$\frac{dy}{dx} = \frac{V \cdot \dfrac{dU}{dx} - U \cdot \dfrac{dV}{dx}}{V^2}$$

$$= \frac{2x^3 \cdot 10x - 5x^2 \cdot 6x^2}{(2x^3)^2}$$

$$= \frac{20x^4 - 30x^4}{4x^6}$$

$$= -\frac{10x^4}{4x^6} = -\frac{5}{2x^2}$$

CONCEPT OF SLOPE

The slope of a line is given by tan θ. The slope is also represented by letter m. θ is the angle of inclination of the given line with the X-axis. The slope thus measures the degree of steepness of a given line. This, as already established, is nothing but the rate of change of a function, i.e. the change in the dependent variable caused by a unit change in the independent variable.

Refer to Figure 2.1. AB is the hypotenuse of the right-angled triangle ABC. Also, dy and dx are the opposite side and base of this triangle, while θ is the angle of incidence, i.e. the angle of inclination of the hypotenuse with the base. The slope of the line AB, in other words, is the marginal change in y associated with a unit change in x.

For any linear function,

$$y = ax + b$$

The slope of the function is given by the coefficient of the independent variable. That is,

$$\frac{dy}{dx} = a$$

Depending upon the relationship of the two variables, the slope of the line may be positive or negative. The slope is positive when an increase in the independent variable causes an increase in the dependent variable or vice versa. But when the increase in the independent variable causes a decrease in the dependent variable or vice versa, the slope is said to be negative. In other words, the slope is positive for all θ between $0°$ and $90°$, while it is negative when $90° < \theta < 180°$. The slope of a line will be zero when the line is parallel to the X-axis, i.e. a horizontal line.

Till now, our discussion has been limited to linear function, i.e. to straight lines. The slope for a straight line, whether it be positive, negative or zero, remains constant at all points on the line. Throughout the length of the line, the ratio of change in y to the change in x will be same. However, for a nonlinear function i.e. a curve, the slope does not remain constant at all points of the curve. It changes from point to point. It is therefore necessary to specify the point at which the slope has to be found out dy/dx is then determined at that point with the same method as above.

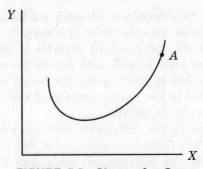

FIGURE 2.2 Slope of a Curve

The slope of a curve at any point *A* can be found by finding the slope of the tangent to the curve at that point.

Practical examples of linear and nonlinear functions are that of demand-price and cost-quantity relationship respectively. The term *derivative of a function* is a generalized expression for the slope of a function. The concept of derivative is very important in managerial economics. Differential calculus is used to explain several concepts in managerial economics, including

- Average and marginal cost
- Average and marginal revenue
- Profit maximization
- Elasticity of demand

CONCEPT OF MAXIMA AND MINIMA

In managerial decision-making, we mostly talk about optimization, which is maximizing or minimizing a given function under certain constraining conditions of resources. Say for example, we aim at profit maximization and cost minimization.

The problems of optimization arise in nonlinear functions. Such functions have both, positive and negative slopes. While a U-shaped curve will focus on minimization, an inverted U-curve will focus on maximization.

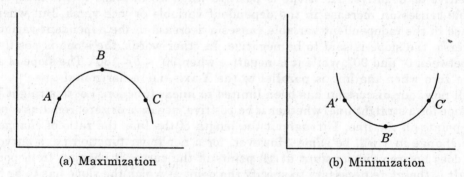

(a) Maximization   (b) Minimization

FIGURE 2.3 Concept of Maxima and Minima

Consider first a case of maximization wherein we have to find out the maxima of the function. The case under consideration is shown in Figure 2.3(a). Here, with the increase in the value of the independent variable *x*, the value of the dependent variable *y* first increases, attains a peak and thereafter decreases for any further increase in *x*. We are interested in finding out the value of *x* where *y* is maximum. A typical example of this case is the determination of that quantity of output which when sold will earn the maximum profit.

The profit, which is equal to the difference between total revenue and total cost (*TR* – *TC*), first increases but later decreases with the increase in quantity. This decrease is accounted for by the decrease in price due to the law of diminishing marginal utility. As we move from point A to C on the curve in Figure 2.3(a), we move from positive slope to negative slope. Somewhere in between A and C there is a point B where the curve, and hence its slope changes direction. This is the point where the slope of the curve is zero. The tangent to the curve at point B is a horizontal line. This is the point beyond which, for any further increase in the independent variable, the dependent variable starts decreasing instead of increasing. Thus, this is the point of maxima where the value of the dependent variable is maximum.

So the necessary condition for maximization is that the slope i.e. dy/dx or the first derivative of a function $y = f(x)$ should be zero.

Note however that merely having a zero slope does not specify whether it is the point of maxima or minima because as seen in Figure 2.3(a) and 2.3(b) both maxima and minima have zero slope. So some other differentiating condition is required for ascertaining the maxima and minima.

On further studying Figure 2.3(a) and 2.3(b), we note that while both have zero slope at point B and B', the manner in which the zero slope is attained is different. In the case of maximization, the slope of the curve changes from positive to negative, i.e. after the point of maxima, the slope dy/dx of the curve becomes negative. In other words, if dy/dx is considered a function of x, the rate of change of dy/dx is negative. It decreases as it moves from A to B to C. Thus,

$$\frac{d}{dx}\left(\frac{dy}{dx}\right) < 0$$

$$\frac{d^2y}{dx^2} < 0$$

That is, the second order derivative should be negative for the condition of maxima.

Similarly for minima, the second order derivative i.e. d^2y/dx^2 should be > 0 or positive, because in this case dy/dx will be an increasing function as it changes from negative to positive with the increase in x.

This can be summed up with the following conditions:

1. Necessary condition for maximization: The first order derivative should be zero. That is,

$$\frac{dy}{dx} = 0$$

2. Sufficient condition for maximization: The second order derivative should be negative. Thus,

$$\frac{d^2y}{dx^2} < 0$$

3. Necessary condition for minimization: The first order derivative should be zero. That is,

$$\frac{dy}{dx} = 0$$

4. Sufficient condition for minimization: The second order derivative should be positive. Thus,

$$\frac{d^2y}{dx^2} > 0$$

 ## CONCEPT OF TOTAL, AVERAGE AND MARGINAL REVENUE

Total revenue: The sum total of the revenue received on selling all the units of the commodity is known as total revenue, that is,

$$TR = P \cdot Q$$

Average revenue: Total revenue divided by the quantity sold is known as average revenue, illustrated as

$$AR = \frac{TR}{Q} = \frac{PQ}{Q} = P$$

Hence, average revenue is nothing but the price of a commodity.

Marginal revenue: Marginal revenue is the change in total revenue due to the sale of one additional unit of the output. This is shown as

$$MR = TR_n - TR_{n-1}$$

where n is the number of units sold.

Geometrically, marginal revenue is the slope of the total revenue curve at a particular output point.

In terms of differential calculus, marginal revenue is the rate of change of total revenue with respect to the output. This is explained by the formula

$$MR = \frac{d(TR)}{dQ}$$

ILLUSTRATION 2.4 A firm sells 320 units of its product in a year at a price of Rs. 8 per unit. However, should it want to sell any more units beyond this level, it will be able to price these units at only Rs. 7 per unit as against the normal price of Rs. 8. Find out the total revenue, average revenue and marginal revenue for the firm.

Solution Here

$$P = \text{Rs. 8 per unit}, \quad Q = 320 \text{ units}$$

$$TR = P \cdot Q$$

$$= 8 \times 320 = \text{Rs. 2560}$$

$$AR = \frac{TR}{Q}$$

$$= \frac{2560}{320} = \text{Rs. 8 per unit}$$

$$MR \text{ upto 320 units} = \text{Rs. 8}$$

$$MR \text{ beyond 320 units} = \text{Rs. 7}$$

ILLUSTRATION 2.5 The price of staplers manufactured by Max Staples Limited varies with the quantity as per the demand equation, $Q = P - 7$. Establish the total revenue, average avenue and marginal revenue functions for Max Staples Limited.

Solution The demand equation for a firm is

$$Q = P - 7$$

We know

$$TR = P \cdot Q \qquad \text{(i)}$$

Given that

$$Q = P - 7$$

i.e.

$$P = Q + 7 \qquad \text{(ii)}$$

Substituting the value of P from Equation (ii) in (i), we get

$$TR = (Q + 7) \cdot Q$$

$$= Q^2 + 7Q$$

∴ The total revenue function is

$$TR = Q^2 + 7 \qquad \text{(iii)}$$

Similarly,

$$AR = \frac{TR}{Q}$$

but,

$$TR = Q^2 + 7Q$$

∴

$$AR = \frac{1}{Q}(Q^2 + 7Q)$$

$$= Q + 7$$

The average revenue function is

$$AR = Q + 7 \qquad \text{(iv)}$$

Marginal revenue is

$$MR = \frac{d(TR)}{dQ}$$

$$= \frac{d(Q^2 + 7Q)}{dQ}$$

$$= \frac{d}{dQ}(Q^2) + \frac{d}{dQ}(7Q)$$

$$= 2Q + 7$$

∴ The marginal revenue function is

$$MR = 2Q + 7 \qquad\qquad\qquad\text{(v)}$$

 ## CONCEPT OF TOTAL, AVERAGE AND MARGINAL COST

Total cost: It is the sum total of the costs incurred on producing all the units of a commodity.

Average cost: The total cost divided by the quantity produced yields the average cost.

$$AC = \frac{TC}{Q}$$

Marginal cost: The marginal cost is the cost of producing one additional unit of the commodity.

$$MC = TC_n - TC_{n-1}$$

where n is the number of units produced.

Geometrically, marginal cost is the slope of the total cost curve at a given output level.

In terms of differential calculus, marginal cost is the rate of change of total cost with respect to the change in output produced.

$$MC = \frac{d(TC)}{dQ}$$

ILLUSTRATION 2.6 The total cost function of a company is $TC = 2Q^2 - 5Q + 8$. You are required to find out the average cost and marginal cost functions.

Solution We know that

$$AC = \frac{TC}{Q}$$

$$= \frac{1}{Q} (2Q^2 - 5Q + 8)$$

$$= 2Q - 5 + \frac{8}{Q}$$

∴ The average cost function is

$$AC = 2Q - 5 + \frac{8}{Q} \qquad (i)$$

The marginal cost is the rate of change of total cost. That is,

$$MC = \frac{d(TC)}{dQ}$$

$$= \frac{d(Q^2 - 5Q + 8)}{dQ}$$

$$= \frac{d}{dQ}(2Q^2) - \frac{d}{dQ}(5Q) + \frac{d}{dQ}(8)$$

$$= 4Q - 5 + 0$$

$$= 4Q - 5$$

∴ The marginal cost function is

$$MC = 4Q - 5 \qquad (ii)$$

QUESTIONS

1. Differentiate the following functions with respect to x:
   (a) $y = x^3$
   (b) $y = 8$
   (c) $y = 3 \log x$
   (d) $y = 2x^2 + 6x$
   (e) $y = 5x^3 - 8x$
   (f) $y = (3x^2 + 4x + 1)(x^2 - 2x + 5)$
   (g) $y = (3x^2 + 5x)/(2x + 1)$

2. What is a function? Explain the different types of functions.

3. Use differential calculus to explain the concept of marginal revenue.

4. Explain the behaviour of total, average and marginal cost.

5. A line AB has coordinates $A(2,3)$ and $B(12,9)$. Find out the slope of this line.

6. Find out the roots of the quadratic equation

$$2x^2 - 15x + 18 = 0$$

7. The demand equation for an ice-cream company, Hot Ice-creams Limited, is given as $Q = 12 - P$. What will be the total revenue, average revenue and marginal revenue functions?

8. State which of the following statements are *true* and which are *false*:

   (a) A derivative establishes the change in one variable due to a change in some related variable.

   (b) A constant function is a power function with zero as the exponent.

   (c) A function is a mathematical relationship between two variables.

   (d) The logarithm of any number to the base 10 is called common logarithm.

   (e) The total revenue always increases with output.

   (f) The rate of change of marginal cost is more than that of average cost.

CHAPTER THREE

Introduction to Managerial Economics

* the nature and scope of managerial economics
* the relation of managerial economics with other disciplines
* the profit maximization model
* the concepts of opportunity cost, marginal analysis and discounting

 ## DEFINITION OF MANAGERIAL ECONOMICS

Managerial economics is the discipline that deals with the application of economic concepts, theories and methodologies to the practical problems of businesses/firms in order to formulate rational managerial decisions for solving those problems.

The basic economic problem viz. resources are scarce and the uses to which they can be put to are unlimited, forces firms to make decisions at every stage of operation, be it sourcing of inputs, conversion of inputs into output or distribution of output. This decision-making involves choosing the optimal solution from the available alternatives. Different alternatives entail different combinations of resources. Had resources been unlimited, one could have utilized all the alternatives and the business could have continued well without any problem. But the scarcity of resources requires managers to analyze and evaluate all the available choices and choose the alternative that produces the result most consistent with the objectives of the firm.

The problems before a firm can be manifold. While the sourcing of inputs could involve deciding whether to make, or buy, how much to buy and from whom to buy, in the conversion process, the problems could relate to deciding on the production technique to be used, how much to produce, what combination of inputs to use and so on. When it comes to marketing the product, questions concerning product pricing, advertisement spend and logistics become paramount.

Finding optimal solutions to all such managerial problems is rendered easy by the concepts and theories of economics and the methodologies of the decision sciences. The basic economic concepts of demand, cost, production and price, along with the theories of consumer behaviour, profit maximization and market structures help in finding out optimal solutions. But for the underlying concepts of opportunity costs, marginal reasoning and discounting, many managerial decisions would have been grossly illogical. The decision-making framework of economics, when applied with the methodologies of decision sciences like statistical estimation, forecasting, optimization, game theory, etc. provides a rational base to managers for solving business problems.

The subject that uses the theories of economics and the methodologies of the decision sciences for managerial decision-making is known as managerial economics.

 ## NATURE OF MANAGERIAL ECONOMICS

The nature of managerial economics is defined by factors such as it

1. is essentially microeconomic in nature
2. is pragmatic
3. belongs to normative economics, i.e. besides being descriptive, it is also prescriptive
4. is conceptual in nature
5. utilizes some theories of macroeconomics
6. is problem solving in nature.

Microeconomics is the branch of economics that deals with the individual units of an economy. These individual units may be either a person or a firm or a group of persons or firms. Since managerial economics is concerned with the analysis of and finding optimal solutions to decision-making problems of businesses/firms, it is essentially microeconomic in nature.

Managerial economics is a practical subject. It goes beyond providing rigid and abstract theoretical frameworks for managers. While at some places it avoids difficult abstract issues of economic theories, at some others, it incorporates complications ignored by economic theory in order to analyze the overall situation in which managerial decision-making takes place. Thus, it is pragmatic.

Economics can also be classified as positive or normative. *Positive economics* describes *what is*, i.e. observed economic phenomenon. Normative economics on the other hand prescribes *what ought to be*, i.e. it distinguishes the ideal from the actual. Managerial economics is prescriptive, not merely descriptive.

Managerial economics is based on a sound framework of economic concepts. Its subject matter is not an arbitrary collection of prescriptions. It aims to analyze business problems on the basis of established concepts. Thus, it is conceptual in nature.

When all individual matters are added up and it becomes a matter of analyzing the problems of the economy or the nation as a whole, we call it *macroeconomics*. An individual economic unit operates in an environment. It affects and is affected by the environment. Most aspects related to this environment are the subject matter of macroeconomics. Managerial economics does not prescribe solutions to business problems in isolation. In order to arrive at logical outcomes, it takes the help of some macroeconomic theories to understand the environment in which the firm operates.

Besides analyzing the managerial problems of business units, managerial economics aims at finding out optimal solutions to the business problems of firms. In other words, it is problem-solving in nature.

SCOPE OF MANAGERIAL ECONOMICS

Managerial economics is a very useful subject. It can be used to explain and understand almost all major business problems. It plays a vital role in managerial decision-making and prescribes specific solutions to the problems of the firm. Managerial economics helps in the following:

- Estimation of product demand
- Analysis of product demand
- Planning of production schedule
- Deciding the input combination
- Estimation of cost of product
- Analysis of cost of product
- Achieving economies of scale
- Determination of price of product
- Analysis of price of product
- Analysis of market structures
- Profit estimation and planning
- Planning and control of capital expenditure

Managerial economics can be used to analyze the demand of a product. Numerous aspects viz. the type of demand, factors on which demand depends and the extent to which the demand of a product will change if these factors are changed by a particular magnitude and in a particular direction, etc. can all be known with the use of the concepts of managerial economics. The subject also suggests several ways and methods for estimating the present and future demand of any product.

The estimation of the likely demand of a product forms the basis for planning how production has to be carried out. This decision is all the more important in the case of products, the usage of which is not uniform over time. While short production may result in the loss of market and opportunity leading to a shedding of the firm's profits, excess production beyond a reasonable level could cause the firm to incur wastage and unnecessary cost. Managerial economics helps in deciding what quantity of goods have to be produced, i.e. how capacity utilization has to be achieved.

A product may be manufactured using different combinations of inputs. For example, handloom produced cloth will require a different combination of input factors—land, labour, capital and technology—than cloth produced on an automatic power loom. Production with different input combinations will involve different costs. One would therefore like to know which combination of inputs will cost least. This job is rendered easy by managerial economics.

Managerial economics and its cost concepts can be employed to analyze the cost of a product. Profits can be maximized either by increasing the revenues or decreasing the costs. While revenue depends on the market, cost is basically a function of the firm. Attempts can be made to reduce the cost only when one knows what the cost is made up of and what are the factors that have a bearing on the cost of a product? It is equally important to know whether or not the output level has any effect on the cost. All such related questions are effectively solved by using the theories of managerial economics.

Besides analyzing cost, a manager would also like to know the exact amount of cost. Managerial economics provides alternative methods for estimating the cost of a product. Also, average cost does not have a unidirectional relationship with output. The increase in output may decrease the average cost only to a certain extent. Any further increase in output increases the average cost of a product thereby creating *diseconomies of scale*. Managerial economics enables one to calculate the optimal level of output where minimum average cost can be obtained.

Another important aspect of managerial decision-making is the price of a product. Besides other factors, it is essential to understand the market structure within which the product is being sold. This also calls for a knowledge of the nature of the product, number of buyers and sellers, entry/exit barriers, etc. so that the product may be priced well. It may also be worthwhile to know whether the product can be priced differently in different markets at the same time. Managerial economics comes handy when choosing between alternative decisions. While helping one to understand the nature of profit, managerial economics presents the logical basis for the various theories that explain the reasons for the emergence of profit. It also enables managers to plan and control profits. *Break-even analysis* is the most important tool for the firm to plan its activities with regard to the choice of production process, expansion/shutdown, make or buy and promotion mix decisions.

Lastly, managerial economics provides a framework for planning the capital expenditure decisions of a firm. It gives the criteria to appraise capital budgeting decisions and choose the best out of the available investment alternatives. It also helps a manager to estimate the cost of the firm's capital and the cash flows associated with a project.

 ## MANAGERIAL ECONOMICS AND OTHER DISCIPLINES

An important feature of managerial economics is its relationship with other disciplines. Although essentially a branch of economics, the subject draws upon a number of other disciplines for propounding its theories and concepts for managerial decision-making.

Economics

The relationship between managerial economics and economics is similar to that of a body and one of its part. The blood running through both is the same. Managerial economics studies the fundamental problem of an economy, i.e. resources are scarce and the uses to which they can be put to are unlimited. As referred to earlier, managerial economics is essentially microeconomic in character. It is economics applied to a firm's decision-making. Various microeconomic concepts such as demand, production, cost, price and profit analysis are of great significance to managerial economics.

Statistics

Statistical tools are of immense use in business decision-making. Managerial economics being prescriptive, aims at estimating the future on the basis of proper analysis of the past and existing structures. Estimation of the future course of action is an essential element in managerial decision-making. Statistical techniques and concepts relating to data collection, data analysis, forecasting techniques and the theory of probability provide the framework for all such analysis and prescriptions of managerial economics. Thus, statistics is closely linked to managerial economics.

Mathematics

Several important methodologies and concepts of managerial economics are based on mathematics. The concept of marginal, which is the slope of the total, that is the rate of change of the total, originates from geometry/differential calculus, while the concept of elasticity uses differential calculus. Similarly, cost-output relationships and pricing decisions are explained on the basis of algebra and geometry. Managerial economics also makes use of logarithms, exponentials, determinants and matrices.

Operations Research

Managerial economics depends heavily on the models and tools of operations research or quantitative techniques. Operations research is a subject that consists of a number of models and analytical tools which are developed on the basis of inter-disciplinary research for solving complex problems of planning and allocation of scarce resources, primarily in defence industries. Managerial economics has generalized and developed the models and tools of operations research for the purpose of business decision-making. Linear programming models, inventory models, game theory, etc. are a few tools that have originated in the works of operation researchers.

Accounting

Accounting is concerned with the recording of the financial operations of a firm. The cost and revenue data that form the basis of all the analyses and computations of managerial economics are quantified through the process of accounting. In other words, accounting information is one of the principal sources of data required by managerial economists for decision-making. The branch of accounting that provides data in a form that can be used by managers to apply the concepts of managerial economics for decision-making is known as *managerial accounting*.

PROFIT MAXIMIZATION

Managements of firms have different objectives for pursuing their operations. While some aim at maximizing the sales revenue or the growth rate or the manager's utility function etc., a majority of the organizations regard profit maximization as the sole criteria for their existence. The primary motivation of such organizations is to increase profits. Had it not been so, there was no reason for Colgate and Britannia to continue spending huge amounts on advertising when both are already well-established household names. Similarly, profit maximization was perhaps the only motivation for Titan to introduce a new model of its wristwatch when the existing ones were highly successful. Maximizing profits involves maximizing revenues while simultaneously minimizing costs. Thus, any managerial decision which is able to increase revenue without a proportionate rise in costs or can reduce costs without a fall in revenue, will increase profits. *Profit maximization* in its most lucid connotation means the generation of the largest absolute amount of profits over the time period being analyzed—short- or long-run. The economic classification of time period as short or long is different from that of accounting. While *short-run* is the period where at least one factor of production is constant, in the *long-run* all the factors are variable.

We will now discuss the costs and revenues associated with any business decision. A company's ability to control its costs varies depending on the time it has to react. As the time increases, the proportion of variable costs also increases. In the short-run, some costs are fixed but in the long-run, all costs are variable. The company must recover all its fixed costs whether or not it produces any output. It should continue producing the output, if it can sell it at a price that covers the additional variable cost that it will have to incur for production. In the long-run, when all the costs are variable, a company must continue in the business only if it can recover the entire costs, including the opportunity cost of the capital.

This phenomenon can be understood with the help of a simple illustration. Consider a printer operating one printing press on a one year lease. He employs three workers on a one-day contract. While the one year lease rental for the press is Rs. 50,000, each worker must be paid Rs. 80 per day. The cost of paper, ink, electricity and other miscellaneous expenses for printing one book is Rs. 100. On any given day, besides the cost of the press, the cost of the workers is also fixed since they have already been employed. For the following day, the cost of the press remains fixed but the wage cost of the workers is variable, as the one-day contract can be allowed to lapse. Similarly, for the following year, all the costs of the printer become variable since then the printer has the option of not renewing the lease on the press and not employing any worker either.

Now suppose the printer receives an order in the short-run, for printing books worth Rs. 400. This will be sufficient to cover the costs of the worker, the raw material and miscellaneous expenses and also contribute Rs. 60 to the fixed overheads, which have to be paid regardless of the order. In this case, the printer should accept the order. If however, the worth of a day's job is less than Rs. 340, then the printer should not take up the order, since he will be better off not hiring any worker or spending on raw material and other expenses and letting his press remain idle. In the long-run, in this case in a year, all the printer's costs are variable. Therefore, he should get out of the business unless he expects to generate enough revenue to cover the costs of the printing press, workers, raw material, other expenses and the opportunity cost of the capital invested in the business.

In the short-run, a firm can only produce more output by working on its fixed factor harder. In our illustration, if the printer were to receive a huge order to be completed the next day, there would not be enough time to increase the number of presses. The only way to meet the new demand would be by increasing the number of workers. In the long-run, however, the firm can alter both—the fixed factor and technology. A firm's choice of technology will determine the cost of production for different levels of output. It also lays down which production costs are fixed and which are variable. Usually there exists some level of output and technology where the economies of scale are exhausted and the minimum unit production cost is achieved.

Besides, achieving the lowest unit cost for any given level of production, the other aim of profit maximization is to earn the highest possible revenues. The extent of profits for a given level of costs depend upon the revenues that a firm can achieve, which in turn is a function of the consumer's willingness to pay for a particular product. How much a consumer is willing to pay will depend on his income, tastes and also on the price of related goods. The maximum price that a consumer is willing to pay for one more unit of a particular good is known as *reservation price*.

A firm must price its product in such a way that the nth ranked consumer pays just this reservation price for the nth unit of output. Given a choice, any firm would want to charge the reservation price from every consumer. But this seems unlikely because it can usually charge only a single price for all the output it sells. Thus, in order to sell to the nth consumer, it must sell to the $n - 1$ consumers at a price below what they will be actually willing to pay. In other words, if a firm lowers its price to expand its market by one additional consumer, it loses the value of price reduction over all the remaining existing customers, but gains the value of the revenue from the last customer. The net of these two values is known as the *marginal revenue*. It represents the change in total revenue due to the sale of one additional unit. While each additional unit brings in additional revenue, it also increases the firm's cost. This increase in the total cost due to the sale of one additional unit is known as *marginal cost*.

Ideally, the firm must choose a price-output combination that yields the highest revenue at lowest cost, for maximizing profits. As long as the marginal revenue exceeds the marginal cost, it will be worthwhile to add that extra customer as then the overall profit will increase. Once the marginal cost equals the marginal revenue, the last consumer makes no additional contribution to the profits of the firm. Beyond this point all successive consumers will actually add more costs than revenue and will thus be no more profitable to serve.

Thus, the key to profit maximization is that firms must choose that price-output combination where the marginal revenue from the last unit sold equals the marginal cost of producing that unit.

The same conclusion can be reached mathematically by constructing a model. The model of profit maximization is based on the following assumptions:

- The firm is owned by .. single person
- The objective of the firm is profit maximization

- The operating market conditions are given to the firm
- The firm acts rationally to achieve its objective

Since, profit is the excess of total revenue over total cost,

$$\pi = TR - TC$$

where, π is the profit of the firm, TR is the total revenue and TC is the total cost. Since both TR and TC are functions of output, that is,

$$TR = f_1(Q) \quad \text{and} \quad TC = f_2(Q)$$

$$\therefore \quad \pi = f_1(Q) - f_2(Q) = f_3(Q)$$

Thus, profit is also a function of output.

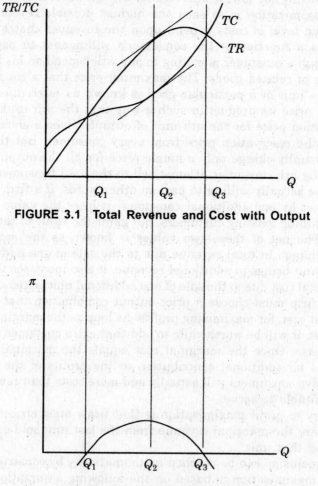

FIGURE 3.1 | Total Revenue and Cost with Output

FIGURE 3.2 Profit and Output

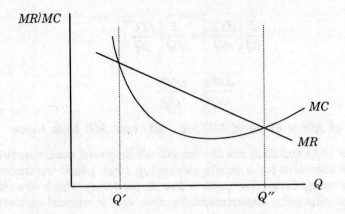

FIGURE 3.3 Marginal Revenue and Cost with Output

We have already learnt the conditions for a function to be maximum. The necessary condition is that the first derivative of the function should be zero. The secondary condition is that the second derivative of the function should be negative.

Hence,

$$\frac{d\pi}{dQ} = 0 \quad \text{and} \quad \frac{d^2\pi}{dQ^2} = -\text{ve}$$

According to the first condition

$$\frac{d\pi}{dQ} = 0$$

$$\frac{dTR}{dQ} - \frac{dTC}{dQ} = 0$$

$$\frac{dTR}{dQ} = \frac{dTC}{dQ}$$

Slope of TR = Slope of TC

$$MR = MC \tag{3.1}$$

The second condition requires that

$$\frac{d^2\pi}{dQ^2} < 0$$

$$\frac{d^2TR}{dQ^2} < \frac{d^2TC}{dQ^2}$$

$$\frac{d}{dQ}\left(\frac{dTR}{dQ}\right) < \frac{d}{dQ}\left(\frac{dTC}{dQ}\right)$$

$$\frac{dMR}{dQ} < \frac{dMC}{dQ}$$

Slope of MR < Slope of MC or MC cuts MR from below   (3.2)

Thus, Equations (3.1) and (3.2) are the conditions for profit maximization. Although the most justifiable objective for a single ownership firm, profit maximization seems an unrealistic motivating factor for quite a few firms today which are characterized by multiple owners, oligopoly, departmentalization and irrational operations.

ILLUSTRATION 3.1   A firm's total cost function is, $C = Q^2 - 22Q$. It faces a demand function of $Q = 14 - P$. Find out the profit maximizing output and price for the firm.

   Solution   Here cost is already given as a function of quantity. The total revenue in terms of quantity, will be

$$TR = P \cdot Q$$

Since, the demand function yields

$$P = 14 - Q$$

$$TR = (14 - Q) \cdot Q$$

$$TR = 14Q - Q^2 \qquad \text{(i)}$$

Given that

$$TC = Q^2 - 22Q \qquad \text{(ii)}$$

The profit function for the firm is

$$\pi = TR - TC \qquad \text{(iii)}$$

Substituting the value of TR and TC from Equations (i) and (ii) in (iii), we get

$$\pi = (14Q - Q^2) - (Q^2 - 22Q)$$

$$= 14Q - Q^2 - Q^2 + 22Q$$

$$= 36Q - 2Q^2$$

$$\therefore \qquad \pi = 36Q - 2Q^2 \qquad \text{(iv)}$$

We know that the necessary and secondary conditions for profit maximization are that the first order derivative should be zero and the second order derivative should be negative. That is,

$$\frac{d\pi}{dQ} = 0 \qquad \text{and} \qquad \frac{d^2\pi}{dQ^2} = -\text{ve}$$

Differentiating Equation (iv) with respect to Q, we get

$$\frac{d\pi}{dQ} = \frac{d}{dQ}(36Q - 2Q^2)$$

$$= 36 - 4Q \qquad \text{(v)}$$

Differentiating Equation (v) gives us

$$\frac{d}{dQ}\left(\frac{d\pi}{dQ}\right) = \frac{d}{dQ}(36 - 4Q)$$

$$\frac{d^2\pi}{dQ^2} = -4 \qquad \text{(vi)}$$

According to Equation (vi), $d^2\pi/dQ^2$ is negative. Hence, this is a case of maximization. The profit will be maximum when $d\pi/dQ = 0$. That is,

$$36 - 4Q = 0$$

$$4Q = 36$$

$$\therefore \qquad Q = 9$$

Substituting this value in the demand equation, we have

$$P = 14 - Q$$

$$= 14 - 9 = 5$$

Thus, the profit maximizing output and price for the firm are $Q = 9$ and $P = 5$, respectively.

BASIC CONCEPTS OF MANAGERIAL ECONOMICS

The various decision-making tools and techniques provided by managerial economics are based on some important concepts. The three most vital concepts are—opportunity cost, marginal analysis and discounting.

Opportunity Cost

Opportunity cost of a decision is the cost of sacrificing the alternatives to that decision. The question of sacrificing arises because of the fundamental economic problem of scarce resources which forces a manager to choose the best out of the available alternatives. Choosing the best automatically means leaving behind all the remaining alternatives. When one employs the resources in one particular course of action, he loses the opportunity of using them in any of the remaining courses of action. The returns of the next best alternative that are foregone when one chooses the best alternative are termed opportunity cost.

Opportunity cost confronts us at every point in life. But most of the times, we don't take this cost into account when making decisions. Common examples of opportunity cost from everyday life are that of a restaurant choosing to make *samosas* instead of *kachoris* and *aloobadas*, a shoemaker making *chappals* instead of shoes and sandals, a company deciding to manufacture product *A* on the lathe machine in place of product *B*, *C* or *D* and so on. Even when a person decides to invest his money in the debentures of a company, he compares the returns on his investment with what he could have earned if the money was kept in a bank as fixed deposit.

Marginal Analysis

Marginal analysis is concerned with finding out the change in the total arising because of one additional unit. Likewise, the change in the total revenue due to one additional unit sold is known as *marginal revenue,* while *marginal cost* is the change in total cost on account of one additional unit produced. Owing to the importance of this concept, it would be worthwhile to discuss the relationship between marginal, average and total in detail.

Revenue. The sum total of the sale proceeds from total units sold is known as *total revenue. Average revenue* is obtained by dividing the total revenue by the number of units of quantity sold.

Marginal revenue, as defined earlier, is the change in total revenue received on selling one additional unit of the good. In terms of differential calculus, marginal revenue is the rate of change of total revenue with respect to the change in output sold. Geometrically, marginal revenue is the slope of the total revenue curve at a given output point. This can be shown in Table 3.1.

TABLE 3.1 Total, Average and Marginal Revenue

Quantity (units)	Price P (Rs./unit)	Total Revenue, TR (Rs.)	Average Revenue, AR (Rs./unit)	Marginal Revenue, MR (Rs.)
1	10	10	10	–
2	9	18	9	8
3	8	24	8	6
4	7	28	7	4
5	6	30	6	2
6	5	30	5	0
7	4	28	4	–2

Graphically, this can be represented by Figures 3.4 and 3.5, respectively.

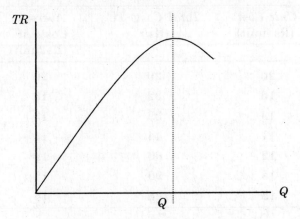

FIGURE 3.4   Total Revenue and Output

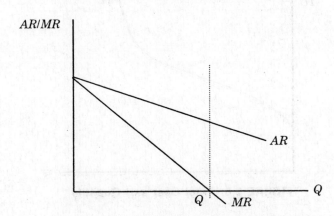

FIGURE 3.5   Average and Marginal Revenue

It can be observed that with an increase in quantity, the total revenue first increases, though at a decreasing rate, then remains constant and finally falls. This is due to the principle of *diminishing marginal utility* that necessitates lowering of prices when quantity is increased. Accordingly, the average revenue and the marginal revenue fall with a rise in output sold. The only difference being that *MR* falls at a faster rate than *AR* and even becomes negative.

Costs.   *Total cost* is the sum total of the costs of total units produced. This total cost, when divided by the number of units produced is termed *average cost*. The change in total cost when an additional unit of the good is produced is known as *marginal cost*. In terms of differential calculus, it is the rate of change of total cost with respect to the change in output produced. Geometrically, marginal cost is the slope of the total cost curve for a given quantity. The behaviour of these costs is detailed in Table 3.2.

TABLE 3.2   Total, Average and Marginal Cost

Quantity (units)	Unit Cost (Rs./unit)	Total Cost, TC (Rs.)	Average Cost, AC (Rs./unit)	Marginal Cost, MC (Rs.)
1	20	20	20	–
2	16	32	16	12
3	13	39	13	7
4	11	44	11	5
5	12	60	12	16
6	15	90	15	30
7	18	126	18	36

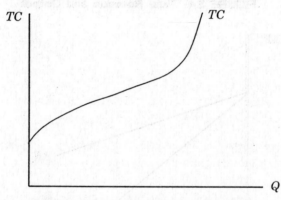

FIGURE 3.6   Total Cost and Quantity

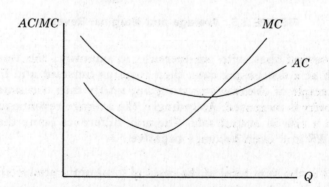

FIGURE 3.7   Average and Marginal Cost

Thus, total cost increases with an increase in quantity. This rise is not uniform, i.e. it first increases at a decreasing rate, then at a constant rate and finally at an increasing rate. This is because of the law of diminishing returns. Accordingly, first both the average cost and the marginal cost fall, then become constant and finally rises. Both the fall as well as rise are more pronounced in the case of marginal cost as compared to average cost. Because of this fact, the marginal cost curve reaches its lowest point first. This point lies lower than the lowest point of the *AC* curve. *MC* then rises above the average cost curve cutting it at the point where *AC* is minimum.

The concept of marginal analysis forms the basis of most managerial decisions. Any decision would be worth taking only when the marginal benefit occurring from it would be more than the marginal cost. A firm would be better off only if this condition holds true. In the short-run, marginal cost relates to the average variable cost and a firm should sell its product even if only the marginal cost is recovered. In the long-run, however, since fixed costs also vary, the average total cost becomes a more useful parameter to consider. Thus, the concept of marginal should be applied keeping in mind the time period.

Discounting

Almost all managerial decisions relate to the future. The value of money today is not the same as it will be at a later point of time. Anything that is received later always involves an element of risk. A rupee received today is more valuable than a rupee that will be received later. This is known as the *time value of money* and it arises because of the following:

Uncertainty of future receipts. Future receipts are always susceptible to risk. One is not sure whether the amount that is due, will be received at the stipulated future date. This places a premium on the money received today.

Urgency of present needs. When the present needs of a firm are urgent and cannot be postponed, then it will like to have money today rather than have it in future. In such cases the firm won't mind even receiving a lesser amount today. For example, suppose a firm needs Rs. 100 today to pay for its variable expenses for sustaining its operations. Then its first priority would be to get Rs. 100 so that it can survive till tomorrow. The firm will deny anything offered, even though it may be manifold, at a future date in lieu of this amount.

Inability to enjoy future consumption. It is always possible that a firm may not be in a position to enjoy and utilize the money received at a later date. For a firm which is running well and carrying out uninterrupted production activities today, the amount received in the future will be of no use if its operations are blocked due to a labour strike at that point in time. This very doubt that a firm may not be in a position to enjoy future benefits, induces it to prefer today's receipts.

Investment opportunities. Everything else remaining constant, a firm would be indifferent to receiving an amount today or later if it is to keep the funds idle. However, if the firm has some investment opportunities available that can generate returns, then it will definitely like to have the money today. Consider a case where a firm can choose to receive Rs. 100 today or after one year. If it does not have any investment option, it will keep this Rs. 100 idle and will be indifferent to receiving it at any time. But if it can invest this Rs. 100 in a fixed deposit with a bank and earn a return of 10% per annum, so that the amount becomes Rs. 110 at the end of the year, the firm would like to have the amount today so that it can have more money at the end of the year.

Due to these four factors, the money received today is more valuable than that which will be received later. In other words, the present value of Rs. 100 received at a later date is less than Rs. 100. This also means that Rs. 100 received at a later date would be equal to Rs. $(100 - x)$ received today. This x is the discounting factor that is incorporated to equate the present value of money received at two different points of time. This x accounts for the time value of money. Such a process of calculating the present value by using mathematical formulae for adjusting the time value of money is known as *discounting*. If the rate of return is r per cent per annum, the present value of an amount A to be received after n years is

$$P = \frac{A}{\left(1 + \dfrac{r}{100}\right)^n}$$

One can now appreciate the magnitude of error that would result if alternatives effecting future cash flows are compared on the basis of their absolute values. The alternatives need to be worked out on the basis of their present values obtained after discounting their absolute future values.

ILLUSTRATION 3.2   A project has a cash outflow of Rs. 1,00,000. It yields cash inflows of Rs. 30,000, Rs. 45,000 and Rs. 55,000 in the first, second and third years respectively. The firm will accept the project if the net present value of cash inflows is more than that of outflow. Should the project be accepted if the cost of capital is 12%?

Solution   The cash flows for the project are as under:

Year 0	1,00,000	Cash outflow (C_0)
Year 1	30,000	Cash inflow (C_1)
Year 2	45,000	Cash inflow (C_2)
Year 3	55,000	Cash inflow (C_3)

Since cash outflow occurs today (year 0) so its present value (*PV*) is same i.e. Rs. 1,00,000

$$PV \text{ of } C_1 = \frac{30,000}{(1 + 0.12)^1}$$

$$= \frac{30,000}{1.12} = Rs.\ 26786$$

$$PV \text{ of } C_2 = \frac{45,000}{(1 + 0.12)^2}$$

$$= \frac{45,000}{(1.12)^2} = \text{Rs. } 35874$$

$$PV \text{ of } C_3 = \frac{55,000}{(1 + 0.12)^3}$$

$$= \frac{55,000}{(1.12)^3} = \text{Rs. } 39148$$

Total present value of cash inflows is

$$= 26786 + 35874 + 39148 = \text{Rs. } 1,01,718$$

Since the present value of cash inflows in more than that of the outflow, the project should be accepted.

QUESTIONS

1. 'Managerial economics uses the theories of economics and the methodologies of the decision sciences for managerial decision-making.' Elaborate.

2. 'Managerial economics is a part of normative economics. It is pragmatic and conceptual in nature.' Discuss.

3. Identify the areas of decision-making where managerial economics prescribes specific solutions to business problems.

4. How does managerial economics relate with and uses other disciplines for propounding its theories and concepts for managerial decision-making?

5. Explain the theory of profit maximization. State the assumptions of the model and derive the necessary and secondary conditions for profit maximization.

6. 'A firm maximizes profit when for every additional unit produced and sold, the incremental revenue received equals the incremental cost incurred'. Comment.

7. The tools and techniques of managerial economics rest on some basic concepts. Explain these concepts.

8. Write short notes on the following:
   (a) Opportunity cost
   (b) Marginal analysis
   (c) Discounting

9. The demand and cost function of a firm are given below:

$$Q = 8 - P$$
$$C = Q^2 - 4Q + 12$$

Find out the output and price at which profit will be maximum.

10. The demand equation for a firm is $Q = 10 - P$. The total cost of the firm is given by the equation $C = 2Q^2 + 2Q + 15$. Find out the price and output under the conditions of

    (a) Profit maximization
    (b) Sales maximization
    (c) Sales maximization subject to a profit of 10

11. Naresh subscribes to 100 debentures of a company. The face value of each debenture is Rs. 100 and the coupon rate is 15% per annum (p.a.). The debentures will be redeemed at the end of three years. Find out the present value of the cash inflows for Naresh at a discounting rate of 12% p.a.

12. State which of the following statements are *true* and which are *false:*

    (a) Managerial economics is a part of normative economics.
    (b) For maximizing profits, the firms must choose the price-output combination where marginal revenue exceeds marginal cost.
    (c) Opportunity cost of a decision is the cost of sacrificing the alternatives to that decision.
    (d) Marginal analysis is a special case of incremental analysis.
    (e) A rupee received today is more valuable than a rupee received later.

CASE STUDY

Case 3.1 Altonative to M800

Maruti Udyog Limited's (MUL) price aggression on Alto seems to be paying off. Last month, for a third time in a row, the Alto pipped MUL's earlier best seller Maruti 800 as the top selling product in the company's stable. And in the first six months of the fiscal, it drove right to the top of the B-segment heap with a cumulative tally of 59009 units.

The Alto's A-segment positioning has brought it within sniffing distance of the largest selling passenger car model in India, the redoubtable M800. In the second quarter of this year, M800 clocked 59871 units, just barely ahead of Alto. In contrast, last fiscal, the Alto's 20000 unit tally was one-fourth of the M800's 82000 unit haul.

The Alto's northward drive has seen some u-turns and speed breakers this fiscal. In the initial few months of the year, the sale of Alto was considerably lower than that of M800. but gradually it picked up speed and pipped the M800 and had no looking back since then, ultimately clocking a 201 percent growth in this quarter.

And all this did not happen on its own. This was the result of a meticulously planned brand positioning by the company. The advertising campaigns, which initially looked to create a pressure on the profit margins, finally paid off well. But the case, for sure, strikes a question in the mind. Why are companies like MUL, already having a best seller, looking out for newer products and promoting them aggressively, so as to not only better others but to even to the extent of overtaking their own best seller?

(*Source:* The Economic Times, October 05, 2004)

CHAPTER | FOUR

Demand Analysis

LEARNING OBJECTIVES

* the basis and types of demand
* the cardinal and ordinal utility approaches to understanding demand
* the important factors affecting demand
* the law of demand
* Giffen goods as an exception to the law of demand

 DEFINING DEMAND

Demand may be defined as the quantity of goods or services desired by an individual, backed by the ability and willingness to pay.

Demand forms the core of almost all the major decisions of a firm. Be it production planning, inventory control, establishing a distribution network, human resource analysis, raising of finance or selection of projects, all managerial decisions ultimately relate to the analysis and forecasting of demand. The market demand for any product is the sum of the demands of individual consumers.

All firms survive on profits. Profit is a function of price and quantity, *ceteris paribus* (the Latin expression for 'other things being equal'). Price and output decisions are guided by the interaction of market demand and supply. Supply can be controlled by the firm. Demand being an external factor, is more difficult to manage.

Before we analyze demand in order to forecast it, it is very important to understand the basis of consumer demand, i.e. why, when and how much does the consumer purchase. *Utility*, i.e. the want satisfying quality of a good or service, is the prime factor that generates demand. Thus, understanding utility is essential for understanding demand. There are two views about utility. One is that utility can be measured, i.e. is *cardinal*, is known as the *Utility Analysis* while the other, which treats utility as something which can only be compared but not quantified, i.e. is *ordinal*, is known as the *Indifference Curve Analysis*.

43

Utility Analysis

The utility analysis was developed by Alfred Marshall to explain consumer demand. This approach is based on the fact that utility is quantifiable, i.e. it can be measured in some units. The unit for measurement of utility is known as *util*. Thus, for example, it can be said that ice cream has 10 utils while *rasgulla* has 6 utils. This holds true for a person who likes ice cream more than *rasgulla*. Since utility can be measured in specific units, so it can also be added. We thus have *total utility* and *marginal utility*. Total utility, which is a measure of the overall satisfaction, is defined as the total satisfaction derived from the consumption of all the units of a good or service. Marginal utility, on the other hand, is the change in total utility when one additional unit of a good or service is consumed. Thus, if the utility derived from the consumption of 1, 2, 3,..., n units of goods or services are U_1, U_2, U_3,..., U_n then

$$
\begin{aligned}
\text{Total utility for 1 unit} \quad & TU_1 = U_1 \\
\text{for 2 units} \quad & TU_2 = U_1 + U_2 \\
\text{for 3 units} \quad & TU_3 = U_1 + U_2 + U_3 \\
\text{for } n \text{ units} \quad & TU_n = U_1 + U_2 + U_3 + \cdots + U_n
\end{aligned}
\tag{4.1}
$$

$$
\begin{aligned}
\text{Marginal utility for the 2nd unit} \quad & MU_2 = TU_2 - TU_1 \\
\text{for the 3rd unit} \quad & MU_3 = TU_3 - TU_2 \\
\text{for the } n\text{th unit} \quad & MU_n = TU_n - TU_{n-1}
\end{aligned}
\tag{4.2}
$$

Assumptions of utility analysis.   The important assumptions of this analysis are:

1. Utility is cardinal.
2. Utility being quantifiable is additive.
3. Various units of a commodity consumed are homogenous. For example, if the case relates to the consumption of 200 ml bottles of a soft drink, then all the units consumed must be 200 ml bottles of the same soft drink.
4. There is no time gap between the consumption of successive units. The consumer goes on consuming the units one by one, without any break.
5. The consumer is rational, i.e. he has perfect knowledge and maximizes utility.
6. The consumer's income is limited and constant.
7. The tastes and preferences of the consumer remain unchanged.
8. The marginal utility of money is constant. Here the marginal utility of money is the change in total utility that results from spending one additional unit of money.

Law of diminishing marginal utility.   The law states that as a consumer increases the consumption of a product, the utility gained from successive units goes on decreasing. In other words, the rate of increase of total utility decreases as more and more units are consumed. Consider the case of a thirsty boy going to a general store on a summer day. Suppose normally a soft drink bottle possess utility of 7 utils. However, under such conditions the utility obtained from the first bottle will be higher, say 9 utils. However, when he consumes a second bottle soon after the first one, he will not get the same level of satisfaction. He may get 7 utils from the second bottle. Likewise, the utility for each successive bottle of soft drink will go on decreasing. A stage may come when he may develop such an aversion for the soft drink that he may even vomit on further consumption. In such cases the utility may even become negative. We can also represent this expample in Table 4.1.

TABLE 4.1   Total and Marginal Utility

Units of Coke	Total Utility, TU (utils)	Marginal Utility, MU (utils)
0	0	–
1	9	9
2	16	7
3	21	5
4	24	3
5	25	1
6	24	–1
7	21	–3

Similar consumptional behaviour will be observed for any product or service. This can also be graphically depicted as shown in Figure 4.1.

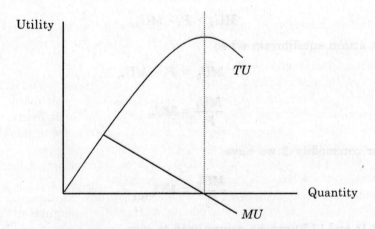

FIGURE 4.1   Total Utility and Marginal Utility

Consumer equilibrium.   A consumer is said to be in equilibrium when he has

    (a) maximized his satisfaction
    (b) spent his entire income
    (c) attained optimum allocation of expenditure and
    (d) consumed optimum quantity of each commodity.

Consumer equilibrium can be better understood by analyzing a situation wherein the consumer consumes a single commodity. This can then be generalized for multiple commodities.

Let a consumer with certain money income consumes commodity 1. If we assume that the money a consumer is willing to pay for each unit of the commodity reflects the marginal utility of that product, we can have the marginal utility curve of a commodity in terms of money units as shown in Figure 4.2.

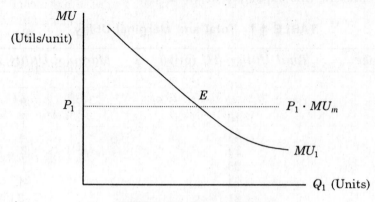

FIGURE 4.2 Marginal Utility

The consumer will continue consuming the commodity and exchanging money income so long as

$$MU_1 > P_1 \cdot MU_m$$

He will thus attain equilibrium when

$$MU_1 = P_1 \cdot MU_m$$

$$\frac{MU_1}{P_1} = MU_m \tag{4.3}$$

Similarly, for commodity 2 we have

$$\frac{MU_2}{P_2} = MU_m \tag{4.4}$$

Equations (4.1) and (4.2) can be generalized to give

$$\frac{MU_1}{P_1} = \frac{MU_2}{P_2} = \frac{MU_3}{P_3} = \cdots = \frac{MU_n}{P_n} = MU_m \tag{4.5}$$

Law of equimarginal utility. The law states that a consumer maximizes his total utility by distributing his entire income optimally among the various commodities consumed by him. This is done in a manner that the marginal utility derived per unit of expenditure, i.e. per rupee is same for all commodities.

$$\frac{MU_1}{P_1} = \frac{MU_2}{P_2} = \frac{MU_3}{P_3} = \cdots = \frac{MU_n}{P_n}$$

The law can be illustrated by simple example. Let a consumer who likes apples more than bananas, consumes apples and bananas. Suppose his income is Rs. 7 and each apple and banana costs him Re.1 (i.e. $P_a = P_b = 1$). The marginal utility derived by the consumer from apples and bananas can be tabulated as in Table 4.2.

TABLE 4.2 Marginal Utilities of Two Commodities

Units	Marginal Utility of apples (MU_A)	Marginal Utility of bananas (MU_B)
1	10	8
2	8	6
3	6	4
4	4	2
5	2	0
6	0	−2
7	−2	−4

For the consumer to spend his entire income of Rs. 7, he can either have 7A and 0B, 6A and 1B, 5A and 2B, 4A and 3B, 3A and 4B, 2A and 5B, 1A and 6B, 0A and 7B, where A stands for apples and B for bananas. Also $MU_a/P_a = MU_b/P_b$ when he consumes 2A and 1B, 3A and 2B, 4A and 3B, 5A and 4B, 6A and 5B, 7A and 6B. The only combination common to both these conditions is 4A and 3B, i.e. 4 apples and 3 bananas. Thus, the consumer will consume 4 apples and 3 bananas.

ILLUSTRATION 4.1 A consumer consumes two commodities, wheat and rice. The marginal utility derived by him from rice is two and a half times the marginal utility of wheat. If wheat is available for Rs. 12 per kg, what price will he be willing to pay for rice in order to maximize his utility?

Solution Here it is given that

$$MU_R = 2.5\, MU_W$$

where MU_R and MU_W are the marginal utilities of rice and wheat respectively.
Also, the price of wheat

$$P_W = \text{Rs. } 12/\text{kg}$$

The law of equimarginal utility states that the consumer will maximize his total utility when

$$\frac{MU_1}{P_1} = \frac{MU_2}{P_2} = \cdots = \frac{MU_n}{P_n}$$

Here,

$$\frac{MU_R}{P_R} = \frac{MU_W}{P_W}$$

$$\therefore \qquad P_R = P_W \cdot \frac{MU_R}{MU_W}$$

$$= 12 \times 2.5 = 30$$

Hence, the consumer will be willing to pay Rs. 30 for every kilogram of rice.

Indifference Curve Analysis

An alternative theory of consumer demand was put forward by J.R. Hicks and R.G.D. Allen. This approach considers utility to be ordinal i.e. it cannot be measured but can only be ranked or compared. Thus, while under the utility analysis it could be said that a person got 10 utils from ice cream and 6 utils from *rasgulla*, under this approach it can only be said that ice cream gives more utility to the person than *rasgulla*.

Assumptions.   The assumptions of the indifference curve analysis are:

1. Utility is ordinal.
2. Utility being subjective is rankable but not measurable.
3. The consumer is rational.
4. The income of the consumer is limited and constant.
5. The tastes and preferences of the consumer remain unchanged.
6. If a consumer prefers a commodity A to B and a commodity B to C then he prefers the commodity A to C.

Consumers generally consume products as part of a group of goods and services rather than as individual products. As a large number of goods and services are available, a wide array of combinations exist. And it is very possible that a number of these combinations will give the same level of satisfaction to the consumer.

Indifference curve.   The locus of points, each representing a different combination of two goods, which provide the same level of utility to the consumer is known as an indifference curve.

The curve derives its name from the fact that a consumer is indifferent to any of these combinations when it comes to making a choice between them. For the sake of simplicity we assume that there is continuous and not incremental variation in consumption. What results then is a smoothened curve. We use Table 4.3 to explain the concept.

TABLE 4.3 Consumer's Indifference

Combination	Apple (X)	Mango (Y)	Total Utility (TU)	MRS = $\Delta Y/\Delta X$
A	1	30	U	–
B	2	24	U	–6
C	3	19	U	–5
D	4	15	U	–4
E	5	12	U	–3
F	6	10	U	–2
G	7	9	U	–1

Thus, the consumer is indifferent to choose between any combination of apples and mangoes as all combinations provide the same level of utility U to him. This data can now be plotted in Figure 4.3.

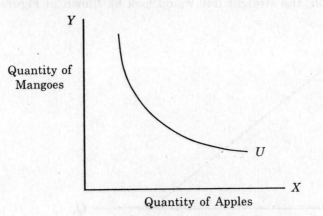

FIGURE 4.3 Indifference Curve

We can now enumerate certain essential characteristics of indifference curves:

1. *Indifference curves are downward sloping:* This is because for the same level of utility if the demand of one commodity increases, the demand for the second commodity has to decrease.
2. *Indifference curves are convex to origin:* This is because two goods cannot be perfect substitutes for each other. As the consumer gets larger quantities of one commodity X at the cost of another commodity Y, marginal utility of X decreases. Due to reduced availability of Y, the marginal utility of Y, i.e. MU_Y increases. Thus, the consumer will be ready to sacrifice lesser quantity of Y for each additional quantity of X.
3. *Indifference curves never intersect each other:* Since the same combination of goods cannot yield two different levels of utility, indifference curves can never cut each other.

4. *Higher indifference curves denote higher levels of utility:* Higher utility can be derived only when the quantity demand either one, or both goods is increased. This would mean a higher indifference curve.

Budget line. A *budget line* represents all the combinations of two products that can be purchased for a given amount of money.

For example, let two goods X and Y be available at prices P_x and P_y and in quantities Q_x and Q_y. For a given budget B, a consumer can make the following purchase:

$$\text{Total Budget} = \text{Spending on } X + \text{Spending on } Y$$

$$B = P_x \cdot Q_x + P_y \cdot Q_y \tag{4.7}$$

If a consumer has an income of Rs. 2000 and the prices of two products X and Y are P_x = Rs. 50/unit and P_y = Rs. 40/unit, then

$$2000 = 50Q_x + 40Q_y$$

When plotted on a graph, the straight line would look as shown in Figure 4.4.

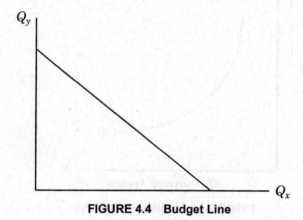

FIGURE 4.4   Budget Line

The changes in any of these three parameters would change the budget line accordingly.

ILLUSTRATION 4.2 Two goods X and Y are available for Rs. 7/kg and Rs. 10/kg. If a consumer has an income of Rs. 35,000, draw the budget line as a graph.

Solution The budget line equation is

$$B = P_x \cdot Q_x + P_y \cdot Q_y$$

Here,

$$B = \text{Rs. } 35000$$

$$P_x = \text{Rs. } 7/\text{kg}$$

and

$$P_y = \text{Rs. } 10/\text{kg}$$

$$7Q_x + 10Q_y = 35000 \tag{i}$$

The budget line can be drawn by plotting the quantities of the commodities X and Y on the x-axis and y-axis, respectively.

The ordinates, where the budget line will intersect the x-axis and y-axis, can be calculated by equating Q_y and Q_x with zero.

When

$$Q_x = 0, \qquad Q_y = 35000/10 = 3500$$

and when

$$Q_y = 0, \qquad Q_x = 35000/7 = 5000$$

Thus, the two axis ordinates for the budget line are (0, 3500) and (5000, 0).

Consumer equilibrium. A consumer is in equilibrium when he has maximized his utility subject to his income/budget. This will happen only when the budget line is tangential to the indifference curve as in Figure 4.5.

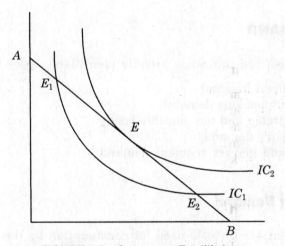

FIGURE 4.5   Consumer Equilibrium

Consider a consumer whose indifference curve is IC_1 and budget line is AB. The budget line cuts the indifference curve at two points E_1 and E_2. Since all points on the indifference curve yield the same level of satisfaction, there is enough scope for the consumer to shift to another indifference curve IC_2, higher and farther from the origin such that it touches IC_2 only at one point. This is the point of tangency. Practically, the consumer now maximizes his utility with respect to his budget.

Marginal rate of substitution (MRS). While discussing consumer indifference we observed that for the same level of utility if the quantity of one commodity was increased, the quantity of the other had to be decreased. In other words, some units of one commodity were substituted for additional units of another.

The rate at which one commodity can be substituted for another, if the utility is to remain unchanged, is known as marginal rate of substitution (MRS). Mathematically,

$$MRS = \frac{\Delta Y}{\Delta X}$$

Thus, marginal rate of substitution is nothing but the slope of an indifference curve. Since quantity of one commodity is increasing while that of the other is decreasing, so *MRS* is always negative, i.e. the slope of the indifference curve is negative/downwards.

Law of diminishing marginal rate of substitution. The convex nature of the indifference curves signifies that the rate of substitution goes on decreasing as more units of a commodity are consumed. In other words, the quantity of a commodity that a consumer is willing to sacrifice for an additional unit keeps on decreasing as he continues substituting one commodity for another. This is the law of diminishing marginal rate of substitution.

TYPES OF DEMAND

Demand can be categorized into some broadly identifiable types as follows:

- Direct and indirect demand
- Derived and autonomous demand
- Demand for durable and non-durable goods
- Firm and industry demand
- Total market and market segment demand

Direct and Indirect Demand

Demand for goods that are directly used for consumption by the ultimate consumer is known as *direct demand*. Since such goods are used for final consumption, such demand is also called *consumer's goods demand*. Demand for all consumer's goods such as bread, tea, readymade shirts, scooters, houses is direct demand. *Indirect demand* is the demand for goods that are not used by consumers directly. They are used by producers for producing other goods. So indirect demand is also known as *producer's goods demand*. Examples of indirect demand are demands for machines, tools, coal, limestone and raw materials. However, the distinction between direct and indirect demand is subjective. When the demand for cloth comes from a consumer for his personal use it is direct demand while when it comes from a garment manufacturer, it is indirect demand. The determinants for both these types of demand are different.

This categorization is helpful in proper analysis of demand. While direct demand depends primarily upon the consumer's income, indirect demand depends upon the concerned producer's output. In the above example, if cloth is a consumer good, then its demand will depend on the consumer's income, while if it is used by a garment manufacturer, then its demand would depend on the demand for readymade shirts and trousers.

Derived and Autonomous Demand

The classification of demand as derived and autonomous is quite similar to its classification as direct and indirect. When a product derives its usage from the use of some primary product, its demand is known as *derived demand*. *Autonomous demand* is the demand for a product that can be independently used. Thus, while the demand for tyres is derived since it depends upon the demand for vehicles, the demand for milk or vegetables is autonomous. However, since almost all products depend on others to some extent, the difference between the two is of more degree.

Durable and Non-durable Goods Demand

Durable goods are those that can be used more than once, over a period of time, as against *non-durable goods* that can be used only once. Both producer and consumer goods can be durable and non-durable. Durable goods are *used* while non-durable goods are *consumed*. Among producer's goods while machines, tools, etc. are durable, others like coal, oil, etc. are non-durable. Consumer's goods such as bread, jam, etc. are non-durable while car, readymade shirts, etc. are durable.

Firm and Industry Demand

As the names indicate, *firm demand* is the demand for the product of a particular firm. On the other hand, demand for the product of a particular industry is known as *industry demand*. For example, demand for pens is an industry demand, while the demand for Parker pens is a firm demand. Similarly, demand for Colgate toothpaste and toothpaste in general are firm and industry demands respectively.

Total Market and Market Segment Demand

Demand analysis requires not only the total demand for a product but also a breakup of the demand for the product in different parts of the market. The market may be segmented on the basis of age, sex, geographical region, etc. Thus, while the demand for Vadilal ice cream in India is *total market demand*, demand for Vadilal ice cream in Rajasthan or demand for Vadilal ice cream by women is a *market segment demand*.

 DETERMINANTS OF DEMAND

There are various factors affecting the demand for a commodity. They are commonly known as *determinants of demand*. The most important of these are:

- Consumer's income
- Price of the good

- Price of related goods
- Consumer's tastes and preferences
- Advertisements
- Credit facilities/discount by sellers
- Multiplicity of uses of goods
- Future expectations of consumers
- Population

The extent to which these factors affect demand varies depending on the kind of goods. We will now discuss the influence of these determinants on the demand for a commodity. The discussion is however partial in the sense that when the effect of any one factor is analyzed, the other factors are assumed to be constant. This is necessary because without such an assumption if all the factors are allowed to vary simultaneously, one would not be able to ascertain whether and to what extent the change is due to a particular determinant. This assumption is also expressed as *ceteris paribus*.

Consumer's Income and Demand

Normally the demand varies proportionately with the income of the consumer. The purchasing power of a consumer increases with a rise in income. With more money, he can buy more goods. With further rise in income and after getting satisfied with the quantity, he will shift to the consumption of better quality goods. Poor quality goods are also known as *inferior goods*. Thus, other things remaining constant, the demand for good quality commodities i.e. *superior goods* increases with the increase in the consumer's income and vice versa. On the other hand, the demand for inferior goods decreases with a rise in income, since then poor quality goods are substituted by better quality goods.

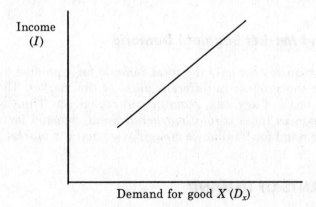

FIGURE 4.6 Engel's Curve

Thus, demand for superior goods varies directly with the consumer's income and inversely with the consumer's income in the case of inferior goods. The income-demand curve is also known as **Engel's curve**, shown in Figure 4.6.

Price of the Goods and Demand

Normally the demand for a commodity varies inversely with its own price. Thus, other things remaining the same, the demand for a good increases as its price decreases and vice versa. This is also known as the *law of demand*.

A graphical representation of the law of demand is known as *demand curve* shown in Figure 4.7. The same data when put in tabular form becomes the *demand schedule* as shown in Table 4.4.

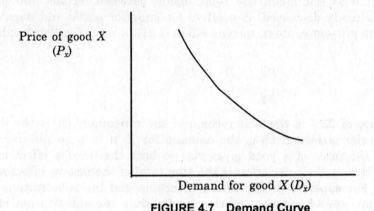

Price of good X
(P_x)

Demand for good $X (D_x)$

FIGURE 4.7   Demand Curve

TABLE 4.4   Demand Schedule

Price of good X, P_x (Rs.)	Demand for good X, D_x (units)
10	100
9	110
8	125
7	140
5	155
5	165

Barring a few exceptions, the law of demand always holds good. This is because of marginal buyers. These buyers start consuming a good if the price falls and stop consumption when its price rises. Such buyers act as though they are sitting on the margin. Exceptions to the law of demand occur because of *intra-marginal buyers*, who do not start or stop consumption with a change in price but merely increase or decrease their consumption.

The effect of a goods price on its demand by intra-marginal buyers can be better explained by dividing this price effect into two parts, the *income effect* and the *substitution effect*. When the price of a good X decreases, *ceteris paribus*, it becomes cheaper in relation to other goods. Thus, consumers shift from other goods to X. In other words, they substitute X for other goods. So the demand for X increases. Similarly, the demand for X will decrease when the price of X increases. This is known as substitution effect.

Also, when the price of a good X decreases, *ceteris paribus*, it implies that the real income of the consumer increases, as the purchasing power rises. This increases the demand for superior goods and reduces the demand for inferior goods. The opposite also holds true. This is known as the income effect.

From the above discussions it is clear that while substitution effect is always negative, income effect is negative for superior goods and positive for inferior goods. Here, income effect does not mean the relationship between income and demand which as we have already discussed, is positive for superior goods and negative for inferior goods. In the present context, income effect is just a way of understanding the price effect. Thus,

$$P\!\downarrow \quad I\!\uparrow \quad D_S\!\uparrow$$

$$P\!\downarrow \quad I\!\uparrow \quad D_I\!\downarrow$$

where, P is the price of X, I is the real income of the consumer, D_S is the demand for X if it is a superior good and D_I is the demand for X, if it is an inferior good.

Any change in the price of a good gives rise to both the income effect and the substitution effect. Hence, the *price effect* is the sum total of the income effect and the substitution effect. For superior goods, both the income and the substitution effects are negative. On the other hand, for inferior goods while the substitution effect is negative, the income effect is positive.

This behaviour of the income and substitution effects gives rise to the following:

1. For superior goods, the price effect is always negative.
2. For inferior goods, the price effect is negative if the negative substitution effect is greater than the positive income effect.
3. For inferior goods, the price effect is positive if the positive income effect is more than the negative substitution effect.

Hence, even for intra-marginal buyers, the law of demand holds good for situations 1. and 2. The only exception is situation 3. which refers to inferior goods, alternatively known as Giffen goods.

These three situations can be diagrammatically illustrated as in Figure 4.8.

Consider the case of a superior good as in Figure 4.8, situation 1. Let the budget line of the consumer be AB. Let IC_1 be the indifference curve for the consumer and E_1 be the equilibrium point where the budget line becomes a tangent to the indifference curve. Now let the price of X decrease. The corresponding new budget line will be AC. The consumer will achieve equilibrium on a higher indifference curve. Let this curve be IC_2 and the point of equilibrium be E_3. So the price effect is $E_1 \rightarrow E_3$. Now we will break this price effect into two parts, i.e. the income effect and the substitution effect. We know that when income changes, the budget line moves parallel to the original line. Draw a line parallel to AC. Label this line $A'C'$. Move it towards the origin until it becomes tangent to IC_1. The point where it becomes tangential to IC_1 is labelled E_2. It may be noted that E_1 and E_2 are on the same indifference curve IC_1. Thus $E_1 \rightarrow E_2$ gives the substitution effect and $E_2 \rightarrow E_3$ indicates the income effect.

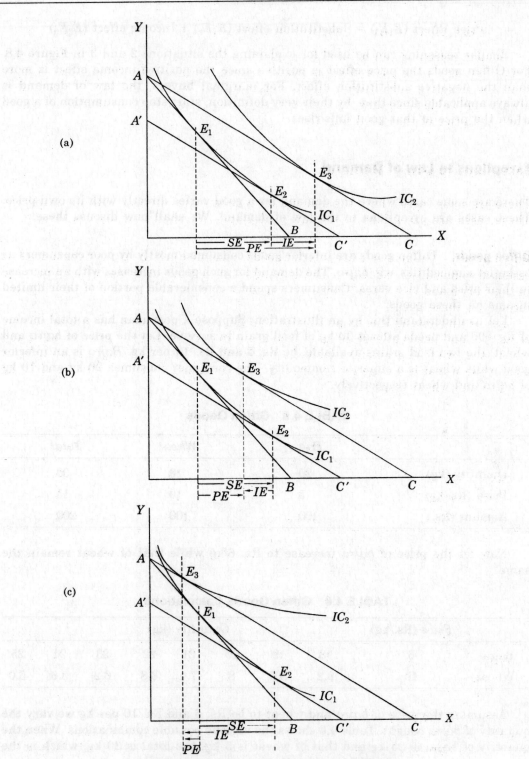

FIGURE 4.8 Income and Substitution Effects

$$\text{Price Effect } (E_1E_3) = \text{Substitution effect } (E_1E_2) + \text{Income effect } (E_2E_3)$$

Similar reasoning can be used for explaining the situations 2 and 3 in Figure 4.8. For Giffen goods the price effect is positive since the positive income effect is more than the negative substitution effect. For marginal buyers, the law of demand is always applicable since they, by their very definition, start/stop consumption of a good when the price of that good falls/rises.

Exceptions to Law of Demand

There are some cases where the demand for a good varies directly with its own price. These cases are exceptions to the law of demand. We shall now discuss these.

Giffen goods. Giffen goods are inferior goods consumed mostly by poor consumers as essential commodities, e.g. *bajra*. The demand for such goods increases with an increase in their price and vice versa. Consumers spend a considerable portion of their limited income on these goods.

Let us understand this by an illustration. Suppose a poor man has a total income of Rs. 200 and needs atleast 30 kg of food grain to survive. Let the price of *bajra* and wheat, the two food grains available, be Rs. 5 and Rs. 10 per kg. *Bajra* is an inferior good while wheat is a superior commodity. The consumer consumes 20 kg and 10 kg of *bajra* and wheat respectively.

TABLE 4.5   Giffen Goods

	Bajra	*Wheat*	*Total*
Quantity (kg)	20	10	30
Price (Rs./kg)	5	10	15
Amount (Rs.)	100	100	200

Now let the price of *bajra* increase to Rs. 6/kg while that of wheat remain the same.

TABLE 4.6   Giffen Goods Calculations

	Price (Rs./kg)		*Quantity* (kg)							
Bajra	6		18	19	20	21	22	23	24	25
Wheat	10		9.2	8.6	8	7.4	6.8	6.2	5.6	5.0

Assuming the price of *bajra* and wheat to be Rs. 6 and Rs. 10 per kg we vary the quantity of *bajra* bought. Table 4.6 shows the various possible combinations. When the quantity of *bajra* is 25 kg and that of wheat is 5 kg, the total is 30 kg, which is the minimum required essential consumption. Thus, as is clear from the example, when the price of *bajra* increases, its demand also increases.

Costly luxury goods.   Luxury goods are those that are not essential for the survival of human beings. Costly luxury goods denote luxury items for rich people. Otherwise, luxury goods can be different for different classes of people. Thus, goods like diamonds, antiques, air conditioners, etc. are luxury goods. For such goods, the demand increases with an increase in price and vice versa. This happens because the utility of such goods is proportional to the price. The higher the price, the greater the utility to the consumer. It is due to this fact that rich people attach a lot of value to costly luxury goods that distinguish them from the common people. These goods have a *prestige value* for the upper strata of society. Whenever the price of such goods rises, their prestige value increases and hence the demand for them goes up.

Speculative goods.   Speculative goods such as shares do not follow the law of demand. For these goods, whenever the prices rise, the traders of such goods expect the prices to rise further. So they buy more such goods in the hope of selling them later at a higher price. The same applies to traders selling speculative goods when their prices fall. Thus, demand varies directly with price.

Outdated goods.   Goods that go out of use due to advancements in the underlying technology are called *outdated goods*. These are generally durable goods such as radio, telephone, etc. With the launch of light push button type telephones the demand for the heavy dial telephones will fall even though they may be available at lower prices. *Seasonal goods*, which are not used during the off-season, will also be subject to similar demand behaviour. For example, the sale of air coolers may go down in winters even if they are sold at reduced prices.

Goods in short supply.   Goods that are available in limited quantities or those whose future availability is uncertain also violate the law of demand. Demand for such goods may shoot up even in the wake of increasing prices. Petrol is one such good.

Prices of Related Goods and Demand

Goods that are related in consumption, i.e. goods whose consumption affects the consumption of other goods, are known as related goods. Goods may be related to each other either as *substitutes* or *complements*. A *substitute good* is one which can be used in place of some other goods. A *complementary good* is used with some other goods. For example, bread and butter are complementary goods while butter and jam are substitute goods.

For understanding the effect of prices of related goods on the demand of a good, consider three goods X, Y and Z, where X and Y are substitute goods and Y and Z are complementary goods. When the price of X falls, it becomes cheaper in comparison to Y and consumers buy more of X. Thus, the consumption of Y decreases. Similarly, when the price of X rises, it becomes costly relative to Y and thus consumers shift their consumption to Y. On the other hand, when the price of Z falls, the consumers buy more of it. With the increased consumption of Z, more of Y will be needed. Likewise, when the price of Z increases, the demand for Z falls. With less of Z the consumers will demand less of Y as well. It can therefore be observed that demand for goods varies directly with the price of its substitute goods and inversely with the price of its complementary goods.

Tea, coffee and sugar are three such goods where tea and coffee are substitutes and tea and sugar are complements. When the price of coffee rises, people will buy more tea. And if the price of sugar rises, consumption of sugar will go down and hence that of tea will also decrease. Thus, demand for tea increases with a rise in the price of coffee and a fall in the price of sugar.

Other Determinants of Demand

Other minor determinants of demand are—tastes and preferences of consumers, population, distribution of population, credit facilities, future expectations and advertisements. Demand for goods will increase if the consumers develop tastes and preferences for it, if the population increases, if sellers provide credit facilities to buyers, if the consumers expect a price rise for the goods in the future and if promotional efforts increase.

| QUESTIONS |

1. What do you understand by *demand*?
2. Depending upon whether utility can be quantified or not, there can be two theories to explain consumer demand. Explain.
3. Explain the utility analysis for understanding consumer behaviour and demand.
4. Explain the indifference curve analysis for understanding demand.
5. What is the law of diminishing marginal utility? Explain the law with the help of an empirical example.
6. What are indifference curves? Write down the properties of indifference curves.
7. Explain the law of diminishing marginal rate of substitution.
8. Categorize demand into its broadly identifiable types with proper examples.
9. There are always certain factors that affect the consumer's demand. Describe the important determinants of demand.
10. Explain the law of demand. What are the exceptions to this law?
11. What are Giffen goods? Explain their price-demand behaviour with the help of an example.

12. 'The law of demand is always applicable to marginal buyers and is usually applicable to intra-marginal buyers.' Comment.

13. State which of the following statements are *true* and which are *false*:
    (a) Indifference curve analysis treats utility as cardinal.
    (b) The indifference curves are convex to the origin.
    (c) A budget line represents all combinations of two products that can be purchased with a given amount of money.
    (d) The consumer is in equilibrium when he has maximized his utility subject to his budget.
    (e) The marginal rate of substitution is the slope of the budget line.
    (f) Shares are an exception to the law of demand.

14. Rajesh consumes two varieties of fruits: apples and mangoes. At a given point of time, mangoes cost twice as much as apples. If he wishes to maximize his utility, how much marginal utility will be derived from mangoes? (It is known that Rajesh derives 8 utils from the consumption of an additional apple.)

15. Shyam is ready to sacrifice 4 pastries for an additional burger in order to maintain the same level of total utility in his breakfast. Find out the marginal rate of substitution for pastries.

CASE STUDY

Case 4.1 Automobiles Riding High

AUTO sector stocks were the darlings of the market during the bull run of 2003–04. The reason for the spurt in investment interest in auto stocks in 2003–04 was quite obvious. After years of teetering growth, punctuated by periods of surge, passenger vehicle sales (including exports) crossed the one-million-unit mark and exports of auto components went past the historic $1-billion level for the first time. Investor interest in auto sector stocks was widespread and companies that were even remotely associated with the automobile industry hit new highs, riding a wave of interest during the year.

With arrival of a new government and its uncertainty over the policies for the auto sector has brought down the valuations of auto stocks. A return to peak valuations will depend on the outlook for the next few years. From the manufacturer's perspective, the challenges will be two-pronged: One will be related to costs and operational efficiencies, and the other to sustaining the demand growth among customers.

From the point of view of sustaining demand growth among customers, manufacturers will face the key challenge of affordability. Affordability is likely to be affected by the increasing fuel prices. Further, interest rates for financing cars are unlikely to go down any further this year. If at all, the lower financing rates can only be offered through subventions that the manufacturer, dealer and financier trio will have to contribute towards. Another factor that will affect the affordability parameter will be the lack of an incentive in the form of a cut in excise duties. The previous two cuts in excise duties, which brought it down to the current 24 per cent, have been nearly erased by the price hikes that car manufacturers effected over the last two years.

A study by the National Council for Applied Economic Research (NCAER) in 2001–02 found that the price elasticity of demand for passenger cars was a high 1.8 units. This meant that for a percentage point reduction in the sticker price of a car, there would be a more than commensurate 1.8 percentage point increase in the demand for the vehicle. So, kick-starting demand in the passenger car segment through a cut in duties is very effective in the short term. The NCAER study on passenger cars and utility vehicles also projected the size of the industry to more than double by the year 2011–12 from 2002–03 levels. From about 7.43 lakh vehicles in 2002–03, the demand for cars and multi-utility vehicles was projected to reach about 15 lakh vehicles by 2011–12.

From being saddled with excess production capacities at the turn of century, the rapid growth in demand in the domestic and export markets has, in just four years, changed the situation to one where many of the leading passenger vehicle manufacturers are looking at a second round of expansion in production capacities to cater to future demand growth.

The growth in demand for passenger vehicles in the next two years will determine the future course of the industry. However, the 27.4 per cent growth in sales of cars and utility vehicles during 2003-04 will be difficult to replicate for the industry during the current fiscal, partly also because the industry's size, at a million vehicles, has now reached a critical position.

As a result, the growth expectations for sales volumes in the domestic market will have to be tempered down for the next two years. However, with India's emergence as a destination for manufacture of quality sub-compact (small) cars, there is a strong likelihood of exports growing at a faster clip than domestic demand. Overall, the industry seems set to witness a doubling of production volumes during the next six years to over two million vehicles by 2010–11. That translates into a compounded annual growth rate of just over 12 per cent.

Studies have shown that in case of USA and Japan there exists a positive correlation between the development of roads and automobile sales especially passenger car sales. In China, car sale grew strongly in the initial stages of country's road development program. India is in a stage of major road development program, with the ambitious Golden Quadrilateral and NSEW corridor underway, and a similar growth in automobile sales can be expected in India also.

As per the estimates of NHAI and CMIE, at the end of FY '04 India had a total road network of 3,300,000 km. Previously also Indian car demand did not respond to its potential, partly because of absence of adequate road infrastructure. Now with the golden quadrilateral almost half-complete and the NSEW corridor coming up at a fast pace, car demand is likely to increase. Broadening of national highways is having a significant effect on the automobile sector and is likely to drive the automobile growth in a significant way. The national highway development program is running on schedule and the timely completion will be a major infrastructural boost for the Indian economy.

The country's weak road network has received a considerable boost from the implementation of the National Highway and related projects. The improving network should improve the speed and comfort of road transportation and also have a benign impact on passenger car demand.

Using the theory of demand analysis, write a note on the demand outlook for the auto sector, substantiating it with appropriate statistics where applicable. What were the reasons for the auto sector stocks to loose their attractiveness? Also identify the major demand drivers for the auto sector?

(*Source:* The Hindu Business Line, June 06, 2004)

Elasticity of Demand

* the concept of elasticity
* various elasticities of demand
* the relationship between total revenue and elasticity

 ## CHANGES IN DEMAND

In the previous chapter, we discussed the determinants of demand. A relationship was established between demand and the factors affecting it. However, the analysis will remain incomplete till we discuss how much demand changes in response to various factors. It is very important for a manager to know the quantitative change in demand due to a given change in the variables influencing demand. It will then be possible to accurately determine demand under a given set of conditions.

 ## DEMAND FUNCTION

A *function* is the mathematical relationship of a variable with its determinants.

$$y = f(x) \tag{5.1}$$

Here, y is a function of x. That is, x determines y. Thus, demand function is the relationship of demand with the determinants that influence it.

$$D_x = f(I, P_x, P_s, P_c, A, ...) \tag{5.2}$$

where

D_x = Demand for the good X

$$I = \text{Consumer's income}$$
$$P_x = \text{Price of the good } X$$
$$P_s = \text{Price of substitute goods}$$
$$P_c = \text{Price of complementary goods}$$
$$A = \text{Advertisements expenditure.}$$

Equation (5.2) is a typical demand function. It shows the dependence of demand on the variables affecting it. These variables can either be under the control of the firm or outside it. Variables that can be controlled by the firm, i.e. those that are internal to the firm, are called *endogenous variables* while those beyond the control of the firm are known as *exogenous variables*.

The demand function must be explicit if the managers are to utilize it for decision-making. An *explicit function* is one where the dependent and the independent variables have a clear and numerically specified relationship. The explicit form of the demand function will then be

$$D_x = aI + bP_x + cP_s + dP_c + eA \qquad (5.3)$$

where, a, b, c, d and e are constants and called the *parameters* of the demand function. Quantifying these parameters with a set of assumed values with $a = 100$, $b = -200$, $c = 50$, $d = -150$ and $e = 75$, we get

$$D_x = 100I - 200P_x + 50P_s - 150P_c + 75A \qquad (5.4)$$

According to Equation (5.4), when the income of a consumer rises by Re. 1, the demand for commodity X increases by 100 units. When the price of X increases by Re. 1, its demand decreases by 200 units. Similarly, the demand increases by 50 units, decreases by 150 units and increases by 75 units when the prices of substitutes, complementary goods and advertisement expenditure increase by Re.1 each. On substituting the value of variables, the Equation (5.4) would give the estimated demand for X under the given conditions.

 ## CONCEPT OF ELASTICITY

The percentage change in a dependent variable resulting from a one per cent change in an independent variable is known as *elasticity*. In other words, elasticity is the measure of responsiveness of a dependent variable to a given change in an independent variable.

For a function

$$Y = f(X)$$

$$\text{Elasticity of } Y = \frac{\text{Percentage change in } Y}{\text{Percentage change in } X}$$

Managerial decision-making is a crucial task. It involves an array of factors each depending on some other variable. Efficient decision-making necessitates a manager's understanding of the extent of this interdependence. This is made easy by the concept of elasticity. Being a ratio of percentage change, elasticity is independent of the unit of measurement.

Elasticity can be measured in two ways, *point elasticity* and *arc elasticity*. The former is used when the change in the independent variable is very small. A large change in the independent variable and its effect on the dependent variable is understood using the latter. While point elasticity measures responsiveness of one variable to changes in another at a given point on a function, arc elasticity computes elasticity over a given range of the function.

$$\text{Point elasticity } e = \frac{\Delta Y/Y}{\Delta X/X}$$

$$= \frac{\Delta Y}{\Delta X} \cdot \frac{X}{Y} \tag{5.5}$$

$$\text{Arc elasticity } e = \frac{\Delta Y/(Y_1 + Y_2)/2}{\Delta X/(X_1 + X_2)/2}$$

$$= \frac{\Delta Y}{\Delta X} \cdot \frac{(X_1 + X_2)}{(Y_1 + Y_2)} \tag{5.6}$$

Study of any change always involves two values. One value denotes the position of the variable before the change and the other after it. Consider Figure 5.1. Suppose the variables change from state 1 to state 2. Since the variables are inversely related, while X increases from X_1 to X_2, Y decreases from Y_1 to Y_2. In Figure 5.1, elasticity will be different when the original position before change is taken to be 1 and when the original position is taken to be 2.

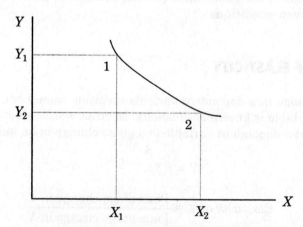

FIGURE 5.1   Point and Arc Elasticity

ILLUSTRATION 5.1 The demand for a product priced Rs. 10/unit and Rs. 8/unit is 200 and 400 units respectively. Compute the point and arc elasticity.

Solution The point elasticity of demand at point 1 is

$$e_1 = \frac{\Delta D}{\Delta P} \cdot \frac{P_1}{D_1}$$

$$= \frac{(400 - 200)}{(8 - 10)} \cdot \frac{8}{400} = -2$$

Similarly,

$$e_2 = \frac{\Delta D}{\Delta P} \cdot \frac{P_2}{D_2}$$

$$= \frac{(200 - 400)}{(10 - 8)} \cdot \frac{10}{200} = -5$$

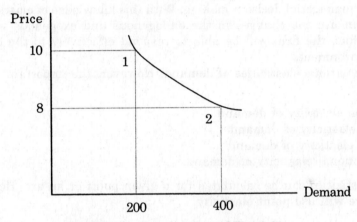

FIGURE 5.2 Computation of Elasticity

In contrast to these, the arc elasticity of demand is:

$$e_a = \frac{\Delta D}{\Delta P} \cdot \frac{(P_1 + P_2)/2}{(D_1 + D_2)/2}$$

$$= -\frac{200}{2} \cdot \frac{(8 + 10)/2}{(400 + 200)/2} = -\frac{200}{2} \cdot \frac{9}{300} = -3$$

It can be seen from the above that point elasticity of demand, between the same two points gives different results when calculated at either of the point. The decision maker thus faces a problem of choosing which value to use. Moreover, arc elasticity, which uses the midpoint of the two extremes on a particular range of a curve, gives an altogether different value than both the point elasticities. This arc elasticity lies between the two point elasticities.

Elasticity of Demand

Now that we have understood the concept of elasticity, let us use the same for establishing the different kinds of demand elasticities. *Elasticity of demand* is defined as the ratio of percentage change in demand to the percentage change in one of the determinants of demand.

$$e_D = \frac{\text{Percentage change in demand}}{\text{Percentage change in determinant of demand}}$$

In other words, elasticity of demand is a measure of the responsiveness of demand to the changes in the variables on which it depends. Demand elasticity shows how sensitive demand is to the changes in the underlying factors in the demand function.

Regardless of whether the underlying factor is within or outside the control of the firm, an effect of its change by a particular amount and in a particular direction is very useful in managerial decision-making. With this knowledge of elasticity of demand, a manager can use the changes in the endogenous and exogenous variables to his advantage. Thus, the firm will be able to respond effectively to the changes in the economic environment.

There are various elasticities of demand. However, the important ones are given below:

1. Income elasticity of demand
2. Price elasticity of demand
3. Cross elasticity of demand
4. Promotional elasticity of demand.

These elasticities can be calculated for a given point or an arc. However, for our discussions we will use point elasticity.

Income elasticity of demand.   The income elasticity of demand is the measure of the percentage change in the demand for a commodity due to a one per cent change in the consumer's income, *ceteris paribus*.

$$e_i = \frac{\text{Percentage change in demand}}{\text{Percentage change in income}}$$

If the demand for a commodity X is denoted by D_x and the consumer's income by I, then,

$$e_i = \frac{\Delta D_x / D_x}{\Delta I / I}$$

$$= \frac{\Delta D_x}{\Delta I} \cdot \frac{I}{D_x} \qquad\qquad (5.7)$$

The income elasticity of demand shows the responsiveness of demand for a particular commodity to the variation in the consumer's income. It enables the firm to foresee the magnitude and direction of the likely change in the demand of its product with the changes in the level of consumer's income in the country.

Income elasticity can either be positive or negative. It is positive when demand has a direct relationship with consumer's income and negative when the relationship between the two is inverse.

From our discussion on the determinants of demand, we know that demand increases with a rise in consumer's income for superior goods and decreases for inferior goods and vice versa. Likewise, the income elasticity of demand is positive for superior or normal goods and negative for inferior goods since a person may shift from inferior to superior goods with a rise in income.

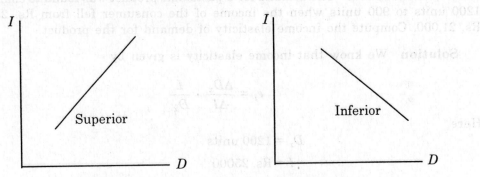

FIGURE 5.3   Demand and Consumer Income

Further, the positive income elasticity of demand can be unity, more than unity or less than unity. It is more than one when the quantity demanded increases at a faster rate than the rise in consumer's income or decreases at a faster rate than the fall in income. For positive income elasticity to be less than one, the relationship will be just the opposite. However, when the rise in consumer's income leads to a proportionate increase in demand of the commodity, income elasticity is said to be unity.

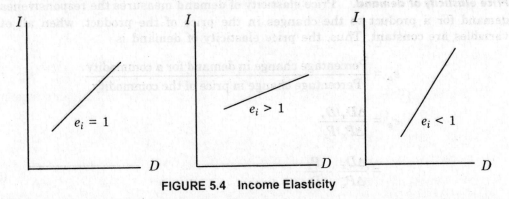

FIGURE 5.4   Income Elasticity

Luxury goods such as cars, air conditioners, mobile phones, etc. are known to take away a larger share of the consumer's income and the consumer buys more of these when his income increases. Necessity goods on the other hand become less important with rising income levels. This behaviour can be seen in goods like food and cloth. Semi-luxury and comfort goods witness a direct and proportionate relationship between demand and income.

The concept of income elasticity of demand is very useful in studying the effects of the changes in national income on the demand for the firm's product. Companies whose products have a high income elasticity will grow faster when the economy will expand. Such firms are very sensitive to the level of business activity. The performance of firms having low income elasticity, on the other hand, will be less affected by economic changes.

ILLUSTRATION 5.2   The demand for a particular product was found to change from 1200 units to 900 units when the income of the consumer fell from Rs. 25,000 to Rs. 21,000. Compute the income elasticity of demand for the product.

Solution   We know that income elasticity is given by

$$e_i = \frac{\Delta D_x}{\Delta I} \cdot \frac{I}{D_x}$$

Here,

$$D_x = 1200 \text{ units}$$

$$I = \text{Rs. } 25000$$

$$\Delta D_x = 1200 - 900 = 300 \text{ units}$$

$$\Delta I = 25000 - 21000 = \text{Rs. } 4000$$

Thus,

$$e_i = \frac{300}{4000} \times \frac{25000}{1200} = 1.5625$$

$$e_i = 1.56$$

Price elasticity of demand.   Price elasticity of demand measures the responsiveness of demand for a product to the changes in the price of the product, when all other variables are constant. Thus, the price elasticity of demand is

$$e_p = \frac{\text{Percentage change in demand for a commodity}}{\text{Percentage change in price of the commodity}}$$

$$e_p = \frac{\Delta D_x / D_x}{\Delta P_x / P_x}$$

$$= \frac{\Delta D_x}{\Delta P_x} \cdot \frac{P_x}{D_x} \tag{5.8}$$

where ΔD_x and ΔP_x are the changes in demand and price of the commodity X, while D_x and P_x are the demand and price of the commodity X at a given point on the demand curve.

But for goods that are exceptions to the law of demand, the price elasticity of demand is negative for all goods. This is because of the fact that the demand for a commodity varies inversely with its own price and vice versa.

Price elasticity varies between 0 and $-\infty$, which will be the respective conditions when the good is completely inelastic or perfectly elastic. Between these two extremes, the values of price elasticity of demand can be clubbed into three ranges using its absolute values. Thus, we can have $|e_p| > 1$ i.e. e_p lies between -1 and $-\infty$ (elastic), $|e_p| = 1$, i.e. $e_p = -1$ (unitary elastic) and $|e_p| < 1$ i.e. e_p lies between 0 and -1 (inelastic demand).

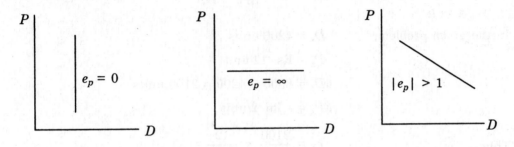

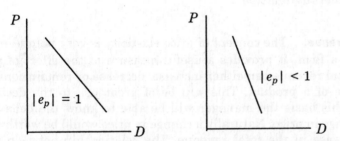

FIGURE 5.5 Price Elasticity of Demand

An elastic demand is where a given change in the price of a commodity induces more than proportionate change in the quantity of the commodity demanded. For example, when $e_p = -4.5$, it is a situation which signifies that for every one per cent change in its price, the demand for that good changes by 4.5 per cent in the opposite direction. Where a price change leads to a less than proportionate change in the demand, it is a case of inelastic demand. For example, $e_p = -0.6$, i.e. for every one per cent price change, there is an inverse demand variation of 0.6 per cent. With unitary elasticity, the quantity demand changes exactly equal to the change in price. While necessities like wheat, milk, have inelastic demand, luxury goods such as cars and fashion items like cosmetics have elastic demand. The price elasticity of demand for cheap goods that are generally consumed in fixed quantities, e.g. salt, is zero.

ILLUSTRATION 5.3 A pen company is able to sell 4,200 units of its latest softgel model pen priced at Rs. 12 per piece. A survey conducted by the company's research team shows that if the price of the pen could be lowered by Rs. 2, the company would be able to sell 6,500 units of this pen. What is the price elasticity of demand for the pen?

Solution We know that price elasticity,

$$e_p = \frac{\Delta D_x}{\Delta P_x} \cdot \frac{P_x}{D_x}$$

In the given problem, $D_x = 4200$ units

$P_x =$ Rs. 12/unit

$\Delta D_x = 6500 - 4200 = 2100$ units

$\Delta P_x = -$ Rs. 2/unit

Thus, $e_p = \dfrac{2100}{-2} \times \dfrac{12}{4200} = -3$

$$e_p = 3$$

as the negative sign is generally omitted.

Price elasticity and total revenue. The concept of price elasticity is very helpful in the total revenue planning of a firm. It provides a useful measure of the effect of price change on revenue. The total revenue can either increase, decrease or remain constant with the decrease in price of a product. This will be of great use to the decision-making process since on this basis the manager will be able to know the behaviour of total revenue with a change in price. Naturally a change in price would be worthwhile only if it leads to an increase in the total revenue. The relationship between total revenue and price elasticity can be calculated as shown below:

$$TR = P \cdot D$$

$$MR = \frac{\Delta TR}{\Delta D}$$

$$= \frac{\Delta(P \cdot D)}{\Delta D}$$

Differentiating partially with respect to D, we get

$$MR = P \cdot \frac{\Delta D}{\Delta D} + D \cdot \frac{\Delta P}{\Delta D}$$

$$= P + D \cdot \frac{\Delta P}{\Delta D}.$$

$$= P\left(1 + \frac{D}{P} \cdot \frac{\Delta P}{\Delta D}\right)$$

We know that

$$e_p = \frac{\Delta D}{\Delta P} \cdot \frac{P}{D}$$

$$\therefore \qquad MR = P\left(1 + \frac{1}{e}\right) \qquad\qquad (5.9)$$

As discussed earlier, the relationships between revenue and demand and price and demand are as given in Figures 5.6 and 5.7.

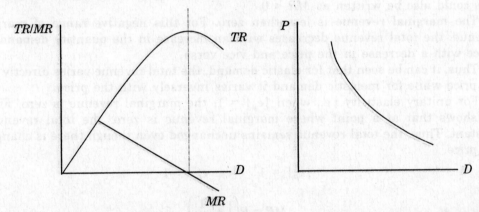

FIGURE 5.6 Total and Marginal Revenue and Demand   **FIGURE 5.7 Price and Demand**

When the demand is elastic, $|e_p| > 1$, the marginal revenue is greater than zero. Thus,

$$|e_p| > 1 \qquad \text{i.e. } e_p > -1$$

For example,

$$e_p = -2$$

$$MR = P\left(1 + \frac{1}{e}\right)$$

$$= P\left(1 - \frac{1}{2}\right)$$

$$= \frac{1}{2}P$$

This could also be stated as $MR > 0$.

For a positive *MR*, as it can be seen from Figure 5.6, *TR* increases with an increase in the quantity demanded. The quantity demanded bears an inverse relation with price, as seen in Figure 5.7 (the Law of Demand). Thus, *TR* increases with a decrease in price and vice versa.

For inelastic demand i.e. $|e_p| < 1$,

$$|e_p| < 1, \quad \text{i.e. } e_p < -1$$

If, $$e_p = -\frac{1}{2}$$

Then, $$MR = P\left(1 + \frac{1}{-1/2}\right)$$

$$= P(1 - 2) = -P$$

This could also be written as $MR < 0$.

The marginal revenue is less than zero. For this negative range of marginal revenue, the total revenue decreases with an increase in the quantity demand and hence with a decrease in the price and vice versa.

Thus, it can be seen that for elastic demand, the total revenue varies directly with the price while for inelastic demand it varies inversely with the price.

For unitary elasticity i.e., when $|e_p| = 1$, the marginal revenue is zero. Figure 5.6 shows that at a point where marginal revenue is zero, the total revenue is constant. Thus, the total revenue remains unchanged even though there is change in the price.

$$|e_p| = 1 \quad \text{i.e. } e_p = -1$$

$$MR = P\left(1 + \frac{1}{-1}\right)$$

$$= P(1 - 1) = 0$$

The above discussion can be summarized as follows:

$|e_p| > 1$, $MR > 0$;   *TR* varies inversely with price
$|e_p| < 1$, $MR < 0$;   *TR* varies directly with price
$|e_p| = 1$, $MR = 0$;   *TR* remains unchanged.

Thus, the concept of price elasticity enables a manager to know the effect of change in price on the total revenue. Depending upon the nature of a product and its elasticity, the firm can now decide whether it should increase or decrease the price of its product in order to increase its total revenue. In other words, the knowledge of price elasticity helps one to understand the fact that an increase in price does not always lead to an increase in total revenue.

ILLUSTRATION 5.4 At a price of Rs. 240 per unit, the shoe company generate an additional revenue of Rs. 336 for every one additional pair of shoes sold. Find out the price elasticity of demand for the shoes.

Solution The relationship between marginal revenue and elasticity is given by

$$MR = P\left(1 + \frac{1}{e}\right)$$

$$1 + \frac{1}{e} = \frac{MR}{P}$$

$$\frac{1}{e} = \frac{MR}{P} - 1$$

$$\therefore \quad e = \cfrac{1}{\left(\cfrac{MR}{P} - 1\right)}$$

Here,
$$MR = \text{Rs. } 336/\text{unit}$$
$$P = \text{Rs. } 240/\text{unit}$$

Thus,
$$e_p = \cfrac{1}{\left(\cfrac{336}{240} - 1\right)}$$

$$= \frac{1}{(1.4 - 1)} = \frac{1}{0.4} = 2.5$$

$$e_p = 2.5$$

Cross elasticity of demand. Demand for a product seldom exists in isolation wherein it may just depend on the price of that product. Often, price of some related product also causes a variation in the demand for a commodity.

Two goods may be related to each other in two ways. Either they can be used together or in place of each other. While the former are known as *complements*, the latter are called *substitute* products. Pen and ink are examples of complements while pen and pencil are substitutes. It would therefore become important for a manager to develop same sort of relationship between the demand for a commodity and the price of related goods. This can be done by knowing the cross elasticity of demand. The *cross elasticity of demand* measures the responsiveness of demand for one product to the changes in price of another.

$$e_c = \frac{\text{Percentage change in demand of } X}{\text{Percentage change in price of } Y}$$

If the demand for the good X is denoted by D_x and price of good Y by P_y, then the cross elasticity between the two can be shown by

$$e_c = \frac{\Delta D_x / D_x}{\Delta P_y / P_y}$$

$$= \frac{\Delta D_x}{\Delta P_y} \cdot \frac{P_y}{D_x} \tag{5.10}$$

The cross elasticity of demand is positive for substitutes and negative for complements. Consider the case of pen and pencil. When the price of pencils will go up, people will replace pencils with pens and will start using fewer pencils and more pens. So the demand for pens will increase. Thus, the demand for pen increases with a rise in the price of its substitute: pencils. The direct relationship between the two renders the cross elasticity positive.

The demand for pens however varies differently with a change in the price of ink. When the price of ink increases, the consumption of ink will decrease and hence the demand for pens will decrease. So the demand for pens decrease with the increase in the price of its complement: ink. Complements thus have a negative cross elasticity of demand.

Looking at the cross elasticity of demand, i.e. its sign and magnitude, one can understand how the two goods are related and to what extent. Zero cross elasticity would indicate that the goods are totally unrelated. Elasticity increases with the increasing strength of the relationship.

The concept of cross elasticity enables a firm to understand how the demand for its product will vary for a given change in the prices of its related products. It thus equips a firm to formulate its pricing strategy in relation to the pricing strategy of its competitors. Thus, cross elasticity also helps in measuring the inter-relation among different industries.

ILLUSTRATION 5.5 Two goods, tea and coffee, are related in such a way that when the price of any one is varied, the demand for the other also varies. It was found that for consumers who are used to consuming tea, the demand for tea fell from 140 kg to 120 kg when the price of coffee was decreased from its current price of Rs. 65/kg to Rs. 60/kg. Find out the cross elasticity of demand for tea and state the relationship between the two.

Solution The cross elasticity between two goods given by

$$e_c = \frac{\Delta D_x}{\Delta P_y} \cdot \frac{P_y}{D_x}$$

Here,

$$\Delta D_x = 140 - 120 = 20 \text{ kg}$$

$$\Delta P_y = 65 - 60 = \text{Rs. } 5/\text{kg}$$

$$P_y = \text{Rs. } 65/\text{kg}$$

$$D_x = 140 \text{ kg}$$

where, x and y denote tea and coffee respectively.

Thus,

$$e_c = \frac{20}{5} \times \frac{65}{140}$$

$\therefore$ $\qquad\qquad\qquad e_c = 1.86$

Since the cross elasticity is positive, the two goods are substitutes.

Promotional elasticity of demand. The promotional elasticity of demand is a measure of the responsiveness of demand for a commodity to the change in outlay on advertisements and other promotional efforts.

$$e_a = \frac{\text{Percentage change in demand}}{\substack{\text{Percentage change in expenditure on} \\ \text{advertisements and other promotional efforts}}}$$

$$e_a = \frac{\Delta D_x/D_x}{\Delta A/A}$$

$$= \frac{\Delta D_x}{\Delta A} \cdot \frac{A}{D_x} \qquad\qquad (5.11)$$

The promotional or advertisement elasticity of demand plays an important role in the marketing decisions of any firm. A low promotional elasticity would indicate that demand changes less as compared to a change in the advertisement outlay of a firm. In such cases, for increasing the demand for its product, the firm will have to incur relatively much higher expenditure on advertisements. The manager should therefore plan for alternative marketing approaches in order to promote sales effectively.

ILLUSTRATION 5.6 Advertisements happen to be a very important factor for pushing up the demand for any product. A company presently sells 6200 units of shoe polish at a price of Rs. 30 per unit. In view of sluggish demand, it decides to increase its outlay on advertising from Rs. 12 lakh to Rs. 20 lakh. If the promotional elasticity of demand for shoe polish is 1.4, find out the new demand for shoe polish.

Solution Promotional elasticity,

$$e_a = \frac{\Delta D_x}{\Delta A} \cdot \frac{A}{D_x} \qquad\qquad (1)$$

We are given,

$$A = \text{Rs. 12 lakh}$$
$$\Delta A = 20 - 12 = \text{Rs. 8 lakh}$$
$$e_A = 1.4$$
$$D_x = 6000 \text{ units}$$

Let the new demand be D

$$\Delta D_x = D - 6000$$

Putting the value of the variables in Equation (i) we get

$$1.4 = \frac{D - 6000}{800000} \times \frac{1200000}{6000}$$

$$D - 6000 = \frac{1.4 \times 800000 \times 6000}{1200000} = 5600$$

$$D = 5600 + 6000$$

$$= 11600 \text{ units}$$

Thus, the resultant new demand for shoe polish will be 11,600 units.

QUESTIONS

1. What is elasticity? How can it be measured?

2. Define *elasticity of demand*. Discuss the important elasticities of demand.

3. 'The concept of price elasticity is very useful in the total revenue planning of a firm.' Comment on the validity of this statement. Derive a relationship between price elasticity and marginal revenue for a firm.

4. Compute the relevant elasticities of demand when the demand for a firm's product increases from 100 to 150 units and when all the other factors remaining constant, the

   (a) Price of the product decreases from Rs. 8/unit to Rs. 6/unit.
   (b) Income of the consumer increases from Rs. 1000 to Rs. 4500.
   (c) Price of the substitute product increases from Rs. 8/unit to Rs. 10/unit.

5. State which of the following statements are *true* and which are *false*:

   (a) Elasticity measures the extent of inter-dependence of two variables.
   (b) The income elasticity of demand is negative for inferior goods.
   (c) The price elasticity of demand is always negative.
   (d) For elastic demand, the total revenue varies directly with the price.
   (e) The cross elasticity of demand is positive for substitutes.

6. The demand for Baggie noodles rises from 6000 kg to 7200 kg when its price is reduced from Rs. 45/kg to Rs. 40/kg. Find out the price elasticity of demand for Baggie noodles.

7. The demand for a particular brand of readymade shirts is found to vary with the consumer's income and its own price in the following manner:

Demand (units)	Price (Rs./unit)	Income (Rs.)
3000	750	5000
3600	650	5000
4500	650	6000

Find out the price and income elasticity of demand for the shirts.

8. The demand for petrol rises from 500 kl to 600 kl when the price of a particular scooter is reduced from Rs. 25,000 to Rs. 22,000. Find out the cross elasticity of demand for the two. What is the nature of their relationship?

9. A firm is able to sell 500 units of its product. Its present outlay on advertising is Rs. 2.50 lakh. The promotional elasticity for the firm's product is 1.65. How much additional expenditure needs to be done on advertising, if it wishes to increase its sales to 850 units?

CASE STUDY

Case 5.1   Reviving Natural Rubber Prices

The natural rubber prices were likely to remain bullish in the next few weeks. Export demand has suddenly revived and so has the post-monsoon seasonal demand from Indian rubber-using industry segments. This month's exports were likely to be in the region of 12,000 tons against 7,000 tons per month in the last quarter of this year.

As the global price of rubber was currently ruling above prices in the Indian market, traders were concentrating on export deals rather than domestic deals. Overseas buyers were also eager to strike bargains. The global price for the RSS 3 grade was around Rs. 57.50–57.75 per kg while the corresponding Indian grade of RSS 4 was selling at Rs. 52 per kg, they said. This price difference had made Indian rubber competitive in the world market.

The demand within the country had also revived as rubber user industries, especially the tyre industry, had stepped up production after the monsoons. Demand from domestic rubber goods manufacturers was around 62,000 tons per month as against the last quarter's demand of 45,000 tons and this demand coupled with export demand would be adequate to sustain rubber growers even through the peak production season.

In tune with the spot market, prices in futures trading had started to rise as well, online traders said. Last month's contracts were done at Rs. 54.40/kg, while current month deals were at Rs 54.70, and deals for the far month at Rs. 55.70/kg.

The increase in rubber production and supply would lead to some selling pressure in the market and this was likely to check any further rise in prices till the production season ended. The rubber crop was likely to be at least 6 per cent larger than the crop size in the last production season, when the yield was 3,20,000 tons. Good monsoon rains and better price realization would lead to improved flow of sap from trees and increased tapping by growers this season.

The development of the past week was in sharp contrast to the slump in natural rubber prices when they nose-dived below Rs. 50/kg and experts had warned of a further fall in prices. Till the first week of the month, both domestic demand and export enquiries were few and far between. The RSS 4 grade was going steady now after peaking at Rs. 67/kg in the last quarter. Rubber growers then were in a state of panic ahead of the main production season, as they feared prices would crash further.

The carry-over stock in the market is expected to be around 25,000 tonnes every month. However, rubber exporters said they were still upset that the central government had slashed the export incentive by 50 per cent. They were of the view that the stock position would be the crucial factor in determining the price level. Unless stocks held by traders and growers came down, any revival in prices would be under threat. It was estimated that a fall in price by Rs. 1/kg would cause a loss of Rs. 30 crore to the rubber farming community.

What concept explains the revival in the export demand of natural rubber? Substantiate your views with relevant computations. How can this concept be used for establishing the future prices of natural rubber?

(*Source:* Business Standard, October 05, 2004)

CHAPTER | SIX

Demand Forecasting

* what is a forecast
* different demand forecasting techniques
* how the least square method is used in regression analysis
* the right choice of a forecasting technique under a given set of conditions

 FORECASTS

Planning is the most important function of managing. In the simplest terms, planning is thinking before doing. It is done to minimize the risks arising out of an uncertain future. The risks associated with an uncertain future can be negated if one tries to make reasonable assumptions about the course that the future is likely to take. Such an estimation of the future situation is known as *forecasting*.

The future can be predicted in two ways. As every variable depends upon some other variable(s), it may be possible to estimate the value of the dependent variables, while disregarding any action of the firm, which will affect the independent variables. Such forecasts are known as *passive forecasts*. On the other hand, if estimates of future situations are made considering the likely future actions of the firm, they are called *active forecasts*. Both the active and passive forecasts are important to a manager in order to ascertain the survival of the firm in the long-run.

Be it the raising of finance, planning of production or setting up of a distribution network, prediction of demand forms the basis of almost all important managerial decisions. *Demand forecasting* essentially involves ascertaining the expected level of demand during the period under consideration. Sales is a function of demand. Likewise, even cost of production depends upon demand. The need for forecasting demand arises because production of any commodity requires time and resources. One thus has to know future demand in order to plan the level of production and make arrangements for the resources to be consumed.

FORECASTING TECHNIQUES

A number of techniques are available for forecasting demand. In view of the important role of demand forecasting in managerial decision-making, it is crucial to use a technique that gives the most accurate forecast with the least possible cost and the minimum use of other resources. Besides accuracy and cost consideration, the choice of a forecast technique is also guided by the urgency of a forecasting technique requirements and the availability of data.

A more accurate forecast will require complex data and be expensive, while a simple forecast will be easy to make, use readily available data and be less costly. Forecasts of greater accuracy will require more resources. The forecasting methods thus range from simple to complex and from relatively inexpensive to expensive. However, the ranking of forecasts is not universal. Which forecast is the best in a given situation, depends upon the nature of the concerned problem. It is very important for a manager to use the right forecasting technique in order to be more effective.

Thus, while choosing a forecasting method, the manager should ascertain the desired level of accuracy, availability of data, the length of the forecast period and the associated costs and benefits. The cost of forecast error also affects the choice of the forecasting method. Where the cost of error is higher, it would be prudent to use a method with a higher degree of accuracy. Less accurate forecasts in such cases would lead to erroneous managerial decisions, which can be critical. Let us now discuss the important forecasting techniques, their advantages and drawbacks. Since a wide choice of forecasting techniques are available and choosing the right technique is crucial, it is important for managers to have knowledge of the whole range of forecasting techniques.

Forecasting techniques can be broadly classified into two categories: *Qualitative techniques* and *Quantitative techniques*. The qualitative techniques obtain information about the likes and dislikes of consumers, while the quantitative ones forecast future demand by using quantitative data from the past and extrapolating it to make forecasts of future levels. These techniques are thus suited to short-term and long-term forecasting, respectively. Forecasts for new products for which no past data is available can be made only by qualitative methods because there is no quantitative data available that can be extrapolated. On the other hand, demand for existing products can be forecasted by employing any of these two methods.

 QUALITATIVE TECHNIQUES

Expert Opinion Survey

This technique of forecasting demand seeks the views of experts on the likely level of demand in the future. Experts are informed persons who know the product very well as they have been dealing with it and related products for a long time. They thus have a rich experience of the behaviour of demand. This personal insight of experts

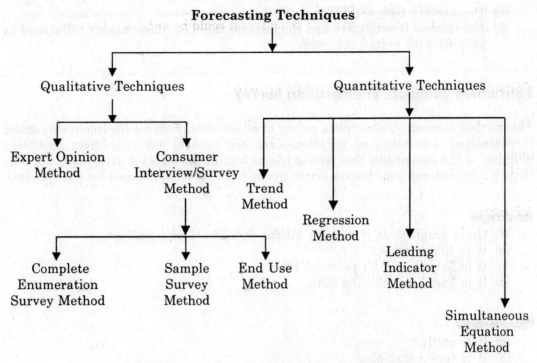

FIGURE 6.1   Overview of Forecasting Techniques

is used for developing future expectations. If the forecasting is based on the opinion of several experts, then it is known as *panel consensus*. This kind of forecasting minimizes individual deviations and personal biases.

A specialized form of panel opinion is the *Delphi Method*. Instead of going in for direct identification, this method seeks the opinion of a group of experts through mail about the expected level of demand. The responses so received are analyzed by an independent body. This method thus takes care of the disadvantage of panel consensus where some powerful individual could have influenced the consensus.

Advantages

(a) It is simple to conduct.
(b) Can be used where quantitative data is not possible.
(c) The forecast is reliable as it is based on the opinion of people who know the product very well.
(d) It is inexpensive.
(e) It takes little time.

Disadvantages

(a) The results are based on mere hunch of one or more persons and not on scientific analysis.

(b) The experts may be biased.

(c) The method is subjective and the forecast could be unfavourably influenced by persons with vested interests.

Consumers Complete Enumeration Survey

This method is based on a complete survey of all the consumers for the commodity under consideration. Interviews or questionnaires are used to ask consumers about the quantity of the commodity they would like to buy in the forecast period. All the data is then collected and added up to arrive at the total expected demand for that product.

Advantages

(a) Quite accurate as it surveys all the consumers of a product.

(b) It is simple to use.

(c) It is not affected by personal biases.

(d) It is based on collected data.

Disadvantages

(a) It is costly.

(b) It is time consuming.

(c) It is difficult and practically impossible to survey all the consumers.

(d) The size of the data increases the chances of faulty recording and wrong interpretation.

(e) Useful only for products with limited consumers.

Consumers Sample Survey

This is a miniature form of the complete enumeration method. Here instead of surveying all the consumers of a commodity, only a few consumers are selected and their views on the probable demand are collected. The sample is considered to be a true representation of the entire population. The demand of the sample so ascertained is then magnified to generate the total demand of all the consumers for that commodity in the forecast period. The selection of an optimum sample size is crucial to this method. While a small sample would be easily managed and less costly, it will be susceptible to larger sampling errors. The converse is true for large samples.

Advantages

(a) An important tool especially for short-term projections.

(b) It is simple and does not cost much.

(c) Since only a few consumers are to be approached, the method works quickly.

(d) The risk of erroneous data is reduced.

(e) This method gives excellent results, if used carefully.

Disadvantages

(a) The conclusions are based on the view of only a few consumers and not all of them.
(b) The sample may not be a true representation of the entire population.

Sales Force Opinion Survey

This method is similar to expert opinion survey method. The difference here is that instead of external experts, employees of the company who are a part of the sales and marketing teams are asked to predict future levels of demand. The sales force, which has been selling the product to wholesalers/retailers/consumers over a period of time, is considered to know the product and the demand pattern very well. Moreover, they being company employees will be less likely to introduce the element of bias in their opinion.

Advantages

(a) Perhaps the simplest of the forecasting methods.
(b) It is less costly.
(c) Collecting data from its own employees is easier for a firm than to do it from external parties.

Disadvantages

(a) Consumer's tastes and preferences keep changing with time. What held good in the past may not necessarily continue to do so in the future as well. The opinion of the sales force may thus be erroneous.
(b) The sales force may give biased views as the projected demand affects their future job prospects.

Consumer's End Use Survey

We have seen in the previous chapter that goods can be either producer's goods or consumers' goods. They can be also a combination of these two wherein they may be used for the production of some other consumer goods and can also be used for final consumption. A commodity that is used for the production of some other finally consumable good is also known as an *intermediary good*.

While the demand for goods used for final consumption can be forecasted using any other method, the end use method focuses on forecasting the demand for intermediary goods. Such goods can also be exported or imported besides being used for domestic production of other goods. For example, milk is a commodity which can be used as an intermediary good for the production of ice cream, *paneer* and other dairy products.

$$D_m = D_{mc} + D_{me} - I_m + x_i \cdot O_i + x_p \cdot O_p + \cdots + x_n \cdot O_n$$

where,

D_{mc} = Final consumption demand for milk

D_{me} = Export demand for milk

I_m = Import of milk

x_i = Per unit milk requirement of the ice cream industry

O_i = Output of the ice cream industry

x_p and O_p notations are similar to x_i and O_i for paneer.

The equation aforementioned can be generalized to calculate the projected demand for any commodity.

$$D = D_c + D_e - I + x_1 \cdot O_1 + x_2 \cdot O_2 + \cdots + x_n \cdot O_n \qquad (6.1)$$

Advantages

(a) The method yields accurate predictions.

(b) It provides sector wise demand forecast for different industries.

(c) It is especially useful for producer's goods.

Disadvantages

(a) It requires complex and diverse calculations.

(b) It is costlier as compared to the other survey methods and is more time consuming.

(c) Industry data may not be readily available.

 ## QUANTITATIVE TECHNIQUES

These are forecasting techniques that make use of historical quantitative data. A statistical concept is applied to this existing data about the demand for a commodity over the past years, in order to generate the predicted demand in the forecast period. Due to this reason, these quantitative techniques are also known as *statistical methods*.

Some important quantitative techniques are discussed below:

Trend Projection Method

This technique assumes that whatever has been the pattern of demand in the past, will continue to hold good in the future as well. Historical data can thus be used to predict the demand for a commodity in the future. In the trend projection method, historical data is collected and fitted into some kind of trend, i.e. repetitive behaviour pattern. This trend is then extrapolated into the future to get the demand for the forecast period. The trend could be linear or curvilinear or have any other complex shape.

Future demand through the trend method can be found by either of the two methods:

- Graphical method
- Algebraic method

In the *graphical method*, the past data will be plotted on a graph and the identified trend/behaviour will be extended further in the same pattern to ascertain the demand in the forecast period. Figure 6.2 shows the past data in bold lines and the forecasted data in dotted lines.

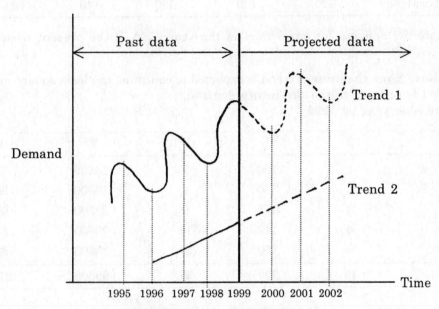

FIGURE 6.2 Forecasting Trends

While trend 1 is curvilinear, trend 2 is linear.

In the algebraic method, also commonly known as the *least square method*, the demand and time data are fitted into a mathematical equation. Some of the most common trend equations are :

1. Linear trend   : $Y = a + bX$
2. Quadratic trend   : $Y = a + bX + cX^2$
3. Cubic trend   : $Y = a + bX + cX^2 + dX^3$
4. Exponential trend : $Y = ae^{b/x}$
5. Double log trend   : $Y = aX^b$

The linear trend is the most widely used mode of time series analysis. It is represented by

$$Y = a + bX \qquad (6.2)$$

where, Y is the demand, X is the time period (number of years), and a and b are constants representing respectively the intercept and slope of the line.

The calculation of Y for any value of X requires the values of a and b. For this two normal equations are to be solved. These are:

$$\Sigma\, Y = na + b\Sigma\, X \qquad (6.3)$$

$$\Sigma\, XY = a\Sigma\, X + b\Sigma\, X^2 \qquad (6.4)$$

ILLUSTRATION 6.1 The following data relate to the sale of generator sets of a company over the last five years.

Year	1996	1997	1998	1999	2000
No. of watches	120	130	150	140	160

Estimate the demand for generators in the year 2005, if the present trend is to continue.

Solution Since the present trend is expected to continue, the least square method is employed here to calculate the future demand.
Let the base year be 1995.

Year	X	Y	X^2	Y^2	XY
1996	1	120	1	14400	120
1997	2	130	4	16900	260
1998	3	150	9	22500	450
1999	4	140	16	19600	560
2000	5	160	25	25600	800
Total	**15**	**700**	**55**	**99000**	**2190**

For a linear equation

$$Y = a + bX \tag{i}$$

The set of normal equations are

$$\Sigma Y = na + b\Sigma X \tag{ii}$$

$$\Sigma XY = a\Sigma X + b\Sigma X^2 \tag{iii}$$

Substituting the table values in Equation (ii) and (iii), we get

$$700 = 5a + 15b \tag{iv}$$

$$2190 = 15a + 55b \tag{v}$$

Solving the set of simultaneous equations by multiplying Equation (iv) by 3 and then subtracting it from Equation (v), we get

$$10b = 90$$

$$\therefore \qquad b = 9$$

Substituting this value of b in Equation (iv), we have

$$700 = 5a + 15 \times 9$$

$$5a = 565$$

$$a = 113$$

Thus, the trend equation is

$$Y = 113 + 9X \qquad \text{(vi)}$$

Since for the year 2005, X will be 10

$$\therefore \qquad Y_{2005} = 113 + 9 \times 10$$

$$= 203 \text{ watches}$$

Advantages

(a) It is a very simple method.
(b) The method provides reasonably accurate forecasts.
(c) It is quick and inexpensive.

Disadvantages

(a) Can be used only if past data is available.
(b) It is not necessary that past trends may continue to hold good in the future as well.
(c) There is no analysis of causal relations between the demand and time series explaining the whys of it.

Barometric Techniques

It has been observed that despite erratic cyclical patterns in most economic time series, the movements of different economic variables exhibit quite a consistent relationship over time. Thus, there is always some time series which is closely correlated with a given time series.

This correlation between two time series can be of three types. Either the second series data can move ahead or move behind or move along with the first series data. Accordingly, when the second series moves ahead of the first series, the second series is known as the *leading series* while the first series is called the *lagging series*. The opposite holds true when the second series moves behind the first series. The series are called *coincident series* if both of them move along with each other.

For example, the Bhuj earthquake in January 2001, led to a massive destruction of property and buildings in Gujarat. This necessitated construction of buildings to rehabilitate the people of affected areas. The construction was followed by a spurt in the demand for cement, fans, tube lights, etc. Thus, one can say that the construction of buildings leads to the demand for cement. In this case, the construction of buildings is the leading indicator or the barometer.

Forecasting techniques that use the lead and lag relationship between economic variables for predicting the directional changes in the concerned variables are known as *Barometric Techniques*. These techniques require ascertaining the lead-lag relationship between two series and then keeping a track of the movement of the leading indicator.

Advantages

(a) It is a simple method.

(b) It predicts directional changes quite accurately.

Disadvantages

(a) It does not predict the magnitude of changes very well.

(b) Finding out a leading indicator for any series is not always feasible.

(c) The lead time is maintained consistently by a very few time series.

(d) The method can be used for short-term forecasts only.

ECONOMETRIC TECHNIQUES

These techniques forecast demand on the basis of systematic analysis of economic relations by combining economic theory with mathematical and statistical tools. While economic theory is used to identify those variables on which other variables depend, the relationship between the dependent and causal variables is estimated through the mathematical/statistical tools. The most commonly used mathematical tool for estimation is the least square method, as discussed earlier.

On the basis of both economic theory and mathematical tools, the equation that best describes the past causal relationship is selected.

Regression Method

Forecasting problems can often be adequately analyzed with single equation econometric models. This is also called the *regression method*. The relevant equation is:

$$D_x = a + bP_x + cI + dA - eP_y$$

Where a, b, c, d and e are constants. D_x is the demand for X, P_x is the price of X, I is the consumer's income, A is the advertisement outlay and P_y is the price of its substitute product Y. Econometric modeling consists of expressing the economic relation in the form of an equation to be followed by estimating the parameters of the system, i.e. the constants a, b, c, d and e. This is usually done with the help of the least square method. Finally the equation is used to forecast the value of demand in the forecast period.

Advantages

(a) As the method is based on causal relationships, it produces reliable and accurate results.

(b) Besides generating the forecast, it also explains the economic phenomenon.

(c) It is neither as subjective as the qualitative techniques nor as mechanistic as the quantitative ones.

(d) This method not only forecasts the direction but also the magnitude of the change.

(e) The method is quite consistent.

Disadvantages

(a) The method uses complex calculations.

(b) It is costly and time consuming.

(c) It requires the use of some other forecasting technique for estimating the value of the causal variables.

ILLUSTRATION 6.2   The following is the price and quantity data of pens sold by a company.

Year	1993	1994	1995	1996	1997	1998	1999	2000	2001	2002
Price (Rs.)	2	1	2	4	5	4	3	8	6	5
Quantity ('000 units)	9	10	8	7	5	6	8	3	4	7

Fit a linear regression line to the data and estimate the demand for pens when the price is Rs. 7 per pen.

Solution   Taking price and quantity as variables X and Y and tabulating them for calculations we get

X	Y	X^2	Y^2	XY
2	9	4	81	18
1	10	1	100	10
2	8	4	64	16
4	7	16	49	28
5	5	25	25	25
4	6	16	36	24
3	8	9	64	24
8	3	64	9	24
6	4	36	16	24
5	7	25	49	35
40	**67**	**200**	**493**	**228**

We then use the least square method to fit the regression line of the form

$$Y = a + bX$$

The set of normal equations for this are

$$\Sigma Y = na + b\Sigma X \tag{i}$$

and

$$\Sigma XY = a\Sigma X + b\Sigma X^2 \tag{ii}$$

Substituting the values of the variables we have

$$67 = 10a + 40b \tag{iii}$$

$$228 = 40a + 200b \tag{iv}$$

For solving this set of simultaneous equations, we multiply Equation (iii) by 4 and subtract it from Equation (iv).

$$40a + 160b = 268$$

$$40a + 200b = 228$$

$$40b = -40$$

$$\therefore \qquad\qquad b = -1$$

Putting this value of b in Equation (iii) we get

$$10a - 40 = 67$$

$$10a = 107$$

$$\therefore \qquad\qquad a = 10.7$$

Thus,

$$Y = 10.7 - X$$

Hence, the regression line is

$$Q = 10.7 - P$$

When, $P = 7$ the demand is

$$Q = 10.7 - 7 = 3.7$$

That is demand

$$Q = 3700 \text{ units}$$

Simultaneous Equations Method

When the inter-relationship between the economic variables becomes complex, the use of single equation regression method becomes difficult. In such cases, forecasting of demand is done using *multiple simultaneous equations*. This is a complex statistical method of forecasting where a complete model is developed explaining the behaviour of all the economic variables.

These variables are of two types. Variables whose values are determined within the system are called *endogenous* while those which are determined outside the model are *exogenous*. The number of equations in such a model equals the number of endogenous variables. The model consists of two basic kinds of equations: *identities* and *behavioural equations*. While the identity equations express relations that are true by definition, the behavioural equations reflect hypotheses about how the variables in a system interact with each other. These equations are solved through methods such as the two stages least square method. A detailed discussion of this method of forecasting is beyond the scope of this book.

QUESTIONS

1. Why is forecasting important to business decisions? Discuss the important qualitative and quantitative techniques of demand forecasting.

2. Explain the various types of survey methods of demand forecasting. How are survey methods superior to statistical methods?

3. Write short notes on:
   (a) Trend method
   (b) Regression method
   (c) Leading indicator method
   (d) A comparative analysis of the various techniques of demand forecasting.

4. The demand for a company's computers has varied with its price in the following manner during the last seven years:

Year	1996	1997	1998	1999	2000	2001	2002
Price (Rs.)	90000	80000	75000	60000	50000	35000	30000
Demand ('000 units)	80	95	110	120	135	150	160

Project the demand for the computers when the price is reduced further to Rs. 20000.

5. The sale of a particular brand of television has been increasing over the years. The demand for these televisions has been 15000, 20000, 30000, 45000 and 55000 for the last 5 years. Estimate the demand for the televisions over the next three years.

6. State which of the following statements are *true* and which are *false*:

   (a) Quantitative forecasting techniques are more suitable for long-term forecasting.
   (b) Delphi method is a special form of panel opinion.
   (c) For products having a large number of consumers, the complete enumeration survey is most useful.
   (d) A large sample is susceptible to larger sampling errors.
   (e) The end use method best forecasts the demand for intermediary goods.
   (f) Regression method combines mathematical techniques with statistical tools.

CASE STUDY

Case 6.1   One billion PC users by 2010

With huge business opportunity that the coming PC boom offers to computer manufacturers, companies are devising plans on a massive scale: the kind normally undertaken by the United Nations. Microsoft has set up an initiative called the Local Economic Development Program for Software, in which the company employees advise government officials on building tech programs. Since the per capita income in these countries, who will be the major growth drivers in the times to come, where those computers will be sold is much lower than in the developed world, a race is on to designing products that are more affordable. Low cost computing is what everyone is looking at to penetrate the new markets.

The IDC says that with a modest PC user base of 200 million in 1995, the market has grown at a rate of 10 percent per year consistently for the rest of the part of the last century. The PCs leaving the factories are expected to grow over time. With almost half of these going to the new users, IDC believes the PC user population will grow to over 1-billion by the year 2010.

Even as the global giants are thinking of ways to design a cheaper PC, local hardware providers are busy trying to capture the markets in countries where the cost is the prime concern of the PC buyer. There is the competition that the hardware manufacturers must fight to get a chunk of the market share. Lower prices are likely to fuel the PC sales further.

In India, HP gave some women in Tamil Nadu solar powered printers and cameras to help them create a business by making ID cards. The women have tended to double their family incomes, not so much through ID cards but rather portraits. In another experiment, HP stocked a van with PCs and wireless connectivity that drives between villages and allows farmers to test their soil, get information about crop prices, or receive advice from agriculture experts in Bangalore.

Meanwhile, global IT research firm Gartner reports that there were 320 million PC users in the beginning of the twenty-first century, which went up to 385 million users within a year i.e. in 2001. The user base thereafter had grown at 20 percent for the next two years and is 655 million in the year 2004. Gartner projected the PC user base to cross the 1.5 billion mark by the year 2010.

Using the concepts that you have learned in the chapter, state which of the two firms is closer to the actual estimate for PC users in 2010.

(*Source:* The Economic Times, October 15, 2004)

Production Analysis

* the concept of production function
* what are isoquants
* how one finds the least cost combination of inputs
* different factor productivities
* the phenomenon of returns to scale

 INTRODUCTION

Production is a process of converting an input into a more valuable output. The analysis of demand is mainly used for planning the production processes and determining the level of production. For equilibrium, supply should be equal to demand. Production is an aspect of the supply side of the market.

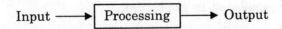

Input ⟶ Processing ⟶ Output

FIGURE 7.1 Production Process

The production theory stresses the efficient use of inputs for producing the desired output. This can be achieved either by using the minimum input to produce a defined level of output or producing maximum output for a given input. Moreover, production does not refer to just the physical transformation of resources. It also covers services. Thus, a production process also includes acquisition of capital resources, efficient employment of these resources, recruitment and training of employees, besides the normal mechanical process of converting raw material into finished goods.

Inputs can normally be combined in more than one way to produce output. Of all the possible combinations, there exists one which is most efficient. Production analysis aims at determining this optimal combination of inputs so as to minimize the costs and hence maximize profits for a given level of revenue. It also studies the inter-relationship between the various factors employed by a firm and their relationship with the output produced.

Production is the process of converting an input into a more valuable output. An input is anything that the firm buys for use in its production process. The goods produced for sale through such a process are known as *output*. The term *processing* includes transportation and storage in addition to its normal meaning of manufacturing activity.

The major production decisions of any firm are related to the budget for the purchase of inputs, the distribution of the budget among the inputs, allocation of inputs to each output and the combination of outputs. However, decisions on inputs and outputs cannot be taken independently. Since they are inter-related, their dependency has to be understood. This is rendered easy by the *production function*.

Production Function

A production function is the technological relationship between the output and its inputs. These inputs are also known as the *factors of production*. For any production process, the factors of production determine the output. Land, labour, capital, management and technology are the five major determinants of any output. The dependent variable, output Q is a positive function of the independent variables, i.e. the factors of production. This can be demonstrated by an equation. That is,

$$Q = f(Ld, L, K, M, T) \tag{7.1}$$

where,

Q = Output
Ld = Land employed in production
L = Labour employed in production
K = Capital employed in production
M = Management employed in production
T = Technology employed in production.

An increase in any of these factors of production, when the other factors are constant, will lead to an increase in output. In other words, all the partial derivatives of the output function, with respect to inputs are positive.

Before moving ahead with the discussion, it will be worthwhile to understand the basic nature of the factors of production. Their meaning is not just limited to what is ordinarily understood. They have a much wider connotation in economic theory. For example, in economics, land does not only mean soil. It comprises of all the natural resources that have exchange value and can be used for producing goods. Such resources include air, light, heat and water, besides the soil surface. These resources can be renewable or non-renewable. Similarly, in economic theory, capital goes beyond money. It is that part of man's wealth, other than land, which yields income. It is not an original factor of production but a man-made instrument of production. It includes a whole stock of wealth consisting of machines, tools, raw material, fuel and consumables. Capital can be *fixed* or *working*. While the former capital can be used for production more than once till it finally wears out, the latter capital is a single-use producers' good. Labour denotes all kinds of work done by man for monetary reward. Management consists of bringing all these three factors of production together, putting them to work and seeking returns while bearing the associated risks.

Generally, the output of any commodity is related to its inputs. Though the determinants may be almost the same, their relative importance varies from commodity to commodity. Consider two commodities, a ballpoint pen and a mobile phone. Production of mobile phones requires larger capital, and technology plays more crucial role in it than compared to a ballpoint pen. Similarly, a diamond polishing process may require larger capital but smaller land as compared to a marble polishing process.

The concept of production function can be better understood by considering two inputs for an output. Although any two inputs can be considered, we take labour and capital since they are the most important variables of all. Thus,

$$Q = f(L, K) \tag{7.2}$$

Different combinations of the two inputs will produce different quantities of output. More inputs should logically produce more output. Say one unit of labour and one unit of capital produce one unit of output. Then more than one unit of labour and one unit of capital or one unit of labour and more than one unit of capital or more than one unit of both labour and capital will definitely produce more than one unit of output. This example can be generalized for X units of labour and Y units of capital producing Z units of output.

Table 7.1 illustrates this reasoning for say, a garment exporting company. The table gives the output matrix for cotton t-shirts for different combinations of inputs. For example, for 2 units of labour and 4 units of capital, the output is 15 t-shirts.

TABLE 7.1 Two Input-One Output Production System

L	K									
	1	2	3	4	5	6	7	8	9	10
1	4	6	7	10	12	14	16	18	19	20
2	7	8	12	15	18	20	28	35	40	44
3	10	14	18	20	25	34	44	52	65	75
4	12	20	30	38	44	55	75	80	90	100
5	14	24	44	53	75	80	92	100	106	110
6	16	28	52	75	90	100	105	110	115	118
7	19	32	60	85	100	106	110	117	122	125
8	20	38	66	92	104	110	116	119	125	130
9	21	44	72	97	105	115	120	124	127	133
10	22	50	75	100	110	118	123	128	132	135

This can also be explained the other way round. A given output of any commodity can be produced employing different quantities of labour and capital. Both the inputs are essential for producing the output and can be substitutes for each other. Different combinations of inputs can be used to produce a particular output. If one input is increased, then the other will have to be decreased in order to maintain the output and vice versa.

From Table 7.1, for an output level of 20 t-shirts, a number of combinations of inputs are possible. 1 unit of labour and 10 units of capital, 2 units of labour and 6 units of capital, 3 units of labour and 4 units of capital, 4 units of labour and 2 units of capital and 5 units of labour and 1 unit of capital all produce the same output of 20 t-shirts. Similarly for the output of 44, 75, 100 and 110 t-shirts there are several possible combinations of inputs. For the same quantum of capital ($K = 10$), the labour increases from 1 to 5 units when the output increases from 20 to 110 t-shirts.

The production function is basically a tool to analyze the input-output relationship. Of all the possible relationships that exist between inputs and output, two are most important to managerial decision-making. They are the relationship between output and variation in one input keeping all others constant and that between output and all the inputs taken together.

RETURNS TO A FACTOR

The *return to a factor* is the relationship between output and variation in one input while keeping the other factor inputs constant. This relationship is also known as *productivity of a factor of production*. It is a short-run relationship. The concept of factor productivity plays an important role in managerial decision-making. It helps in finding out the optimal input combination for a production system.

Factor productivities are of three types: *total, average* and *marginal*. The *total physical product (TPP)* of a factor of production is defined as the total production obtained by employing different quantum of that factor input, while all the other factors are constant. It denotes the total output from a production system. The *average physical product* (APP) of a factor of production is the total physical product of that factor divided by the quantity of that factor while all the remaining factors are held constant.

$$APP_x = TPP_x/X$$

Marginal physical product (MPP) of a factor is the change in total physical product obtained due to the use of one additional unit of that factor of production, while all other inputs are kept constant.

$$MPP_x = \frac{d}{dx}(TPP_x)$$

From the input-output matrix of Table 7.1, we can draw another table for five different output levels of a particular commodity.

The concept of total physical product shows the relationship between output and change in only one factor input, while other factors are kept constant. As seen in Table 7.2, when the capital is held constant at 10 units and labour is increased from 1 unit to 5 units, the output increases from 20 units to 110 units.

TABLE 7.2   Input Combinations for Different Output Levels

Q = 20		Q = 44		Q = 75		Q = 100		Q = 110	
L	K	L	K	L	K	L	K	L	K
1	10	2	10	3	10	4	10	5	10
2	6	3	7	4	7	5	8	6	8
3	4	4	5	5	5	6	6	7	7
4	2	5	3	6	4	7	5	8	6
8	1	6	2	10	3	10	4	10	5

For $K = 10$, we can calculate the total, average and marginal physical product. The results, when different units of labour are used are shown in Table 7.3.

TABLE 7.3   Factor Productivities

Labour	TPP_L	APP_L	MPP_L
1	20	20	—
2	44	22	24
3	75	25	31
4	100	25	25
5	110	22	10

When this data is plotted on a graph, it yields the *TPP*, *APP* and *MPP* curves. It can be seen in Figure 7.2 that the total physical product of labour (TPP_L)

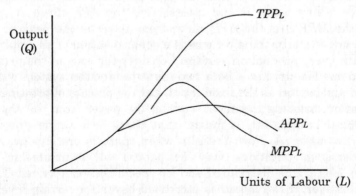

FIGURE 7.2   Total, Average and Marginal Physical Product

increases with an increase in the quantum of labour, when capital is held constant at 10 units. However, the increase is not linear. The TPP_L first increases at an increasing rate up to 3 units of labour beyond which its rate of increase starts decreasing. The APP_L first increases, attains a peak value at 3 units of labour and then decreases thereafter.

The behaviour of MPP_L has also been found to be similar to that of APP_L. But although it moves in the same direction, the rate of rise and fall is more pronounced in the case of MPP_L as compared to the APP_L curve. Thus, it first remains above the APP_L curve, achieves a higher peak of 31 units of output as compared to 25 units of output for APP_L at 3 units of labour. Finally, it falls faster so as to fall below the APP_L at 5 units of labour.

The above behaviour of factor productivities can be generalized. The total physical product increases with an increase in one factor input, when the other factors of production are held constant. However, the rate of increase is not uniform. It first increases at an increasing rate and then after a certain level, it increases at a diminishing rate.

This behaviour of total physical product is due to the *law of diminishing returns*. The law states that as the quantity of a variable input increases, all other factors of production being constant, the resulting output increases, but at a diminishing rate beyond a certain point. In other words, it states that the marginal physical product first increases and then decreases beyond a certain level of variable input, when all other factor inputs are kept constant.

The logic behind the law of diminishing returns is obvious. Initially, as more of a variable input is used, the fixed factor inputs are utilized more efficiently. This phenomenon continues up to a level where there is optimum utilization of fixed factors. Beyond this point, any increase in the variable factor would be useless as the fixed inputs would be inadequate to keep the total physical product from rising at an increasing or fixed rate.

The average physical product and marginal physical product first increase, attain a peak for some value of the variable factor and then finally decrease. The only difference between the two is that the slope of the marginal physical product curve is greater than that of the average physical product curve. Initially, the *MPP* curve remains above the *APP* curve, attains a higher peak but then starts falling faster than the *APP* curve falling below it and intersecting the *APP* curve at some point. This point where the *MPP* cuts the *APP* curve from above is the peak of the *APP* curve.

Thus, the law of diminishing returns is a generalization of an empirical observation associated with every production system. Consider the case of the printing press with one press and one labour. Let it be a two-input production system with labour as the variable input and capital as the fixed input. Let the process of printing a paper include plate preparation, printing the sheet, cutting the paper from the sheet and packing.

If the capital is constant, it means that there is a single press and a defined quantum of raw material. Now, initially when there is one labour, he has to do all the jobs. Under such conditions, very few papers will be printed in a day. As more labour is used, jobs can be distributed and job specialization attained. This will increase the output. However, if the labour is increased beyond a certain level, it will lead to confusion, repetition and excess of manpower. This will lower the efficiency and the benefits received from the employment of additional labour will not be as large as before. The fixed inputs grow much more slowly as compared to the variable input and hence the additional units of labour will be disadvantageous to production. As more and more of labour is employed, but not provided with additional paper, ink and other related inputs, every addition will be less productive. Consequently, the rate of increase in the number of papers printed per additional unit of labour will fall. However, the total output will increase. Thus, we observe that the factor productivity increases due to increased specialization and better utilization of fixed factors, but only up to a certain level.

 ## RETURNS TO SCALE

All our discussions till now have been confined to studying the production function, when one of the inputs is increased while the other input factors are kept constant.' The next question we have to deal with is what happens to the output and how it behaves when all the input factors are increased together, i.e. when the production is expanded exactly to scale. The relation between the output and variation in all the inputs taken together is known as *returns to scale*. It may be noted that all the factors of production are changed *in the same proportion* and *in the same direction*. In contrast to the concept of returns to a factor, returns to scale is a long-term phenomenon. It affects the optimum scale of operation of a firm and its production facilities.

Returns to scale are measured by comparing the percentage change in output with the percentage change in all inputs. The returns to scale implicit in a two-input, single- output production system can be examined through the *isoquant analysis*.

Returns to scale can be of three types: *increasing returns to scale, decreasing returns to scale* and *constant returns to scale*.

In Figure 7.3, when labour and capital are increased from L_1 to L_2 and K_1 to K_2, respectively, the output increases from Q_1 to Q_2. The returns to scale will be increasing if $Q_2 > 2Q_1$, decreasing if $Q_2 > Q_1$ but $< 2Q_1$ and constant if $Q_2 = 2Q_1$.

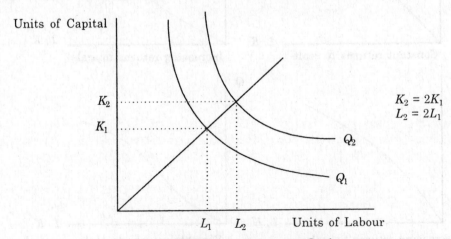

FIGURE 7.3 Returns to Scale

Thus, returns to scale are said to be *increasing* if there is more than proportionate increase in output when compared to increase in inputs. If the output increases in the same proportion as the increase in inputs, it is a case of *constant* returns to scale. Since here the relationship between inputs and output is in exact proportion, the production function is known as *linearly homogenous function*. For *decreasing* returns to scale, the output increases in smaller proportion than the increase in inputs.

For a 20% rise in all the inputs, if the output increases by more than 20%, there is increasing returns to scale. If the output also increases by exactly 20%, the returns to scale are said to be constant. Diminishing returns to scale occur when there is a less than 20% rise in the output corresponding to a 20% rise in all the inputs.

The returns to scale concept can be practically understood by re-examining the production system explained by Table 7.1. Let the system now operate by employing 2 units of labour and 2 units of capital. The output produced is 8 t-shirts.

Now, if the inputs are increased by 100%, i.e. to 4 units of labour and 4 units of capital, then the output increases by 375% to 38 t-shirts. This is a case of increasing returns to scale. Thus, the output is increasing more than the proportion of increase in the productive factors. However, if the inputs are increased from 8–4 (8 unit of labour and 4 units of capital) by 25%, to 10–5 (10 units of labour and 5 units of capital), the output increases to 110 t-shirts from 92 t-shirts, showing a rise of 19.5% only. This increase in output is less than proportional to the increase in inputs, thus representing decreasing returns to scale.

This means that returns to scale vary over different levels of input use. Another interesting phenomenon that can be noted from the analysis is that different percentage

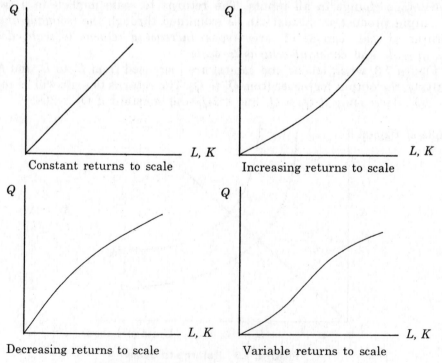

FIGURE 7.4   **Various Returns to Scale**

increases in output result in different types of returns to scale. For example, suppose the firm is currently operating at 5–5, producing an output of 75 t-shirts. If from this level, the inputs are increased by 20% to 6–6, the output is seen to increase to 100 t-shirts, a rise of over 33%. This exhibits increasing returns to scale. But if the inputs are increased by 100% from the same level of 5–5 to 10–10, the output is found to increase by only 80% to 135 t-shirts, exhibiting decreasing returns to scale. The returns to scale can also be demonstrated graphically.

There is yet another way of understanding the behaviour of output in response to a change in all the inputs. That is the concept of *output elasticity*.

Output Elasticity (e_0)

Output elasticity is defined as the percentage change in the output associated with a one percentage change in all the inputs. It is a measure of the responsiveness of output to the changes in all the inputs taken together.

$$e_0 = \frac{\text{Percentage change in output } (Q)}{\text{Percentage change in all inputs } (X)}$$

$$= \frac{\Delta Q/Q}{\Delta X/X}$$

$$= \frac{\Delta Q}{\Delta X} \cdot \frac{X}{Q} \tag{7.3}$$

where,

Q = Output

X = Complete set of input factors = $[L, K]$ (for a two input-one output production function).

It is evident that when output elasticity of any production system is more than unity ($e_0 > 1$), then the percentage change in output is more than the percentage change in all the inputs taken together, i.e. the production function exhibits an increasing returns to scale. Likewise, $e_0 < 1$ and $e_0 = 1$ will represent decreasing and constant returns to scale respectively. Compared to the graphical representation of returns to scale, the analysis of output elasticity is more accurate and precise.

ILLUSTRATION 7.1 Output is always a function of inputs. The output for a product changes by 8%, when its inputs are changed by 6%. If the output to input ratio is 1:4, calculate the output elasticity.

Solution

$$e_0 = \frac{\text{Percentage change in output } (Q)}{\text{Percentage change in all inputs } (X)}$$

$$= \frac{8}{6} = 1.33$$

$$e_0 = 1.33$$

ISOQUANTS

The variation in inputs and the resultant behaviour of output can be understood in greater depth if we are able to determine the output when the inputs are substituted. We shall now examine the role of input substitutability in the analysis of the production function and hence in the selection of an optimal combination of inputs.

The earlier illustration in Table 7.1 had some combinations of inputs which produced the same output of t-shirts. It was also shown that one input can be substituted for another to maintain the same level of output.

If we plot the points representing different combinations of inputs for a given output and join these points, the resultant curve is known as an *isoquant*. Thus, an isoquant is defined as the locus of all those combination of inputs, which when combined efficiently, produce the same quantity of output. In our example, the isoquant is the locus of different combinations of labour and capital that produce the same number of t-shirts. Isoquants are also known as *isoproduct curves* or *production indifference curves*. The word isoquant is derived from its Greek base where *iso* means same and *quant* means quantity. The family of all isoquants represents all the possible combinations of inputs that produce different output levels. The family can therefore also be called the *geometric representation of production function*.

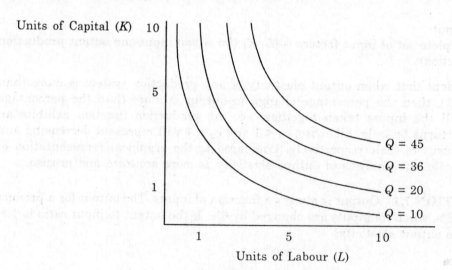

FIGURE 7.5 Isoquants

Isoquants have the following characteristics:

1. *Isoquants have a negative slope, i.e. they are falling curves.*

This can be explained from the fact that for maintaining the same output, if one input is increased than the other will have to be decreased as represented in Figure 7.6.

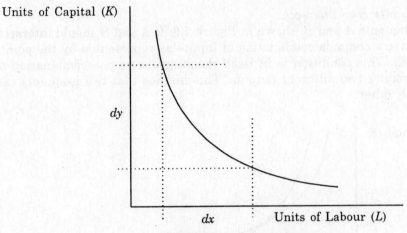

Units of Capital (K)

dy

dx   Units of Labour (L)

FIGURE 7.6   Slope of Isoquant

It is not possible to have the other input constant or increasing when one input is increased. The isoquant would be horizontal or vertical in the former case and rising in the latter. Thus, an isoquant can never be constant or rising because output will always increase when one input is increasing while the other is constant or both the inputs are increasing.

2. *An isoquant, which is farther from the origin, represents higher output.*

Consider two isoquants *A* and *B* plotted in Figure 7.7.

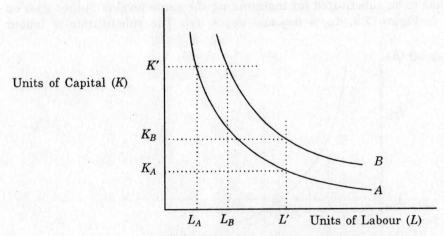

Units of Capital (K)

K'

K_B

K_A

B

A

L_A L_B L' Units of Labour (L)

FIGURE 7.7   Isoquants and Output

Let A be closer to the origin and the B be further away. For the same constant level of one input, it may be noted that value of the second input will be higher for the second isoquant. For L' units of labour, $K_B > K_A$ and for some K' units of capital, $L_B > L_A$. Following the same logic we can say that the higher isoquant or the one that is farther from the origin denotes higher output.

3. *No two isoquants ever intersect.*

Consider two isoquants A and B, shown in Figure 7.8. If A and B should intersect, then they should have a common combination of inputs as represented by the points of intersection (L, K). This condition is in itself meaningless as one combination of inputs can never produce two different outputs. This implies that two isoquants can never intersect each other.

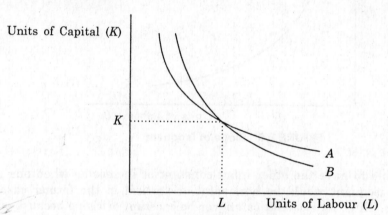

FIGURE 7.8 Intersecting Isoquants

4. *Isoquants are convex to the origin.*

Our earlier discussion on indifference curves had highlighted the law of diminishing marginal rate of substitution. Accordingly, for every successive unit of labour, the unit of capital that has to be substituted for maintaining the same level of output goes on decreasing. As in Figure 7.9, $dx_1 = dx_2$ and $dy_2 < dy_1$. The substitution of labour

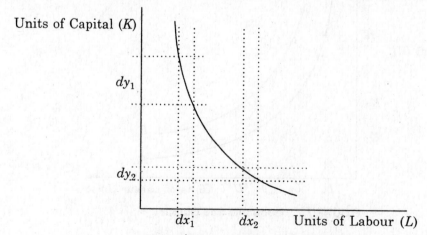

FIGURE 7.9 Shape of an Isoquant

becomes more and more difficult as more units of labour are substituted for capital. Had this not been so, the isoquants would be falling straight lines with labour and capital as perfect substitutes.

Thus, isoquants are convex to the origin. The slope of an isoquant is a measure of the marginal rate of technical substitution. The *marginal rate of technical substitution (MRTS)* is defined as the amount of one input factor that must be substituted for one unit of another input factor in order to maintain a constant output.

$$MRTS = \frac{\Delta Y}{\Delta X} = \text{Slope of an isoquant} \qquad (7.4)$$

The marginal rate of technical substitution usually diminishes as the amount of substitution increases. Our earlier discussion on marginal physical product has shown that

$$MPP_x = \frac{\Delta TPP_x}{\Delta X}$$

$$\Delta TPP_x = MPP_x \cdot \Delta X$$

Similarly, $\qquad \Delta TPP_y = MPP_y \cdot \Delta Y$

For substitution of inputs X and Y along an isoquant the total physical products absolute value must be equal for both the inputs. That is,

$$\Delta TPP_x = \Delta TPP_y$$

$$\therefore \qquad \frac{\Delta Y}{\Delta X} = \frac{MPP_x}{MPP_y} \qquad (7.5)$$

Thus, the slope of an isoquant is also equal to the ratio of the marginal physical product of the inputs. Different points on an isoquant denote different combinations of inputs. As we move along an isoquant, from one combination of inputs to another, one input is substituted for another (Figure 7.10).

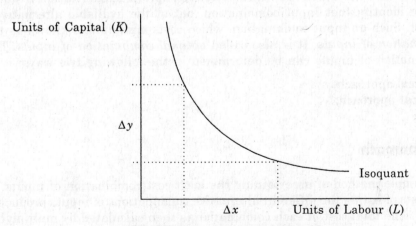

FIGURE 7.10 **Substitutability of Inputs**

Thus, the slope of an isoquant, which is simply the ratio of the change in the capital (*y*-axis input) to the change in labour (*x*-axis input), is the basic determinant of the substitutability of inputs.

5. *Isoquants never touch the axes.*

The isoquants show different input combinations for the same output (Figure 7.11).

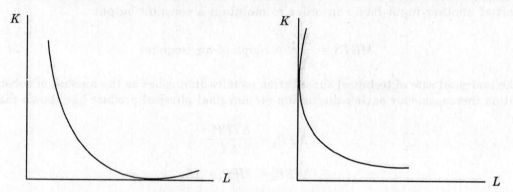

FIGURE 7.11 Isoquants and Axes

However, in none of these combinations is an input equal to zero because both labour and capital are necessary for producing any output.

For similar reasons, isoquants also cannot cut the *x*- or the *y*-axis (depicting labour or the capital).

 LEAST COST COMBINATION OF INPUTS

The ongoing discussions on isoquants have shown us that there can be a number of combinations of inputs for producing any given output. Each input combination, however, would have a different cost. Since the firm's objective is profit maximization it would naturally like to identify that input combination, out of the available alternatives, which costs least. Such an input combination, which costs minimum is known as the *least cost combination of inputs*. It is also called *optimal combination of inputs*. The least cost combination of inputs can be determined in the following two ways:

1. Arithmetical approach
2. Geometrical approach.

Arithmetical Approach

This is a very simple method of ascertaining the least cost combination of inputs. It essentially consists of listing the different alternative combinations of inputs producing the same output. The total cost of each combination is then calculated by multiplying the quantity of each input by its respective price per unit. These costs are then compared and the alternative with the minimum total cost is chosen as the least cost combination.

The process can be illustrated through the example we used in Table 7.1. Table 7.4 shows the various possible combinations for producing 100 t-shirts.

TABLE 7.4 Two-input Combination for Production of 100 T-shirts

L	K
4	10
5	8
6	6
7	5
10	4

Let the prevailing price of labour and capital be Rs. 10 per unit and Rs. 7 per unit respectively. Further, assume as many units of these inputs as desired can be bought at these rates, i.e. they are sufficiently available. The cost of each of the five combinations can now be calculated as illustrated in Table 7.5.

TABLE 7.5 Cost Combinations for Different Input Combinations

Combination	Inputs (units)		Cost (Rs.)		Total cost
	Labour (L)	Capital (K)	Labour	Capital	(Rs.)
1	4	10	40	70	110
2	5	8	50	56	106
3	6	6	60	42	102
4	7	5	70	35	105
5	10	4	100	28	128

Combination number 3 with a total cost of Rs. 102 represents the least cost or optimal combination of inputs for an output level of 100 t-shirts.

Geometrical Approach

An understanding of this approach requires knowledge of isocost lines. An *isocost* (*iso* = same) may be defined as the locus of all those combinations of input which have the same cost, i.e. which can be purchased for a given expenditure level.

In our two-input, one-output production function, the cost equation for inputs can be written as

$$C = L \cdot P_L + K \cdot P_K \qquad (7.6)$$

where

    C = Total cost of inputs
    L = Quantity of labour
    P_L = Price of labour
    K = Quantity of capital
    P_K = Price of capital.

Thus, a linear equation can be obtained for a given level of expenditure and prevailing prices of inputs. For labour costing Rs. 10 per unit and capital costing Rs. 7 per unit, the cost equation becomes

$$C = 10L + 7K$$

If the company has a budget of Rs. 70,

$$10L + 7K = 70$$

i.e. it can buy 10 units of labour with no capital or 7 units of capital with no labour or some in between combination of labour and capital. By joining the two extreme points, we get an isocost (Figure 7.12).

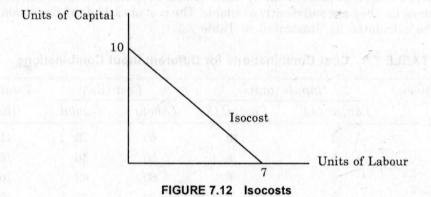

FIGURE 7.12 Isocosts

The higher the budget, the farther will be the resultant isocost from the origin. Isocosts are always straight lines with a negative slope. If a number of isocost lines are drawn, all will be parallel, as factor prices are the same in all cases. Each point on the isocost represents a combination of inputs, the total cost of which equals a constant budget. Isocosts are also known as *budget lines*. The prices of labour and capital will indicate the capital-axis and labour-axis intercepts of the isocost line.

Once the isocost has been developed for a particular budget, we can draw the isoquant for the required output level on the same graph as shown in Figure 7.13.

When the isoquant curve is superimposed on the isocost line and lines drawn parallel to the isocost line so as to approach the isoquant, the point of tangency between the isoquant and the isocost is the point of the least cost combination of inputs. At that point A, labour and capital are combined in a proportion that maximizes the output for a given budget. The budget of such an isocost can be found from the intercept.

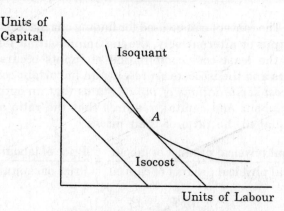

FIGURE 7.13   Isoquant and Isocost

Alternatively, if the entire family of isoquants is superimposed on the isocost for a given budget, then we just have to find the isoquant that is tangent to the isocost line. Any other combination of inputs on that isoquant will have a cost higher than the budget as they will lie on higher isocosts.

Expansion path.   When a family of isoquants is superimposed on the various possible budget lines, all the isocosts will be tangential to some particular isoquant. We will thus have a number of least cost combinations, one each for every output level.

If all the points of tangency between the isocosts and isoquants, representing different output levels are joined, the resultant curve is known as an *expansion path*. Thus, expansion path is the locus of all possible least cost combinations of input for a production function (Figure 7.14). In other words, it depicts the optimal combination of inputs for increasing output levels. Since it covers the entire scale of operation, it is also called a *scale line*.

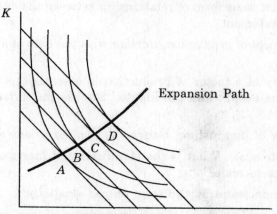

FIGURE 7.14   Expansion Path

With an understanding of isocosts, the behaviour of output, for a given change in input, can be used for managerial decision-making. The production function or the isoquants represent only technological information. Isocosts supplement this with commercial information. The concept can be used for finding out the least cost combination of inputs for a given output or alternatively, the maximum output for a given budget.

The condition that the least cost combination of inputs occurs at the point of tangency of the isoquants and the isocosts represents an important economic principle. The *principle for least cost combinations of inputs* states that an optimal combination of any two inputs, say labour and capital, requires that the ratio of their marginal physical products be equal to the ratio of their prices.

$$\frac{\text{Marginal physical product of labour}}{\text{Marginal physical product of capital}} = \frac{\text{Price of labour}}{\text{Price of capital}}$$

$$\frac{MPP_L}{MPP_K} = \frac{P_L}{P_K} \tag{7.7}$$

The above equation is a simple representation of the fact that at the point of tangency, the slope of an isoquant is equal to the slope of an isocost. The left side of the equation is the ratio of marginal physical products and it measures the slope of an isoquant. Similarly, the ratio of prices of inputs, on the right, represents the slope of an isocost. At a point where the inputs are combined optimally, the isocost is a tangent to the isoquant i.e. their slopes are equal. Thus, for the input combination to be optimal, the ratio of marginal physical product of inputs must be equal to the ratio of prices of those inputs. Any combination of inputs that does not satisfy this condition is sub-optimal. Managers in such cases should look for some other input combination that can produce the same output at a lower cost.

QUESTIONS

1. 'Since production is a process of converting input into a more valuable output, there always exist some form of relationship between the output and its inputs.' Elucidate the statement.

2. Explain the concept of *production function* with the help of a two-input and one-output case.

3. 'The productivity of a factor of production is essentially a short-run relationship between the output and the inputs.' Discuss the different types of factor productivities.

4. What is the law of diminishing returns as applied to any production system?

5. Define returns to scale. What is the significance of increasing, decreasing and constant returns to scale?

6. What do you understand by the term *output elasticity*?

7. What are isoquants? Describe the characteristics of isoquants.

8. There can be a number of input combinations for producing a given output. A firm would always be interested in finding the combination that has the least cost. Suggest a mechanism to determine the least cost combination of inputs.

9. What are *isocost lines*? How do they help in finding the least cost combination of inputs?

10. What do you know about expansion path? Discuss.

11. Combinations of two factor inputs, labour and capital, produce different outputs of a particular commodity as given below:

Q = 50		Q = 70		Q = 95		Q = 117		Q = 130	
L	K	L	K	L	K	L	K	L	K
1	20	2	20	3	20	4	20	5	20
2	12	3	14	4	13	5	13	6	15
3	7	4	9	5	9	6	8	7	11

where, Q = output, L = labour and K = capital.

Determine the marginal physical products of labour for 20 units of capital.

12. The input-output matrix for a firm's product is as follows:

L\K	1	2	3	4	5	6
6	36	40	45	52	59	64
5	30	38	42	48	55	59
4	24	36	40	45	49	54
3	19	30	36	40	45	47
2	14	24	30	33	36	40
1	10	16	24	30	32	35

Draw any two isoquants from the given output data. Also suggest the input pairs, which exemplify the increasing and decreasing returns to scale.

13. The various possible combinations of two inputs, labour and capital, which can produce 100 units of output are given as under:

L	2	3	4	5	6
K	20	15	12	10	9

If the prevailing prices of labour and capital are Rs. 15 per unit and Rs. 12 per unit, find out the least cost combination of these inputs.

14. State which of the following statements are *true* and which are *false*:

(a) Inputs can be combined in more than one way to produce the output.

(b) Returns to a factor are also known as productivity of the factor of production.

(c) The rate of change of *APP* is higher than that of *MPP*.

(d) Output elasticity is the responsiveness of output to the changes in all the inputs taken together.

(e) Isoquants are concave to the origin.

(f) The ratio of marginal physical product measures the slope of an isoquant.

CASE STUDY

Case 7.1   *Mitsui Steel Plant*

Mitsui & Co, the $6 billion Japanese conglomerate, is keen to set up a five million tonne steel plant in Orissa. "We are now exploring the possibilities and gathering information on the prospects of putting up a steel plant here, before coming out with a concrete proposal", said Takao Miyachi, chairman, Mitsui & Co India Pvt Ltd. He said, the most significant aspect of the proposed venture is that for the first time in the country, it will use the latest technology developed by an associate company of Mitsui, which uses non-coking coal for production of steel. This technology will not only help the venture to overcome the crisis faced by many steel industry due to short-supply of coking coal, but also is very cost effective.

Mitsui already owns a chunk of mining lease in Orissa through its Indian subsidiary Sesa Goa Ltd (in which the Japanese company has 51 per cent stake) at Thakurani sector in Keonjhar district. Orissa has one of the richest iron ore reserves in the country, which account for a major share of the cost of production of steel.

Though Miyachi did not specify the cost of the project saying it is still in an exploratory stage, he hinted that the cost could be less than the present industry standard of Rs. 2,000 crore per tonne of steel because of the use of new technologies. Striking a cautious note, Miyachi remarked that Mitsui does not want to join the current rush by various domestic and international steel majors to set up steel projects in Orissa. It will wait and watch and ascertain the atmosphere here before making the move. Besides, steel industry being cyclic in nature, we have to see there is enough demand for the product when the new project comes up, he added.

However, globally one of the key business areas of Mitsui is iron and steel product and raw material trading. The expansion of capacities and volume of business has a priority of place in the company's goal of attaining 100 billion yen income mark within the next two years.

Among other international players, BHP Billiton is also planning an investment of Rs. 7,000 crore in the state for mining and production of steel among other things. South Korean steel giant Posco is also in talks with the Orissa government to setup a 3 million tonne plant in Orissa. Non-ferrous metals major Vedanta Resources— holding company of Sterlite Industries has also lined up an investment of Rs. 12,500 crore to set up a 5 million tonne steel plant in the state, along with development of iron ore mines. Meanwhile, Tata Steel, the country's largest private sector steel company has also announced a plan to setup a 6 million tonne steel plant in Orissa. The company has envisaged an investment of around Rs. 15,000 crore for this project.

Why are so many major international steel manufacturers planning to set up steel plants in Orissa? Analyze the production function for steel and critically comment on the production strategy as envisaged by Mitsui & Co.

(*Source:* Business Standard, September 01, 2004).

Cost Analysis

 ## INTRODUCTION

Profit maximization is different from wealth maximization. While the former is concerned with profits, that is, the excess of revenues over cost, the latter aims at maximizing the net present value of future cash flows that are derived from costs and benefits. Whatever may be the firm's objective, the analysis of costs and benefits is the central concern of all managerial decisions. This chapter will highlight a number of cost concepts and then develop a relationship between cost and output, both in the short-run and the long-run. While on the one hand, cost is the charge on revenue from which profits are found out, on the other, it also forms the basis of price, which is a component of revenue. Thus, cost plays a pivotal role in determining the profits of a firm.

 ## COST CONCEPTS

There are various prevalent cost concepts. Cost is understood differently for different purposes. The definition of cost thus varies from decision to decision. Cost may include price to be paid for a good, its transportation, storage and handling expenses besides other miscellaneous outflows. Since different decisions are affected by different types of costs, it is essential for a manager to understand which decision should consider which cost, that is, he must identify the relevant cost. A cost which may be relevant for one particular type of decision is very likely to be meaningless for arriving at some other decision. *Relevant cost* is defined as the cost that actually affects a given business decision and should therefore be considered in the decision-making process. In order to ascertain the relevant cost to be considered for a particular situation, we need to discuss the various possible cost concepts in detail.

Actual Costs and Opportunity Cost

Costs that are actually incurred in acquiring or producing a good or service are known as *actual costs*. Since these costs are real cash outflows and are generally recorded in the account books, they are also called *acquisition* or *accounting costs*. Any process of production requires input factors to be used for producing an output. Each factor of production has its price. For land, it is rent, for labour it is wages, for capital it is interest and so on. All these costs form the actual costs. Cash outflows in the form of the expenditure/payments made by the firm to the suppliers. Factors of production, are only recorded by the accountant in the account books of the firm.

Resources seldom have a single use. Normally they can be put to use in a number of alternative ways. A firm selects the best alternative and implements it. In doing so, it rejects all the other uses of the resource. Had the resources not been put to use in the best alternative, they would have gone to the second best alternative. Thus, the price of the resource (cost to the firm) must be at least equal to the value of the resource in the next best alternative use. The *opportunity cost* is the notional cost of sacrificing the alternatives. In other words, it is the value of a resource in its best alternative use, i.e. the value that must be foregone in putting a resource to one particular use.

Consider a firm that has Rs. 100. With this amount it can either make a fixed deposit with a bank and earn an interest of 10% per annum (p.a.) or can purchase the factors of production for producing t-shirts. Let the cost of land, labour, capital and management be Rs. 20, 35, 30 and 10, respectively. Thus, the actual cost of this production activity will be Rs. 95. The opportunity cost will however be 10% p.a.

Since opportunity cost is a notional concept, it is not recorded in the books of account. However, it should be considered in decision-making. It should be used as a break-even cost. A firm should continue to be in business only till the time it is able to generate more profits than what it would have made in an alternative business, in case of two alternatives, or the next best alternative, in case of many alternatives.

Fixed Costs and Variable Costs

Costs of different kinds behave differently with the output. Some remain fixed over a range of output, while others vary with the output. *Fixed costs* are defined as the costs that remain constant with respect to the output. They might exist even if no output is produced. On the other hand, costs that vary with the changes in output are known as *variable costs*. The rent of building and factory, interest on borrowed capital, cost of plant and machinery, etc. are all fixed costs, while the costs of raw material, wages, etc. are all variable costs. In other words, costs of fixed assets are all fixed costs and those of current assets are variable costs.

However, there are some costs which cannot be so easily distinguished into fixed or variable costs. They are fixed to some extent and variable thereafter. Such costs are known as *semi-variable costs*. They neither remain constant nor vary with the changes in output. For example, the charges for electricity and telephone are semi-variable costs. There is always some fixed charge that has to be paid in these bills regardless of the extent of use, i.e. the number of units consumed/calls made. Besides this fixed charge, the units/calls are also charged on a per unit basis. Similarly, the incentive based salary package of a marketing professional is also a semi-variable cost.

Although in practice the precise distinction between fixed and variable costs is not always realistic, this cost concept is quite useful in managerial decision-making. It may be noted that fixed costs don't remain fixed over the entire period of production but only for a range of production. The behaviour of fixed costs can be compared to a flight of steps.

Explicit Costs and Implicit Costs

Explicit costs are out-of-pocket costs for which a cash payment is made. However, there are some costs that don't involve a cash outlay. They are known as *implicit costs* or *book costs*. While the payment for raw material, utilities, wages, etc. constitutes explicit costs, depreciation and salary of owner, manager etc. are implicit costs. If a building is owned by a firm, then the rent that would have been received had it been rented would become the implicit cost. However, if the building was taken on rent by the firm, then the rent would be an explicit cost. It can thus be inferred that if a factor of production is owned by a firm, its cost is implicit cost while if it is hired or rented then it is an explicit cost. Thus, ownership differentiates between the two types of costs.

Since implicit costs do not involve cash payment, they are often ignored by firms, especially the smaller ones. But it must be recognized for efficient decision-making that both explicit and implicit costs need to be considered. The implicit costs can be measured using the opportunity cost concept. Failure to consider the implicit costs may lead to wrong decisions and over-estimation of profits.

Total Costs, Average Costs and Marginal Costs

The sum total of all the costs: fixed, variable, explicit and implicit for the entire output, is known as *total cost*. *Average cost* is the cost per unit of output and is computed by dividing the total cost by the number of units produced. *Marginal cost* is the change in total cost due to the production of one additional unit of output.

Let the cost of producing 10 units be Rs. 5000 and that for 11 units be Rs. 5050. In this case, the average cost of each unit is Rs. 500 and the marginal cost of producing the eleventh unit is Rs. 50. However, since it is not possible to have small divisible units of output, the incremental cost concept is preferred over the marginal cost concept. *Incremental cost* is the change in total cost due to the production of additional output. Mathematically, marginal cost is:

$$MC_n = TC_n - TC_{n-1}$$

where, TC_n and TC_{n-1} are the total costs for producing n and $n-1$ units of output.

Historical Costs and Replacement Costs

The *historical cost* is a past cost that is actually incurred at the time of acquisition of that asset. On the other hand, *replacement cost* is the current cost of purchasing that asset now. Depending upon the nature of the commodity or asset, the replacement cost will be more than or less than the historical cost. For assets that appreciate with time, the replacement cost will be more than the historical cost. The opposite holds good for depreciating assets. For volatile assets, that is, assets with large price variations, the replacement costs will be quite different from the historical costs.

A machine costing Rs. 2 lakh was purchased 5 years ago. Over time it has depreciated at the rate of 10% per annum. It is presently worth Rs. 1.18 lakh. Here, Rs. 2 lakh is the historical cost of the machine and Rs. 1.18 lakh is its replacement cost. Suppose, the current market price of a company's shares is Rs. 240 per share, as against Ram's acquisition price of Rs. 400 per share, two years ago. Then, Rs. 400 and Rs. 240 are the historical and replacement costs of the share of the company.

Historical costs are useful for accounting and recording purposes. Managerial decisions are for the present and the future. Therefore, they rely on replacement costs. If a manager has to plan his investment it would be absurd if he values his portfolio at the acquisition price. He can liquidate his holding only at the current prices.

Short-run Costs and Long-run Costs

Before we discuss costs in the short-run and long-run, it would be worthwhile to define short- and long-run. *Short-run* is a period during which one or more inputs of the firm are fixed. In the *long-run* all the factors inputs are variable. The fixed factors in the case of short-run are the plant and equipment. Thus, in the short-run, the decisions of a firm are constrained by prior financial commitments and capital expenditure. No such restrictions exist in the long-run. The actual duration of a short-run is affected by the economic life of the firm's assets, the time required to install new assets and the associated degree of specialization in the assets.

Corresponding to these periods, there are short-run costs and long-run costs. A *short-run cost* is that cost that varies with output when plant and equipment remain the same. In contrast, *long-run cost* is that cost which varies with output when all the factor inputs change. While decisions relating to production with a given plant size use short-run costs for analysis, those concerning increasing plant size require an analysis of long-run cost curves.

Accounting Costs and Economic Costs

Some cost concepts are used by accountants for record keeping, financial analysis and control and auditing purposes, while others are used by managers for decision-making. Costs that are recorded in the books of account and are used for accounting, auditing and financial control and are known as *accounting costs*. On the other hand, costs that help in managerial decision-making for achieving the economic objectives of a firm are called *economic costs*.

The basic difference between these two types of costs is of being recorded in the books of account. The concepts of actual cost, fixed cost, variable cost, explicit cost, implicit cost, etc. are all accounting costs. The concepts of average cost, marginal cost, short-run cost, long-run cost, opportunity cost and replacement cost are economic costs. There are no airtight compartments of accounting costs and economic costs. Both these costs are closely related and use each other for decision-making. The development and inter-dependence of managerial accounting and managerial economics substantiates this view.

Accounting is confined to record keeping and control. It takes into account whatever has happened in the past and what is happening in the present. Decision-making, on the other hand looks towards the future. It tries to predict the likely levels of profitability in the times to come and helps the firm to plan its operations accordingly. It thus tends to have a futuristic view of costs.

 DETERMINANTS OF COST

There are many factors that determine the cost behaviour. In different firms there are different factors that affect the costs. In the following discussion we shall attempt to arrive at some general determinants of costs.

Prices of Factors of Production

Total cost comprises of the cost of factors of production and the cost of raw material. When the price of any one or more factors of production increases, while every thing else is kept constant, the total cost of production increases. The nature of this increase will vary from case to case. It will depend upon the extent to which the factors of production can be substituted for one another. If the factor inputs are readily substitutable, it is possible for the firm to replace a costly input by a relatively cheaper input. In this case, the increase in cost will not be as large as what it would have been if the substitution was not possible. Thus, the cost of production varies directly with the prices of the factor inputs.

Productivity of Factors of Production

The productivity of a factor of production may be defined as the unit contribution of that factor to the output. Productivity, in a sense, is a measure of the efficiency of the input factor. A factor with higher productivity will be able to produce a larger output, when other things remain the same. In other words, the same output can be produced by using smaller quantities of the factor inputs which have higher productivity. Naturally, the cost of production in such cases will decrease. Thus, cost of production varies inversely with the productivity of factor inputs.

Technological Advancement

Technological advancement improves the efficiency or productivity of a factor of production. The cost of production is inversely related to technological advancements.

Output

Output is the most important determinant of cost. A larger output requires more of the factor inputs and the raw material. *Ceteris paribus*, larger quantities of raw material and factors of production would mean higher costs of production. Thus, cost varies directly with the output.

The two components of total cost, fixed cost and variable cost, behave differently with the output. As their names indicate, fixed costs remain constant over a range of output while variable costs vary with output. However, this distinction between fixed cost and variable cost holds good only in the short-run, as in the long-run all costs are variable. We thus need to study the cost-output relationship separately for the short- and long-run.

 SHORT-RUN COST-OUTPUT RELATIONSHIP

The short-run cost-output relationship explains the behaviour of costs with varying levels of output in the short-run, i.e. for a particular plant size. It helps to determine the costs for different output levels for a given scale of operations. Since in the short-run we have both fixed costs and variable costs, so the total cost is equal to the sum of both, the fixed costs and variable costs. Plants of varying sizes will display different cost-output behaviour.

The total cost (*TC*) for the short-run is given by

$$TC = TFC + TVC$$

Average cost,
$$AC = \frac{TC}{Q}$$

$$= \frac{TFC}{Q} + \frac{TVC}{Q}$$

$$= AFC + AVC$$

Marginal cost, $MC = \dfrac{\Delta TC}{\Delta Q} = \dfrac{\Delta TVC}{\Delta Q}$ since *TFC* is constant

where

TFC = Total fixed cost
TVC = Total variable cost
Q = Output
AFC = Average fixed cost
AVC = Average variable cost.

As the fixed costs and variable costs vary differently with the changes in output, we shall first discuss them individually and later together to understand the behaviour of total cost. The relationship between the two is explained in Table 8.1.

TABLE 8.1 Computation of Costs

Q	TFC	TVC	TC	MC	AFC	AVC	ATC
0	240	0	240	–	–	–	–
1	240	70	310	70	240	70	310
2	240	130	370	60	120	65	185
3	240	180	420	50	80	60	140
4	240	220	460	40	60	55	115
5	240	250	490	30	48	50	98
6	240	270	510	20	40	45	85
7	240	294	534	24	34	42	76
8	240	360	600	66	30	45	75
9	240	495	735	135	27	55	82
10	240	700	940	205	24	70	94

The total fixed cost remains constant with an increase in output. Accordingly, the average fixed cost decreases. But this decrease is not linear. The rate of fall of average fixed cost goes on decreasing as the output increases. The total variable cost increases with the increase in output. It increases in variable proportions, first at a diminishing rate for a certain range of output and then at an increasing rate. The law of diminishing returns forms the basis of this behaviour.

A practical example will better illustrate the behaviour of total variable costs. Consider the case of a shirt manufacturing company. Let the fixed cost comprise the cost of land, building and machines for cutting, stitching and packing. Initially, even for producing one shirt, one person each will have to be employed for cutting, stitching and packing. Assume that raw material like cloth, thread, etc. are available in the least divisible quantities. The labour will be under utilized in the beginning. Each labour can complete at least ten jobs per day. In that case, the firm doesn't need any additional labour for producing two shirts. However, the requirement for raw material would accordingly double. The other variable costs such as water, power, etc. will also increase. In all, the total variable cost increases for producing two shirts as compared to one shirt but it does not double. Thus, up to a certain level of output, the total variable cost increases, but at a decreasing rate. Beyond ten shirts per day, the firm will require more labour and raw material. This will lead to a spurt in the total variable cost. It will thereafter increase at an increasing rate. Taking the behaviour of total fixed cost and total variable cost as given in Table 8.1 and Figure 8.1, average fixed cost, average variable cost, total cost, average total cost and marginal cost can easily be calculated using simple mathematics.

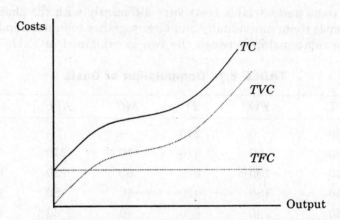

FIGURE 8.1 Short-run Total Cost-output Relationship

The resultant curves for all these costs have been plotted in Figure 8.2. The average total cost decreases with an increase in the output, although at a diminishing rate. The average variable and average total costs first fall, form a bottom and then rise beyond a certain output level. The average variable cost remains below the average total cost. The marginal cost also behaves in a similar fashion with the only difference being that its rate of fall and rise is greater than the average variable and average total costs. Thus, the marginal cost attains a lower bottom than the average variable cost and the average total cost. It also becomes minimum at a lower output level as compared to the average variable cost which in turn achieves its lowest point before the average total cost. The marginal cost curve cuts the average variable curve and average total cost curve from below at their minimum points and rises above them.

In other words, if *MC*, *AVC* and *ATC* attain their lowest values at output levels of Q_1, Q_2 and Q_3, respectively, then $Q_1 < Q_2 < Q_3$ and *MC* cuts *AVC* from below at Q_2 and *ATC* from below at Q_3 output level.

It may be noted that the shape of the total cost curve in the short-run is a function of the productivity of the variable input factors. The productivity of variable factors increases up to a certain output beyond which it decreases. When the productivity of variable inputs increases, each additional unit of output will require less of the variable input factors. Keeping all the other factors constant, this would mean less cost. Thus, the total cost will change by a smaller amount for every additional unit of output. In other words, the marginal cost will decrease. For similar reasons, when the productivity

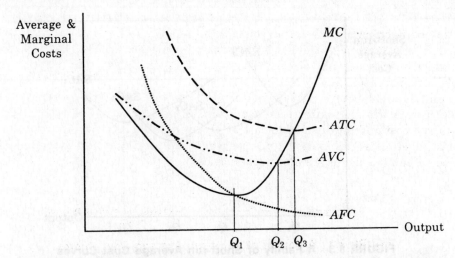

FIGURE 8.2   **Short-run Average Cost, Marginal Cost-output Relationship**

of the variable input factors decreases after a particular output level, the marginal cost increases.

 ## LONG-RUN COST-OUTPUT RELATIONSHIP

So far our discussions centered on the condition that at least one of the input factors (here we have taken plant size) remained fixed. Long-run cost-output relationship explores the behaviour of cost to the changes in output when even the plant size is varying, i.e. all the factors inputs are variable. There is no cost that remains fixed in the long-run. Thus, the long-run cost curve will be a composite for several short-run cost curves, one each for a different plant size. In each of the short-run average total cost curves shown in Figure 8.3, the lowest point of the curve denotes the optimal combination of inputs for a particular plant size or scale of operations. All such points when joined will again give a curve of similar nature but of course flatter than the individual short-run curves. This is termed as the *long-run average cost curve*. It can be observed that the long-run average cost curve is an envelope of the family of short-run average cost curves.

While Q_1, Q_2, Q_3 and Q_4 are the least cost-input combinations for different plant sizes 1, 2, 3 and 4, Q_5 is the least cost plant size for a given technology. As is evident from Figure 8.4, Q_5 is the minimum point of the long-run average cost curve. As against a limited number of operating options available with the firm in the short-run, when it is constrained to operate with a given plant size; in the long-run since even the plant size is variable, the firm has a wide range of output levels on which it can operate.

The U-shaped long-run average cost curve shows that the production system first witnesses an increase and then a decrease as it returns to scale. The long-run total cost also has a varying relationship with output.

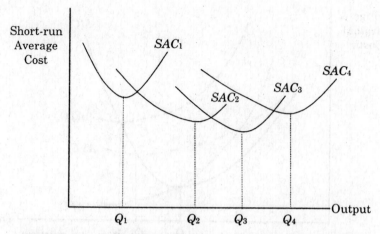

FIGURE 8.3 A Family of Short-run Average Cost Curves

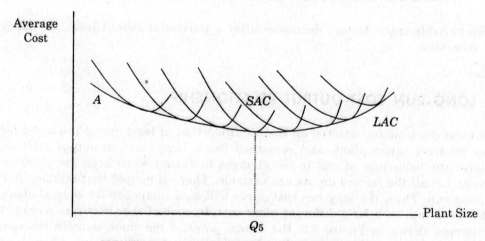

FIGURE 8.4 Long-run Cost-output Relationship

 ECONOMIES AND DISECONOMIES OF SCALE

The economies and diseconomies of scale are a phenomenon relating to the long-run cost-output relationship. As is evident from Figure 8.5, the long-run average cost first decreases with an increase in output, reaches a minimum point and then finally increases beyond a certain plant size. In the first part, when the long-run average cost decreases with an increase in plant size, *economies of scale* are said to exist. *Diseconomies of scale* arise when the long-run average cost increases with the increase in plant size. At the optimal plant size, economies of scale equal the diseconomies of scale.

When we say that there are economies of scale, it does not mean that there are advantages in all the aspects. Normally, it shows that there are advantages in a

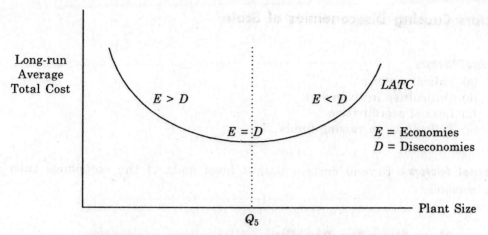

FIGURE 8.5 **Economies and Diseconomies of Scale**

majority of factors. Thus, economies and diseconomies of scale co-exist in all plant sizes. Neither of them is absolute. A decreasing long-run average cost with increase in plant size signifies that economies of scale are more than diseconomies. The opposite happens when the average cost increases with an increase in plant size. Economies and diseconomies may arise out of factors, both external and internal to the firm. These factors can be related to production, market or any other factor of production. Some major factors are listed below:

Factors Causing Economies of Scale

Internal factors
    (a) Specialized labour
    (b) New better quality machines
    (c) Quantity discounts in the purchase of inputs
    (d) Low-cost funds
    (e) Marketing and distribution.

External factors
    (a) Better transportation facilities
    (b) Better repairs and maintenance
    (c) Common research and development
    (d) Recreational and educational facilities for families of employees
    (e) Training and development.

Factors Causing Diseconomies of Scale

Internal factors
    (a) Labour unions
    (b) Difficulties in teamwork
    (c) Loss of coordination
    (d) Difficulties in raising funds.

External factors   Beyond certain output level most of the economies turn into diseconomies.

Larger Plant Size—The Benefits

We shall now attempt to discuss these factors in detail. Up to a certain level, an increase in plant size provides advantages with respect to several internal factors affecting the cost of a product. The increased activity makes it possible for the firm to employ specialized labour for various jobs as it now has sufficient production levels to sustain the same economically. This improves the quality of jobs, which were till now performed by unskilled or general labour. In other words, more and better output can be produced by using the same input with the introduction of specialized labour.

Larger plant size also facilitates the use of newer and better quality machines. Such machines increase the productivity and in turn decrease the cost of production. Increasing output levels also require larger quantity of inputs. The firm can now be in a better position to bargain for the price of input from its suppliers. It can avail quantity discounts for its purchases. They will reduce the cost of the input.

A larger plant size will normally have a larger capital base. Every thing else remaining the same, it will be safer for a lender to lend to a bigger firm. As returns are proportional to risks, the lender will be ready to provide funds to such firms at a lower interest rate. Similarly, increased output up to a certain level can be marketed/distributed with the same distribution infrastructure. This would translate into lower selling expenses, leading to economies of scale.

Increased plant size would also bring advantages to the firm from external factors. Since a larger plant requires the movement of larger quantities of men and material from and into it, cheaper transportation facilities will be available. Such plants will be better connected by rail and road. More machines will mean greater need for maintenance. Larger plants require adequate and specialized maintenance and repair facilities in the near vicinity. These measures ensure reduced costs and economies of scale. Increasing the plant size leads to the development of common research facilities, better recreational and educational facilities for employees and improved training and development. However, these internal and external factors create economies of scale only for increasing plant size up to a certain level. Beyond that level, any further increase in the plant size increases the long-run average cost. For instance, while an initial increase in labour facilitates the use of specialized labour, too many labourers would result in the loss of coordination, delayed decision-making and formation of trade unions. This will result in duplication of work, wastage of time and an increase in the average cost. Similarly, raising funds beyond a certain level would prove to be difficult and costly and create diseconomies of scale.

ESTIMATING COST-OUTPUT RELATIONSHIP

Till now we have discussed the behaviour of cost with the changes in output. While decision-making requires a knowledge of the way in which costs vary with the changes in output, it is more important to know the exact magnitude of cost for a given output. Profit maximization is the most common objective of firms. Profit is the difference between total revenue and total cost. Hence, ascertaining the price and cost of a product and its demand becomes the primary job for any manager.

As we have seen earlier, economies turn into diseconomies beyond a certain plant size, at which the average cost is the minimum. The cost behaves differently with changes in the output on either side of this optimum plant size/output level. One would thus like to know the exact magnitude of change in cost for a given change in output. These can be calculated by finding the exact relationship between cost and output. This relationship can be estimated by any of the following methods:

1. Accounting method
2. Engineering method
3. Econometric method.

Accounting Method

This method consists of estimating the components of total cost separately. For this, the total cost is first classified into fixed, variable and semi-variable costs. Each of these is then measured individually. They are then added up to arrive at the total cost. Average and marginal costs for each output are found making simple arithmetical calculations as we know that $AC = TC/Q$ and $MC = TC_n - TC_{n-1}$.

This method of estimating cost is perhaps the simplest of all the three methods. However, the calculation of various costs for different output levels is a very tedious, cumbersome and complicated task. This requires a detailed breakdown of accounts.

Engineering Method

The engineering method of estimating the cost-output relationship is based on the relationship of the physical units of inputs and output in any production process. In other words, it relates directly to the physical expression of a production function. All plant and equipment have a *rated production capacity*, also known as the *installed capacity*. This denotes the maximum output that can be produced on a particular machine under a given set of conditions. Also, the input-output norms for any production process can be deduced from the practical experience of operators who have been operating the machine over a reasonable period of time. Based on the knowledge of the installed capacity and the input-output norms, the physical units of input required to produce a rated output can be worked out. Once this is done, the cost curve is formulated by multiplying the quantity of each input by its price and summing them up to yield the cost estimates for a particular level of output and repeating the same exercise for different output levels. The prices of factor inputs can either be the current prices or the expected prices over the period under consideration. In this manner the cost-output relationship can be obtained.

Though an effective method for estimating the cost-output relationship, the engineering method has its own limitations. The input-output norms, which are based on the judgement of operators could quite possibly be inaccurate, if not carefully formed. It is also difficult to extend the engineering production function beyond the range of existing systems. Further, the method is susceptible to variations in the factor prices. Despite these drawbacks, the engineering method is superior to the accounting method since it is not based on historical data but on the current price data. It is also a better approach for estimating the cost-output relationship for production processes where significant technological changes are expected.

Econometric Method

The econometric method uses statistical techniques for estimating the cost-output relationship. It consists of three stages:

(a) Collecting historical data on cost and output.
(b) Fitting a functional form with cost as the dependent and output quantity as the independent variable. The commonly used forms are linear, quadratic and cubic.
(c) Applying the least square method to estimate the form chosen in the second stage.

Our earlier analysis of cost and the related changes in output has shown that both the average and marginal cost curves are U-shaped, i.e. they first fall, attain a bottom and then finally rise. The slope of the marginal cost curve on either side is more than that of the average cost curve. This behaviour of average and marginal costs where both are U-shaped holds true only if the total cost is a cubic function of the output.

$$TC = aQ^3 + bQ^2 + cQ + d$$

where, TC is the total cost, Q is the output, and a, b, c and d are constants.

In case of a linear function, the average cost will fall linearly while the marginal cost will remain constant for all output levels, while in the quadratic form, the average cost curve will be U-shaped but the marginal cost will rise in a straight line.

The econometric method can be used to determine both the partial and the comprehensive cost function. While the partial function allows only the output to vary while all the other determinants of cost remain constant, the comprehensive cost-output relationship represents variations in all the factors that affect cost. The accuracy of this method is directly proportional to the size of historical data. The more the data, the better are the chances of finding the most consistent form that fits it. The econometric method is the most systematic of all the three approaches of estimating the cost-output relationship. But it is more appropriate for use at macro level than at the level of the firm where the accounting and engineering methods are more suitable.

QUESTIONS

1. Since different decisions are affected by different forms/types of costs, it is essential for a manager to understand which decision considers which cost concept. Comment in detail.

2. 'The behaviour of costs is determined by several factors.' Elucidate the statement.

3. Explain the short-run cost-output relationship with the help of a hypothetical example. How do the different costs behave with the changes in output?

4. Long-run cost-output relationship is an envelope of the family of short-run cost curves. Give your views.

5. Explain *economies* and *diseconomies of scale*? Are these short-run or long-run phenomena?

6. Discuss in details the factors that cause economies and diseconomies of scale.

7. The estimation of cost-output relationship is a critical task. What are the different methods that can be used to establish this exact relationship?

8. State which of the following statements are *true* and which are *false*:
   (a) Opportunity cost of a decision is the cost of sacrificing the alternatives to that decision.
   (b) Implicit costs are also known as book costs.
   (c) Historical costs are always more than replacement costs.
   (d) Cost of production varies directly with the productivity of factor inputs.
   (e) In the short-run, all the factor inputs are variable.
   (f) The engineering method of cost estimation uses statistical techniques.

CASE STUDIES

Case 8.1 Cutting Costs, Changing Mindsets

'Together we can' was the new maxim being heard across Ranbaxy Laboratories Limited, India's largest pharmaceutical company. The promise was made more than a year back when Project Crusoe was born. Project Crusoe, which stands for Creatively Releasing, Unleashing Substantial Operating Efficiencies, began as a small cross-functional team in Ranbaxy, but soon took the shape of a people's revolution.

Though initially conceived as a cost-efficiency exercise, Project Crusoe has now positioned itself as a change enabling HR exercise in the company. The pharma major had initiated the exercise for real business benefits and hence took the task in the most methodical and scientific manner, identifying broad areas of the business that needed a re-look and getting the right talent within it to overhaul it.

The team was given a clear brief—challenge everything that has come to be accepted as a norm. The team members, working as internal consultants, were to benchmark, question, ponder, suggest and implement better systems within established time frames. The result was ideas that veered clear of current practices, but ingrained in practicality and the current business context. Idea banks, constant brainstorming, weekly reviews and debates made the entire idea generation process into one that gave birth to concepts that could be applied to business, not just discussed and shelved.

Today, the project is delivering in scale and proportion that has surprised the teams as well. Over 15 different areas of spend were addressed in four waves and around 425 projects were identified which are likely to generate savings up to 10 percent.

A director in the company was appointed as the team leader for the project on a full-time basis. Each wave comprised 20–25 executives drawn from various functions across geographies, across layers and functions with the youngest member aged 21 and the oldest 50, which gave a perfect blend of fresh ideas and experience. The cumulative experience of the teams in each wave was close to 300 years.

The project experimented with new technologies and leveraged them to acquire substantial benefits for the company. Two such tools used were online reverse auction and forward auction by the freight team and stores, spares and repairs team. The results re-affirmed that e-business delivers cost-reduction and efficiency and improves velocity of transactions, thereby delivering an improved performance.

What was initially understood to be a euphemistic term for cost cutting has today grown to the size and stature of a regular business function. The company realized very early that cost cutting was no way to define what may ultimately change the way it does business. It was decided to approach the task with the objective of making a cultural change at the organization.

The core focus of each wave was to challenge the costs of business operations, but the third wave also worked aggressively on bringing in a cultural change in the ways of doing business. The fourth wave went a step ahead and brought about a change in the business models. A greater visibility and involvement at the employee level was generated to bring in a change of mindset and attitudes. The first initiative was taken by the Power and Fuel team who created innovative posters to communicate to every Ranbaxian the benefits of saving power and fuel, even in their personal lives.

The company has already implemented around 150 projects so far and the rest are under various stages of implementation. Each Crusoe crusader is responsible for taking ownership of the implementation of the project through the operational cross-functional team, required in the identified projects.

Various communication tools such as thought provoking colorful posters, screen savers across locations have brought in high visibility and participation from all Ranbaxians. The Crusoe team's journey so far was aided by the success of the Crusoe Contest, which generated around 800 unique cost-saving suggestions. The success of the project shows that Ranbaxy has been able to use the power of its people to charter the competitive waters that today's businesses strive in.

Identify the mainstay of Project Crusoe. How did the Crusoe team members implement the project? Discuss the success of the project in the short run and the long run.

(*Source:* Business Standard, February 20, 2004)

Case 8.2 Kwality Restructuring

Realizing the changing needs of the market in the new era, the Kwality group of companies had planned to restructure manufacturing operations across the country. Under a plan being chalked out with the help of Hindustan Lever, with which it had a marketing joint venture, Kwality planned to close small, uneconomical plants and expand capacity at the larger plants. The number of plants in each region would be cut to reduce overheads and operating expenditure.

The Kwality plants were set up when government restrictions were in force, and ice creams were still reserved for the small-scale sector. Now, most of the restrictions are gone, and ice creams have been dereserved. The company doesn't see any reason for three plants in the same area or state. It thus started a process of consolidation through which it hoped to reduce the overheads costs.

The Kwality group was divided into four factions for the four different zones. The northern faction of the Kwality group, led by the Lamba family, had three plants in Punjab. The western faction, led by the Ghai family, had two plants in Maharashtra and one in Goa. There was also another factory in Ahmedabad controlled by the Ghai family.

Some years ago, Hindustan Lever signed four joint venture agreements with each faction. Under these agreements, Lever took over the marketing and distribution of these companies' brands, and formed a strategic alliance for the manufacture of ice creams under the Kwality-Walls brand name. Lever had a frozen desserts plant at Nashik, Maharashtra. However, a good portion of Lever's ice cream sales comprised purchases from the Kwality group. Hindustan Lever was helping them out in forming a strategic plan for the operations.

One would like to have just one large plant for each region. But the decision had to be taken keeping the ground realities in view. For example, a single plant for the western region would find it difficult to service the entire Maharashtra and Gujarat, which are two of the biggest ice-cream consuming states in the country. The Kwality group was also preparing to move out of its Mumbai factory, housed in Worli, in south Mumbai. Sources said it is an expensive location, and the company was looking for a place either in the suburbs or in Pune.

Under a plan being chalked out with the help of Hindustan Lever, Kwality planned to close small, uneconomical plants and expand capacity at the larger plants. The number of plants in each region would be cut to reduce overheads and operating expenditure

Discuss the underlying issue in this case. What did Kwality want to achieve from the restructuring of its manufacturing operations? Outline the considerations involved in the aforesaid restructuring exercise of Kwality.

(*Source:* Business Standard, October 21, 2004).

CHAPTER | NINE
Pricing

LEARNING OBJECTIVES

* the determinants of price and their effect on the pricing decisions of a firm
* pricing for different objectives
* the characteristics of major market structures
* pricing under major market structures
* the rationale for MRTP
* the commonly used pricing methods in practice

 ## THE IMPORTANCE OF PRICING

Of all the managerial decisions, pricing is of utmost importance. Profit maximization continues to be the guiding objective of most firms. Pricing effects profit by affecting both, total revenue and total cost. It affects revenue which is the product of price and quantity sold and cost, which depends upon the volume of production which in turn is guided by demand, a function of the price of the product. Moreover, pricing is a highly volatile decision. One just cannot decide a particular price and sleep on it. The price of a product needs to be monitored continuously. There are several factors that have a bearing on the price and any change in these factors may cause a change in the price. Some prominent *determinants of price* are:

1. Demand
2. Cost of production
3. Objective of the firm
4. Government policy
5. The nature of competition.

The extent to which price is affected by a unit change in these determinants varies from factor to factor. Let us now examine the role of each of these factors in determining the price of a commodity.

Demand

The price of a commodity depends on its demand. Traditionally, price is determined where demand and supply are equal. Keeping all the other factors constant, the greater the demand for a commodity, the more highly priced it can be. This flows from the logic that if the consumer has high utility for a product or a greater number of consumers develop utility for it, the demand for the product will increase. A higher utility will induce the consumer to pay a higher price for the same product. Thus, an increase in the demand of a commodity will lead to a higher price. In other words price is directly related to demand.

Cost of Production

The cost of production is generally the basis on which the price of a product is defined. It is an important criterion even when firms do not adopt a cost-plus pricing method. After all, no firm likes to incur losses in the long-run. It will thus always try to recover at least the cost of production. It thus follows that the higher the cost of production, the higher will be the price of the product. Hence, price is directly related to the cost of production.

Objective of the Firm

Firms with different objectives will price their products differently. Those pursuing the profit maximization objective will price their product in such a manner that they are able to earn maximum profits. On the other hand, those striving for maximizing their sales may settle for a comparatively lower price. The difference in pricing can be demonstrated by a numerical illustration. Suppose a firm has the following demand and cost functions:

$$Q = 20 - P$$
$$C = Q^2 - 28Q + 2$$

When the firm pursues the objective of profit maximization,

Profit, $\quad\quad\quad\quad \pi$ = Total revenue – Total cost

$$= P \cdot Q - C$$
$$= Q(20 - Q) - (Q^2 + 10Q + 2)$$
$$= 20Q - Q^2 - Q^2 + 28Q - 2$$
$$= -2Q^2 + 48Q - 2$$
$$\frac{d\pi}{dQ} = -4Q + 48 = 0 \quad\quad Q = 12 \quad\quad P = 8$$

However, if the firm maximizes its sales

$$\text{Total revenue,} \qquad TR = P \cdot Q$$
$$= Q(20 - Q)$$
$$= 20Q - Q^2$$
$$\frac{dTR}{dQ} = 20 - 2Q = 0 \qquad Q = 10 \qquad P = 10$$

Thus firms with the same demand and cost function price their products differently when they are pursuing differnt objectives.

Government Policy

Pricing decisions are also affected by the prevalent government policies from time to time. Government controls the prices of commodities either directly or indirectly. While rationing of essential commodities is the best example of direct control, taxes and subsidies are the means of indirect control. Imposition of taxes and duties, respectively on finished products and raw material will cause price rise. On the other hand, provision of subsidies will lead to lowering of prices, *ceteris paribus.*

Let the supply function for the firm be,

$$Q = 8 + 2P$$

Under equilibrium conditions, the price of a commodity can be obtained by equating demand and supply,

$$20 - P = 8 + 2P$$
$$P = 4$$

If the government imposes a sales tax of Rs. 3 per unit, the new supply function will be

$$Q = 8 + 2(P - 3)$$
$$= 2 + 2P$$

The price in this case will be,

$$P = 6$$

The Nature of Competition

The nature of competition that a firm's products face is perhaps the most important factor governing the price of that product. The competition is an indication of the relative positioning of a product in the market vis-a-vis its competitive products. It is an aggregate of the number of buyers, number of sellers, degrees of product differentiation and entry-exit barriers. Different combinations of these characteristics yield different types of market structures. Some important market structures are perfect competition, monopolistic competition, monopoly, oligopoly, monopsony, oligopsony, etc. These divisions are on the basis of the extent of competition. The first four structures are most commonly found. We shall now discuss pricing in these four market structures.

MARKET STRUCTURES

Perfect Competition

Of the different kinds of market structures, the maximum competition happens in perfect competition. Monopoly has the least competition (Figure 9.1).

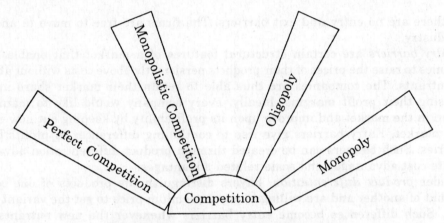

FIGURE 9.1 Market Structure Spectrum

The major characteristics of a perfect competition market are as follows:

(a) There are a large number of buyers.
(b) There are a large number of sellers.
(c) The product is homogeneous.
(d) There are no entry and exit barriers.

In a perfectly competitive market, since there are a large number of buyers and sellers, no particular buyer or seller has any significant impact on the market. Individual trade transactions are extremely small in comparison to the total number of transactions or the aggregate of the goods exchanged and hence unable to affect the existing price-output structure. Thus, the price, as determined by the industry demand and supply equation remains constant. All the market participants have to take the price that is given to them, i.e. individual buyers and sellers are price takers.

As the product sold in a perfectly competitive market is homogeneous, it does not matter to the buyer who the seller is. In other words, the consumer is indifferent to the seller and the seller also has no special preference for a particular consumer. All the buyers and sellers have complete knowledge of the market. Complete information about the demand, supply, cost, price and quality is available freely to all participants.

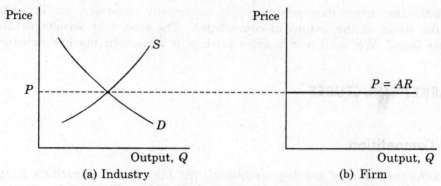

FIGURE 9.2 Perfect Competition—Price Determination

Also, there are no entry and exit barriers. The firms are free to move in and out of the industry.

Entry barriers are certain structural features of a market that enable existing companies to raise the prices of their products persistently above costs without attracting new entrants. The companies are thus able to retain their market share inspite of increasing their profit margins. Ideally, every company would like to maintain its position in the market and improve upon its profitability by keeping out new entrants to the market. Entry barriers give rise to continuing differences in profits between industries. Such barriers can be created through product differentiation advantages, absolute cost advantages and scale related advantages.

Under *product differentiation*, buyers distinguish the products of one company from that of another and are willing to pay a premium price to get the variant of their choice. Such differences become entry barriers whenever the new entrants fail to realize the same prices for an identical product. Although consumers will normally prefer low price for identical products, they may be ready to pay a premium for a product if switching costs are associated with it. *Switching costs* are the costs that occur to the consumers for changing from purchasing one product to purchasing another. These may arise due to several reasons. Habits are an obvious source of switching costs, wherein companies design their marketing campaigns to reinforce the purchasing patterns of existing customers and raise their resistance to change. Consumers also incur costs in gathering information about new products and once satisfied, they are likely to resist making further investments. Switching costs also arise when consumption involves the purchase of highly specific complementary products that lock the consumers into existing purchasing patterns.

Absolute cost advantages arise whenever the costs of the products of existing companies are lesser than those of new entrants. They are thus able to undercut the prices of new entrants up to the point of this difference in prices without sacrificing profits. Privileged access to scarce resources, investments in research and development, government tariffs, subsidies, trade quotas are some of the factors responsible for absolute cost advantages.

Scale related advantages create the most effective entry barriers. These are economies of scale that arise whenever a company's cost per unit falls as the volume of production and sales rise. We have already discussed the details in an earlier chapter. Scale advantages impede small-scale entry. They require the new entrants to either enter in a similar, large-scale or not enter at all. Very few markets develop natural entry barriers and even when they do so, very few companies rely on the structural features of markets alone to protect them from new entrants. They usually need strategic entry deterrents such as sunk costs, squeezing entrants and raising the costs of the products of their rivals to create such barriers.

The market price in a market with pure competition is determined by the intersection of the aggregate industry supply and demand. While the aggregate demand curve for an industry refers to the sum of the quantities that the individual consumers will buy at different prices, the industry supply curve is obtained from the sum of quantities that individual firms are willing to supply at different prices.

A firm may make profits, losses or break-even in the short-run. But because of the condition of free entry and exit, in the long-run firms break-even, i.e. they are neither able to make profits nor do they incur any losses. In the short-run, a firm may make profits if it is able to produce at a favourable cost, low enough in comparison to the market price, in order to generate profit. However, if its cost of production is higher than the price level, it might incur losses and break-even if the cost is equal to the price. In the long-run, the firm can only break-even or make normal profits. If the firms make abnormal profits, then they will attract new firms into the industry. The increased supply will then lower the price. The opposite happens when firms make heavy losses. The loss making firms will close shop and exit from the industry. This will restrict the supply and cause the price to rise.

Figure 9.3(a) represents the case of a firm making profits in the short-run in a perfectly competitive market. Such firms have such a cost curve that the lower part of the average cost curve lies below the average revenue curve. The average revenue curve in this case is a straight line and is equal to price and also the marginal revenue. That is, $P = AR = MR$, because price remains constant. This horizontal straight line depicts the price and is a result of the intersection of the industry demand and supply curves. As we have already seen, the shapes of the average cost and marginal cost curves are such that, they both first fall, attain a bottom and then eventually rise. The only difference is that the rate of the rise and the fall of the marginal cost curve are more than the average cost curve and MC cuts AC from below at its lowest point.

The point of intersection of the marginal cost and marginal revenue curve gives the equilibrium point E. When we drop perpendiculars from this point E on the x-axis and y-axis, we get the equilibrium output and price at points Q and P respectively. Drawing horizontal lines from the point of intersection of the perpendiculars and the average revenue and average cost curves gives us the revenue and cost points on the y-axis, as shown by points P and A. One may note that point P is common to both the price and revenue. This is because price remains constant in this market structure. Here, the area of the rectangle $OPEQ$ represents the total revenue while that of rectangle $OACQ$ shows the total cost. In this case, total revenue is more than total cost. The difference in the two areas, as given by rectangle $PECA$ is the profit made by the firm in the short-run.

Similar logic holds good in the case of Figure 9.3(b). The total revenue and total cost are determined by the areas of the rectangles $OPEQ$ and $OBCQ$ respectively. The

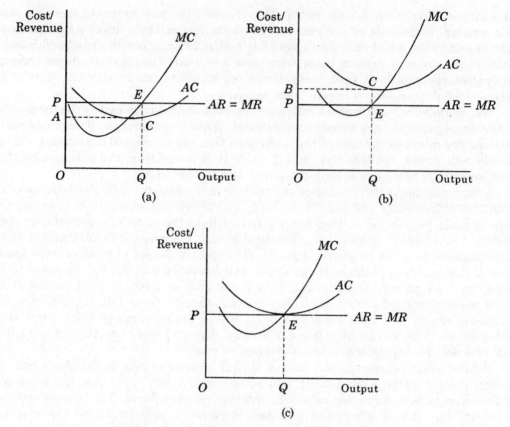

FIGURE 9.3   Pricing under Perfect Competition

difference between the two, i.e. the area of rectangle *BCEP* gives the loss incurred by the firm. The firm breaks even in the conditions shown in Figure 9.3(c), where the *AC* curve is tangent to the *AR* line. Both, total revenue and total cost are the same and are given by the area of the rectangle *OPEQ*. In this condition, there is neither any profit nor loss, i.e. the firm breaks even.

Whether the firm makes profits or incurs losses in the short-run will depend on its cost structure. It will be a measure of the efficiency of production. While efficient firms will be able to make profits by cutting down on the costs of production, inefficient firms will end up incurring losses. And this happens only in the short-run. In the long-run no firm makes profit or loss. They all break even as shown in Figure 9.3(c).

Practically speaking, it is difficult to find a product that could belong to a perfectly competitive market. However, a few products, approximate to quite an extent to such a market structure. Milk, sugar, food grains, etc. are some such products. Take the case of milk. When we go to a new place, the first thing that we want to ensure for the next morning is milk. We do not wish to go into the intricacies of whether the milkman comes on a motorcycle or on a bicycle. We simply ask the neighbour to send us his milkman. The same holds good in the case of sugar. Most of us don't specify at the provision store what brand of sugar we want. We simply ask for the desired quantity without bothering about which company has produced the sugar. There are a large number of buyers and sellers of these products. The products are not differentiated and so the customer is not brand-specific. Nor does the price change frequently. An individual firm or the consumer has nothing to do with the price of these products, which is determined by industry demand and supply.

ILLUSTRATION 9.1   The cost equation for Sweet Sugars Limited is $C_1 = 75Q_1 - 8Q_1^2 + Q_1^3 - 85$. It sells in a perfectly competitive market. The sugar industry's demand and supply curves are $Q = 360 - 2P$ and $Q = 10 + 3P$ respectively. Here P and Q are the price and quantity demanded/supplied and C_1 and Q_1 are the total cost and quantity supplied by the firm. Find out the:

(a) Equilibrium price and quantity of sugar
(b) Profit maximizing output of Sweet Sugars
(c) Profit made by Sweet Sugars in the short-run.

Solution   (a) We know that in a perfectly competitive market, the point of intersection of the industry demand and supply curves determines the equilibrium price and quantity for a product.
Given that

Industry demand, $\hspace{5em} Q = 360 - 2P \hspace{5em}$ (i)

Industry supply, $\hspace{5em} Q = 10 + 3P \hspace{5em}$ (ii)

Equating (i) and (ii), we get

$$360 - 2P = 10 + 3P$$
$$5P = 350$$
$$\therefore \hspace{5em} P = 70$$

Substituting this value of P in either of these two Equations (i) or (ii) we get the value of Q

$$Q = 10 + 3 \times 70$$
$$Q = 220$$

Thus, the equilibrium price and quantity of sugar are Rs. 70 and 220 kg respectively.

(b) For a firm in a perfectly competitive market, the price of its product has to be taken as given by the market. If P_1 is the price of sugar of Sweet Sugars Limited, then

$$P_1 = \text{Rs. } 70/\text{kg}$$

Total revenue, $\hspace{4em} TR = P_1Q_1 = 70Q_1$

The profit of Sweet Sugars is given by

$$\pi = TR - TC$$
$$= 70Q_1 - (75Q_1 - 8Q_1^2 + Q_1^3 - 85)$$
$$= 70Q_1 - 75Q_1 + 8Q_1^2 - Q_1^3 + 85$$
$$= -Q_1^3 + 8Q_1^2 - 5Q_1 + 85$$

The necessary condition for profit maximization is

$$\frac{d\pi}{dQ_1} = 0$$

i.e.

$$\frac{d\pi}{dQ_1}(-Q_1^3 + 8Q_1^2 - 5Q_1 + 85) = 0$$

$$-3Q_1^2 + 16Q_1 - 5 = 0$$

$$3Q_1^2 - 16Q_1 + 5 = 0$$

$$3Q_1^2 - 15Q_1 - Q_1 + 5 = 0$$

$$3Q_1(Q_1 - 5) - 1(Q_1 - 5) = 0$$

$$(3Q_1 - 1)(Q_1 - 5) = 0$$

$$Q_1 = 1/3 \quad \text{and} \quad 5$$

Assuming the quantity to be an integer value

$$Q_1 = 5$$

The secondary condition of $\dfrac{d^2\pi}{dQ_1^2}$ = –ve is also true

Thus the profit maximizing output is 5 kg.

(c) Profit made by Sweet Sugars in the short-run is:

$$\pi = -Q_1^3 + 8Q_1^2 - 5Q_1 + 85$$

$$= -(5)^3 + 8(5)^2 - 5 \times 5 + 85$$

$$= -125 + 200 - 25 + 85$$

$$= \text{Rs. } 135$$

Monopolistic Competition

Next in the market structure spectrum, in order of decreasing competition, is monopolistic competition. The degree of competition in a monopolistic market is less than that in a market with perfect competition but more than that in an oligopoly and of course a monopoly. The characteristics of a market with monopolistic competition are as follows:

(a) There are a large number of buyers.
(b) There are a large number of sellers.
(c) The product is differentiated only due to branding.
(d) There are no entry and exit barriers.

Like in a purely competitive market, since in monopolistic competition there are a large number of buyers and sellers, the prices of the products are similar. They are not exactly the same because of product differentiation. Product differentiation arises not because of the quality but only due to packaging/branding. Though the product is the same, each manufacturer places his product in the market as though it is unique and does not have any substitute. This of course is not the reality. Each firm tries to present the same/similar product differently to the consumer. Accordingly, there might be some variance in the price of such products due to the perceived brand image. But this variance will not be large.

Complete information about the market is available to all the participants at nominal charges. Although there are no entry and exit barriers, the existing strong brands act as deterrents, i.e. as entry barriers to the prospective industries.

Prices of products in a monopolistic market will thus tend to cluster in a close range. This difference in the prices will be based on a relative quality assessment by the consumer of a particular product. Accordingly, consumers will value a particular brand more than others. Due to such product differentiation, the demand curve of an individual firm will be downward slopping. As the firm reduces the price of its product, its product becomes relatively less costly in comparison to that of the products of its competitors. The consumers thus buy more of it leading to an increase in demand. It may be noted here that firms make their decisions independently and thus any change in the price of the product by one firm does not affect the prices of the products of other firms.

This perceived differentiation eliminates the perfect elasticity of the demand curves for the firms. Unlike the perfectly horizontal demand curve of a firm in a perfect competition market, the demand curve here is falling. The firm here is not a price taker. It determines its own price-output combination. The degree of price flexibility and slope of the curve depend on the strength of the firm's product differentiation and the relative brand preferences of the consumer. Higher product differentiation leads to strong brand preference by the consumer and hence, more control of the firm on the price of its product. In Figure 9.4, the demand curve of X is more price sensitive and elastic than that for Y and thus reflects stronger product differentiation.

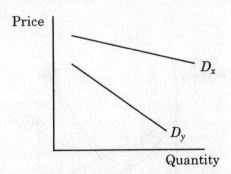

FIGURE 9.4   Product Differentiation

The price-output decisions in monopolistic competition are a mix of that in monopoly and perfect competition.

The average revenue and marginal revenue curves in this market will be downward sloping, with the marginal curve lying below the average revenue curve. The average and marginal cost curves will be functions of the firms and hence of the same nature for all market structures. They will both be U-shaped and the rate of rise and fall of the marginal cost curve will be more than that of the average cost curve.

A firm may make profits, incur losses or break even in the short-run. This will depend on its cost structure and the strength of its brand in the minds of consumers. It will make profits if it is able to produce at a competitive cost and/or is able to position its product in the market as a premium product that can attract customer loyalty and thus command higher price. Figure 9.5(a) is the diagrammatic representation of a firm making profits in a monopolistic market. Let the marginal cost curve cut the marginal revenue curve from below at the point of equilibrium E. Draw a vertical projection from this point E on the x-axis and on the average revenue and average cost curves. Let these points be Q, R and C respectively. Also, draw horizontal perpendiculars from points R and C on the y-axis. Let them intersect the y-axis at point P and G respectively. As explained in the case of perfect competition, the area of the rectangle $OPRQ$ represents the total revenue, while the area of the rectangle $OGCQ$ indicates the total cost. The difference between the two is the measure of profit or loss. In Figure 9.5(a), since the average revenue curve lies above the average cost

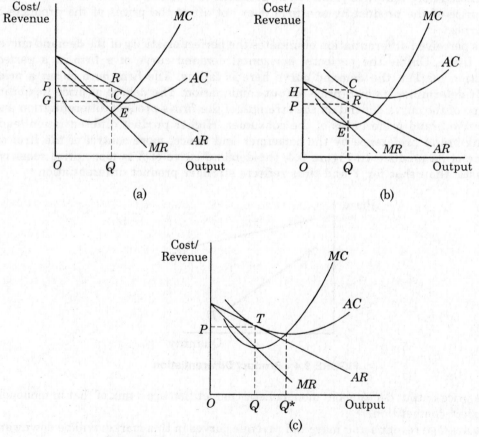

FIGURE 9.5 **Pricing under Monopolistic Competition**

curve at the point of equilibrium, the area of rectangle *OPRQ* is more than that of *OGCQ*. So the firm makes profits as shown by the area *GPRC*.

Similarly, we can explain the firm incurring losses or breaking even in the short-run as shown in Figure 9.5(b) and 9.5(c) respectively. The firm will incur losses if the average revenue curve lies below the average cost curve at the point of equilibrium. The area *PHCR* represents the loss in Figure 9.5(b). If however, the average revenue curve becomes tangential to the average cost curve at the point of equilibrium, the points *R* and *C* of the Figure 9.5(a) and (b) will merge into a single point *T*. The area of total revenue and total cost will be exactly equal to the area of rectangle *OPTQ*. Thus, the firm will break even i.e. it will neither make profits nor incur losses. It will only make nominal profits.

The above phenomenon occurs only in the short-run. In the long-run, no firm makes abnormal/excess profits or losses. It only makes normal profits. This is because of the condition of free entry and exit. Excessive profits in the short-run will attract new firms to join the industry, while abnormal losses will cause the loss making firms to move out of the industry.

Figure 9.5(c) represents long-run monopolistic competition. Perfect competition and monopoly rarely exist in the real world. Monopolistic competition is perhaps the most commonly found market structure. Most of the things that we consume daily fall into this category. The markets for pens, toothpastes, soaps, perfumes, clothes, shirts, trousers, floppies, etc. are all characterized by monopolistic competition. The same quantity packs of all toothpastes whether they be Colgate, Cibaca, Promise, Forhans or Close-up are priced almost similarly. Slight differences may exist for the different brands as consumers are made to believe that one has cloves inside it or another promotes togetherness and so on. No consumer normally tests such products to find out if they really have what has been promised in the advertisements. All the products are essentially the same with just some minor differences.

Although most firms compete with a large number of firms producing similar products, many still have some control over the price of their product. There is one more peculiar characteristic of monopolistic competition as seen in Figure 9.5(c). In the long-run, the equilibrium output *OQ* is less than the optimum output *OQ**. Society desires the optimum output at the lowest cost. But a monopolistic firm produces less than what it can. There is always some *excess capacity* left in such market structures. This excess capacity arises because of the nature of the average revenue and average cost curves. Since the average cost curve is U-shaped and average revenue is a falling straight line, the average revenue can be a tangent to the average cost curve only when the average cost curve is falling too. Since the average cost curve falls before it reaches its minimum point, the equilibrium output will always be lower than the optimum output.

Oligopoly

Such a market structure is characterized by a few sellers. The price-output decisions are interdependent. The degree of competition here is less than monopolistic competition but higher than that in monopoly which has almost no competition. The main characteristics of an oligopoly market situation are:

(a) There are a large number of buyers.
(b) There are only a few sellers.
(c) There are entry and exit barriers.
(d) The product can be homogeneous or heterogeneous, i.e. similar or differentiated.
(e) The price-output decisions of one firm are highly dependent on those of others.

In an oligopoly there are only a few sellers, so the pricing decisions of the firms are interdependent. An individual firm's action will cause its competitors to react. Such interdependence is the major characteristic of an oligopoly. Any action of a firm leads to a series of actions and reactions by the other firms. Thus, before taking any decision for the revision of the price of its product, a firm must carefully consider the potential reactions of its competitors. This is not a simple exercise as a large number of reactive behaviours are possible. This renders the understanding of the demand curve and price-output equation difficult unless some assumptions regarding the probable reactions of firms are made.

Pricing in an oligopoly has been explained on the basis of several models. These models suggest the assumptions of rival firms. Here we will briefly discuss the three most such prominent models.

Cournot's model. This model assumes that rival firms do not react to the change in prices of goods of other firms. Each firm makes its price-output decisions independently of the price-output decisions of its competitors. All the actions and decisions of the firm are geared towards profit maximization. The firm feels that it is not worthwhile to take into account the counter moves of its competitors. This model is more specifically applicable to routine day-to-day decision-making where it does not make much difference whether the firm takes into account or ignores the interdependence among the firms. Since in this model, interdependence disappears from decision-making, the price-output decisions are simply based on a standard analysis of the theory of the firm. The demand curve is determinate and can be found out. Since this model was put forward by Augustin Cournot, it is known as Cournot's model. As per this model, firms will decide their output assuming that the output of rival firms remains constant. Practically however, the model has doubtful applicability because it makes pricing decisions of oligopoly firms by negating the most important characteristic feature of such competition, i.e. the interdependence of pricing decisions.

Collusion model. This model recognizes that oligopoly firms depend on each other for their price-output decision-making. Thus, they enter into some sort of agreement for the price and output levels. When this agreement is formal and overt, the group of firms that operate under it for determining their price and output levels, form what is known as a *cartel*. Such formal agreements are however not possible in all countries. Where they are illegal, firms operate under a covert and informal agreement to decide their price-output levels. Such an informal agreement is termed *collusion*.

A cartel or collusion is probably the best way to price products in an oligopoly. This is because when firms are under an agreement for defining their price and output levels, they act almost like monopolist entities. The firms can then extract the maximum from their customers. In the process, almost all the firms will be benefitted and will be able to price their products so as to maximize the total profits of the industry. Decision-making under such an arrangement, whether formal or informal, will be centralized. Firms will dissolve their individual decisions into a joint decision that will be applicable to all firms. The combined centralized authority, i.e. cartel or collusion will decide the price-output levels in a manner that the total profits of the industry may be maximized.

The price-output determination under a cartel is as shown in the Figure 9.6. Figures 9.6(a) and (b) show the price-output and cost-revenue relationships for two individual firms 1 and 2, while Figure 9.6(c) on the extreme right is a representation of the entire industry.

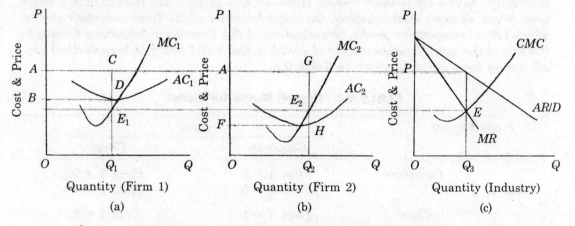

FIGURE 9.6   Price-output Determination for a Cartel

The industry's combined marginal cost curve (*CMC*) is obtained from the horizontal addition of the marginal cost curves of the individual firms. The point of intersection of this *CMC* with the industry's marginal revenue *MR* is the point of equilibrium *E* for the cartel. The vertical projection from point *E* on the x-axis gives the total output of the industry. The price will be determined by the horizontal projection on the y-axis from that point on the average revenue or demand curve, where the vertical projection drops on it from the equilibrium point. Once the total industry output is determined, the cartel allots the output quota to be produced by each firm such that the marginal cost of each firm is the same. For determining the output of individual firms, a horizontal projection from *E* is dropped on the marginal costs curves of those firms. Vertical projection from these points of intersection E_1 and E_2 on the x-axis of respective firms 1 and 2 give the output for these firms. These are the output levels where the firms equate their individual marginal costs to the previously determined profit maximizing marginal cost level for the industry. The profits are generally divided among the firms on the basis of the share of their individual outputs in the total industry output. They can also be determined on the basis of the historical market share of each firm in the industry.

Although the most profitable oligopoly structure, cartels are difficult to sustain. This may be due to various reasons like changing products, entry of new firms and disagreement among the members. Firms subvert or cheat the cartel agreement. They rarely agree on the allocation of profit amongst themselves. Each firm feels that it has got a bad deal and could have made higher profits otherwise. In our illustration, firms 1 and 2 will be making profits equal to the area of the rectangles $ABDC$ and $AFHG$ respectively. Here the points D and H are the points of intersection of the vertical projections from E_1 and E_2 on the average cost curves AC_1 and AC_2 respectively.

When one of the firms cheats, it will be extremely profitable for that firm. The profit made by it will be higher than what it would have made under the cartel. With the industry operating at monopoly price-output levels, this subverting firm will be secretly lowering its price and offering concession to customers. The other firms will accordingly bear a cut in their profits. However, this greed is not restricted to a single firm. When all firms start cheating, the cartel fails and all the firms lose their profits, which fall to competitive levels. Organization of the Petroleum Exporting Countries (OPEC) is the most prominent case of cartel in the world today. A hypothetical pay-off matrix for a cartel is given in Table 9.1.

TABLE 9.1 Pay-off Matrix for Cartel

Profit Pay-off		Firm 1	
		Cooperate	Cheat
Firm 2	Cooperate	Firm 1 = 5 Firm 2 = 5	Firm 1 = 9 Firm 2 = 1
	Cheat	Firm 1 = 1 Firm 2 = 9	Firm 1 = 2 Firm 2 = *2

Under the cartel, when both firms cooperate, they make a profit of say Rs. 5 lakh each. However, if one of them cheats, it is able to make profits of Rs. 9 lakh leaving just Rs. 1 lakh for the other firm, which cooperates. When both the firms cheat, the cartel breaks and the individual firms just make nominal profits of Rs. 2 lakh each.

Leader-follower model. This model suggests a less formal yet effective arrangement for ascertaining the behaviour of member firms in an oligopoly. Price leadership is a situation where one firm is recognized as the industry leader and all the other firms in the industry follow and accept its pricing policy. This generally happens when one of the firms in the industry is very big and strong and has an excellent brand image and sales. The others are relatively small and weak. The product of the big firm is so strong that its brand stands distinctly apart and is taken as a synonym for the product. For example, Bajaj Auto in the scooter industry, Tisco in steel and Camlin in writing ink are a few cases of industry leaders.

This leadership may result from size, strength, quality, product, cost efficiency and/or other related factors. The leader's price-output decision is made as though it is a monopolist, while the follower firms face a competitive scenario for the price-output decision. The followers, like the firms in a perfectly competitive market are merely price takers. The price-output decisions of the leader-follower model are illustrated in Figure 9.7.

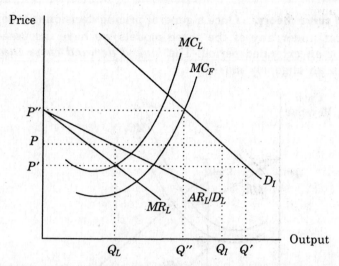

FIGURE 9.7 Price-output Decision under Leader-follower Model

Here MC_L, AR_L and MR_L are the marginal cost, demand and marginal revenue curves for the leader firm. D_I is the demand curve of the industry as a whole. MC_F is the curve representing the horizontal summation of the marginal cost curves of all the price followers.

Since the follower firms are price takers, they will operate at output levels where their individual marginal cost curves intersect the price line, just like in a purely competitive market. Thus, MC_F represents the supply curve for the follower firms. This implies that at price P'', the followers will cater to the full demand leaving nothing for the leader. At any price below P'', the followers would supply till MC_F, while the residual horizontal difference between D_I and MC_F will be the leader's demand. Plotting all residual demand quantities at prices below P'' will yield the demand curve for the price leader, AR_L/D_L and the related marginal revenue curve, MR_L. The demand curve for the price leader is thus:

$$AR_L = D_I - Q_F$$

Since the price leader has a demand curve AR_L, similar to that of a monopolist, it maximizes profits by operating at the point of equilibrium, i.e. where $MR_L = MC_L$. At this output for the leader Q_L, the followers will supply a combined output of $Q_F = Q_I - Q_L$ units. The market price will be P.

From the above discussion it becomes clear that it is not possible to arrive at a logical price-output decision without taking into account the interdependent behaviour of the firms. All oligopoly firms therefore use one model or the other to deduce the behaviour of rival firms. When no such attempt is made and each oligopoly firm chooses to work out its price-output strategy on its own, there will be *price wars* in the market and each firm will try to cut down its price in order to have a greater market share. In such a situation nobody wins.

Kinked demand curve theory. Once a general pricing decision is taken by a firm in an oligopoly market under any of the three models we have discussed, it is found to remain fixed for an extended period. The *kinked demand curve theory* explains this price rigidity in an oligopoly market.

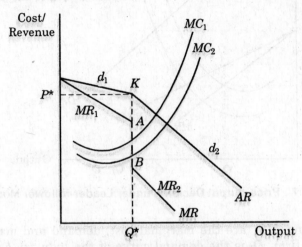

FIGURE 9.8   Kinked Demand Curve

It is often noted that in an oligopoly rival firms show one behaviour when there is an increase in the price, and another when the price is decreased by a firm. When a firm increases its price, the rival firms do not follow it by increasing their prices as well. By continuing with the existing price they are able to increase their market share. On the other hand, when a firm decreases its price, rival firms immediately follow it by decreasing their prices. If they will not do so then their customers will go to the firm that decreases its price.

In other words, the demand curve for a firm operating under oligopoly comprises of two parts having different elasticities, one for price increase and the other for price decrease. The former is more elastic than the latter. Thus, there happens to be a kink in the demand curve at the point where the firm operates. The firm continues to operate at that point. This rigidity in the pricing decision arises because the firm has no reason to either increase or decrease its price. If it increases its price to increase the profits it does not gain. Rather it loses revenue since the other rival firms do not follow its price increase. It also does not decrease its price because if it does so then the rival firms follow suit immediately, and there is neither appreciable increase in revenues nor in profits.

The average revenue or demand curve of an oligopoly firm thus has a kink at the point at which it operates. Corresponding to this kink in the demand curve, there is a vertical break in the marginal revenue curve. This point of discontinuity in the marginal revenue curve signifies a gap in it at the current price-output level, which leads to price rigidity.

The price-output level that maximizes the profits for a firm is derived from the equilibrium point, which lies at the intersection of the marginal cost and the marginal revenue curves. The price-output combination can remain optimal at the kink even though the marginal cost fluctuates because of the associated gap in the marginal revenue curve. Thus as shown in Figure 9.8 the profit maximizing price-output combination remains unchanged as long as the marginal cost fluctuates between MC_1 and MC_2 i.e. between the gap.

Monopoly

The last kind of market structure that we shall discuss in this chapter is monopoly. It lies at the opposite extreme of perfect competition in the market structure spectrum. It is a market characterized by the following:

(a) There is a single seller.
(b) There are a large number of buyers.
(c) The product does not have any close substitute, i.e. it is highly differentiated.
(d) There are high entry and exit barriers.

Monopoly exists when there is a single firm selling a product that has no close substitute. Hence, the firm itself is the industry. However, in practice, pure monopoly like pure competition is rare to find. But an understanding of price-output decisions in these two markets provides a valuable basis for explaining the pricing strategies of firms in monopolistic competition and oligopoly markets, which comprise the major market structures in any economy.

The demand curve of the monopolist firm will be downward sloping and its slope will be more than that of a firm in monopolistic competition. Since the firm and the industry are one and the same, the demand function and hence the demand curve of a monopolist firm will be same as the industry demand function and curve. This is why the curve will be falling. The marginal revenue curve will naturally behave in a similar manner. The cost curves will be U-shaped, with the marginal cost curve cutting the average cost curve at its lowest point from below.

Figure 9.9 is a diagrammatic representation of the pricing decision under monopoly. As is the case in monopolistic competition, E is the equilibrium point under the conditions of profit maximization. It is the point of intersection of the marginal revenue and marginal cost curves. Figures 9.9(a), (b) and (c) are the situations of profit, loss and break-even respectively, with the area of the rectangle $PRCL$ being the profit and the area of the rectangle $PMCR$ representing the loss. In break-even conditions, the points R and C merge into a single point T, i.e. the average revenue curve becomes a tangent to the average cost curve.

As the demand curve is downward sloping, the incremental price for each additional unit sold will go on decreasing. Thus, the marginal revenue will be equal to the price only for the first unit of output. For all the other output units, the marginal revenue will always be less than the price or the average revenue. So the marginal revenue curve will lie below the average revenue curve. For convenience, the AR and MR curves are drawn as straight lines.

The monopoly firm will have price OP and output OQ. Such a firm could make profits, incur losses or break-even with nominal profits in the short-run. But in the

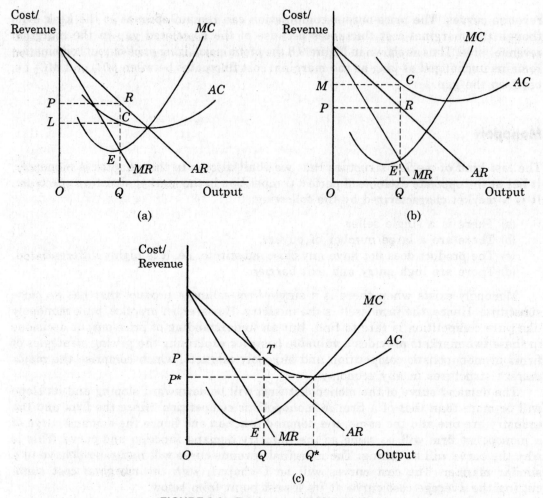

FIGURE 9.9   Pricing under Monopoly

long-run also it could make profits unlike a firm in monopolistic competition. This is because of the entry and exit barriers. Due to such barriers, neither can new firms easily enter the industry nor can the existing ones move out.

A monopolist firm will generally produce less than the optimum output. We have already discussed the reason when studying monopolistic competition. We know that a falling demand curve has to be tangential to the average cost curve. So here also the equilibrium output *OQ* at which the monopolist will operate will be less than the optimum output where society would want him to operate. It is for this output that the average total cost will be minimum. The magnitude of the gap between the equilibrium output and the optimum output is more in the case of a monopolist firm than that for monopolistic competition because the slope of the demand curve is more in the former. Accordingly, the price for a monopoly firm will also be higher than the minimum average total cost.

In contrast to free markets, monopolies need to be supervised and regulated. The two major characteristic features of free markets are that the economies of scale are modest and that it is relatively easy to enter the market as a supplier. The modest economies of scale indicate that in such markets, the long-run average costs begin to rise quite sharply as the output increases while the firm is still supplying a relatively small share of the market. Food processing, textiles, garments and furniture-making companies fall in this category. Secondly, low capital requirements and low sunk costs make entry for new entrants easy. Most of the service industries fall under this category. Given these two conditions, the markets will offer consumers the maximum attainable satisfaction, i.e. the highest possible output at the lowest possible prices without the firms incurring losses. The threat of entry ensures that the prices never exceed the long-run average costs. Moreover, competition also ensures that the price equals the long-run marginal cost. Thus, the price of a good accurately reflects the opportunity cost of manufacturing it.

Monopoly is, however, a market structure where these two conditions are not satisfied. In this kind of market, the unit costs fall as the production increases until it is economical for a single company to satisfy the entire market. There are economies of scale for the one company which meets market demand. Such markets are also characterized by entry barriers. Thus, in contrast to a perfectly competitive market, a monopoly offers the lowest possible output at the highest possible prices, a situation which is highly detrimental to the interests of society.

Monopolies thus need to be regulated by policy-makers. Otherwise, left to themselves, they will charge monopoly prices and restrict output. The absence of any competitive threat may also make them wasteful, inefficient and sluggish. Since all the costs can be passed on to consumers, managers will have little incentive to keep them under control. There will be no motives for innovation and change.

Thus, the firm will sell lesser output at a higher price as compared to a firm operating under perfect competition. The difference between the two gives a measure of monopoly power. The greater the difference, greater is the monopoly power. Although the firm profits in a monopoly, society, consumers, suppliers and even employees suffer due to higher prices and shortage of desired products. The monopoly market enhances the economic efficiency by restricting the number of firms to one. But at the same time, it also provides an incentive to under produce and earn economic profits. This is the reason why monopolies need to be regulated for their prices and output quantities. The Monopolistic and Restrictive Trade Practices (MRTP) Act owes its existence to this fact. Further, a monopolist can set either price or quantity, but not both. Given one of these, the value of the other is determined by the demand curve.

 ## PRICE DISCRIMINATION

Price discrimination is a pricing phenomenon wherein the same product is sold by a firm in different markets at different prices at the same time. This difference in prices in the two markets is not related to the differences in costs of production and distribution. Every price sustains a particular level of demand. The total demand for a product at a given price is the aggregate of the demands of individual consumers. This demand is a function of the consumer's preference, price of close substitutes and complements to the product, and the level of income of each individual consumer.

The pricing of a product is one of the most important decisions for a firm. Different companies use different methods at different times to price their products. A lot of money is spent by most companies on market research for ascertaining the possible prices that consumers will be willing to pay for their products. The aim behind all such exercises is to find out the maximum amount that different consumers are willing to pay.

Such a pricing scheme that makes each consumer pay the maximum amount that he is willing to pay is known as *first degree price discrimination*. Under this method of pricing, the full benefit of the trade between buyer and seller goes to the seller. At the same time, business is not lost by charging such a high price that consumers do not wish to buy the product. Auctions are perhaps the best example of first degree price discrimination. They enable the seller to identify those consumers who are willing to pay the maximum possible price for their product. Given a choice, every firm would want to sell its product through the auction approach. But this is not practically possible for all products. Auctions are possible only for very special products such as works of art, antiques, mining rights. These are cases where the sale volumes are low and there are many potential buyers for the scarce product. These buyers have all the information about the product but are unable to cooperate. Since most of the products of common use do not satisfy these conditions, so auctions are found to have limited use.

Where auctions are not feasible, firms try their best to approximate the first degree price discrimination. There are two ways of doing this. The first approach is based on the law of diminishing marginal utility. Accordingly, it believes that the satisfaction that an individual consumer derives from each successive unit of a commodity goes on diminishing as he consumes more of it. The incremental value that a consumer perceives in a product gets lower with each additional unit consumed. A thirsty Coke-loving consumer will pay the maximum amount possible for the first can of Coke. His willingness to pay for all additional units will gradually decrease. The amount that he will be willing to pay for the fifth can, will not be as much as he did for the first can. All the assumptions of the law of diminishing marginal utility hold good in this case.

Even the price paid for the first unit will be different for different consumers depending upon their love for Coke. The price at which one consumer buys Coke may not attract other consumers. So the seller comes up with a scheme wherein he offers Coke at a lower unit price in packs of six cans each. The consumer gets the benefit of reduced prices only if he buys the full pack with six cans. Thus, the consumer who needs Coke badly but needs just one unit, can have it by paying a higher price, while the other consumer who is not that much desperate can get a lower price by buying a pack of six cans. In neither of the two cases does the firm lose business.

Such a form of price discrimination, which is based on the volume of consumer purchase, is known as *second degree price discrimination*. It is quite commonly found in everyday life. Quantity discounts on products is a classic illustration of this pricing practice. Still another example is that of two-tier pricing wherein there is a fixed access and a variable use component as in the cases of club fee, transport charges, etc. In the case of transport charges for instance, a frequent traveller will be able to reduce his average cost of travel by paying a fixed amount for a monthly pass.

The second way of approximating first degree price discrimination is where products are priced according to the type of buyer and not the volume of purchases. Such a pricing mechanism where pricing is based on the characteristics of buyer is known as *third degree price discrimination*. Student concessions in rail/road/air travel, cinema halls, etc. is the best example of third degree price discrimination. In such practices, a particular section of society is provided a better deal than the rest of the society. The reasons for such beneficial treatment are varied.

Pricing practices can even be *complex*, combining the second and third degree price discrimination, as in the case of discounted students travel passes. Whatever may be the case, price discrimination is only possible in imperfectly competitive markets, which can be segmented and where there is no resale. Only when the market can be distinguished into two or more different parts that different prices can be charged. Further, if resale is allowed, then the price-sensitive class of consumers, which buys the product at cheaper rates will sell it to those who can buy only at higher rates from the sellers. The price would then be the same for all consumers and discrimination will no longer be possible.

The prices in different markets can be related to one another through their respective elasticities. From our knowledge of the price elasticity we have

$$MR = P\left(1 + \frac{1}{e}\right) \tag{9.1}$$

For any two markets 1 and 2,

$$MR_1 = P_1\left(1 + \frac{1}{e_1}\right) \quad \text{and} \quad MR_2 = P_2\left(1 + \frac{1}{e_2}\right) \tag{9.2}$$

The condition for profit maximization is

$$MR_1 = MR_2 = CMR = MC \tag{9.3}$$

where
P_1 = Price in market segment 1
P_2 = Price in market segment 2
e_1 = Elasticity in market segment 1
e_2 = Elasticity in market segment 2
MR_1 = Marginal revenue in market segment 1
MR_2 = Marginal revenue in market segment 2
CMR = Combined marginal revenue
MC = Marginal cost.

Equating Equations (9.2) and (9.3), we get

$$P_1\left(1 + \frac{1}{e_1}\right) = P_2\left(1 + \frac{1}{e_2}\right)$$

$$\frac{P_1}{P_2} = \frac{1 + \dfrac{1}{e_2}}{1 + \dfrac{1}{e_1}} \tag{9.4}$$

$$e_1 = e_2, \qquad P_1 = P_2$$

$$|e_1| > |e_2|, \qquad P_1 < P_2$$

$$|e_1| < |e_2|, \qquad P_1 > P_2$$

Thus, price discrimination would be profitable if, and only if, different market segments have different price elasticities. If they have the same elasticity then the profit-maximizing price in each segment would also be the same. Firms will be able to price their product higher in that market segment which is less elastic since sales will be less sensitive to price variations in such markets.

Figure 9.10 is a diagrammatic representation of price discrimination. AR_1, MR_1 and AR_2, MR_2 are the average revenue and marginal revenue curves relating to any two market segments 1 and 2, which have price elasticities, e_1 and e_2. Let $e_2 > e_1$, CMR represents the combined marginal revenue, which is obtained by summing up MR_1 and MR_2 horizontally. Till point N, $CMR = MR_1$, since $MR_2 = 0$. The point where MC cuts CMR is the point of equilibrium for the firm as a whole. For finding out the profit maximizing price and output in both the market segments, draw horizontal projections from the point E on MR_1 and MR_2 curves. Let these points be denoted as E_1 and E_2. Vertical projections from E_1 and E_2 on the x-axis give the output in the two segments, i.e. Q_1 and Q_2. Draw horizontal lines from the vertical projection of points E_1 and E_2 on AR_1 and AR_2. These will give the profit maximizing prices in the two market segments, i.e. P_1 and P_2. It may be noted in the diagram that $P_1 > P_2$ when $e_1 < e_2$.

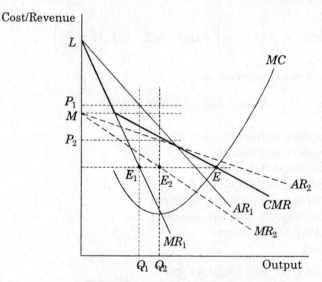

FIGURE 9.10   Price Discrimination

ILLUSTRATION 9.2   A movie theatre Dreamlok has a fixed cost of Rs. 700 and an average variable cost of Rs. 200 per movie show. Suppose the theatre is able to separate its customers into two separate markets; general public and students, with the following demand functions:

For general public   : $100\ P_G = 2000 - 3Q_G$
For students   : $100\ P_S = 1200 - Q_S$

where, P and Q are the price and quantity demand of show tickets respectively. If the theatre was allowed to discriminate,

(a) How many movie show tickets would it sell in the two segments and what will be the price of a ticket for general public and students?
(b) Compute the total profit made by the theatre.

Assume that the objective of the theatre is profit maximization.

Solution   (a) The total cost function is

$$TC = 700 + 200(Q_G + Q_S) \tag{i}$$

Total revenue is the sum of revenues in individual markets. That is,

$$TR = R_G + R_S$$

$$= P_G \cdot Q_G + P_S \cdot Q_S$$

Profit, $\pi = TR - TC$

$$= P_G \cdot Q_G + P_S \cdot Q_S - [700 + 200\ (Q_G + Q_S)]$$

Substituting the values of P_G and P_S from the demand equation for the general public and students in this equation, we get

$$\pi = (2000 - 3Q_G)Q_G + (1200 - Q_S) \cdot Q_S - 700 - 200Q_G - 200Q_S$$

$$= 2000Q_G - 3Q_G^2 + 1200\ Q_S - Q_S^2 - 700 - 200Q_G - 200Q_S$$

$$\pi = -3Q_G^2 + 1800Q_G - Q_S^2 + 1000Q_S - 700 \tag{ii}$$

The necessary conditions for profit maximization are that the partial derivatives of Equation (ii) with respect to Q_G and Q_S be zero. That is,

$$\frac{d\pi}{dQ_G} = 0 \ \text{ and } \ \frac{d\pi}{dQ_S} = 0$$

Here,

$$\frac{d\pi}{dQ_G} = -6Q_G + 1800 = 0$$

$$Q_G = 300$$

Here,

$$\frac{d\pi}{dQ_S} = -2Q_S + 1000 = 0$$

$$Q_S = 500$$

The secondary conditions for negative second derivative also hold true. That is,

$$\frac{d^2\pi}{dQ_G} = -6 \quad \text{and} \quad \frac{d^2\pi}{dQ_S} = -2$$

Putting these values of Q_G and Q_S in the demand equations, we get

$$100P_G = 2000 - 3Q_G = 2000 - 3 \times 300 = 1100$$

$$\therefore \qquad\qquad\qquad\qquad P_G = 11$$

$$100P_S = 1200 - Q_S = 1200 - 500 = 700$$

$$\therefore \qquad\qquad\qquad\qquad P_S = 7$$

Price of a general ticket = Rs. 11
Price of a student ticket = Rs. 7
Quantity of general tickets = 300
Quantity of student tickets = 500

(b) Total profit $\pi = TR - TC$

$$= -3Q_G^2 + 1800Q_G - Q_S^2 + 1000Q_S - 700$$

$$= -3(300)^2 + 1800 \times 300 - (500)^2 + 1000 \times 500 - 700$$

$$= 450000$$

$$\therefore \quad \text{Total Profit} = \text{Rs. } 4,50,000$$

ILLUSTRATION 9.3 With the help of the above data prove the validity of the proposition 'Under price discrimination, price is lower in more elastic markets than in less elastic markets'.

Solution From the solution to the above illustration, we have

$$P_G = \text{Rs. } 11 \qquad P_S = \text{Rs. } 7$$

$$Q_G = 300 \qquad Q_S = 500$$

From our knowledge of price elasticity we know that,

$$e_{PG} = \frac{\Delta Q_G}{\Delta P_G} \cdot \frac{P_G}{Q_G}$$

With P_G and Q_G given, the value of $\Delta Q_G/\Delta P_G$ can be found from the demand equation for general public:

$$100PG = 2000 - 3QG$$

$$Q_G = \frac{2000}{3} - \frac{100}{3} \cdot P_G$$

Differentiating w.r.t. P_G, we get

$$\frac{\Delta Q_G}{\Delta P_G} = -\frac{100}{3}$$

Thus,

$$e_{PG} = -\frac{100}{3} \times \frac{11}{300} = -\frac{11}{9} = -1.22$$

$\therefore$
$$e_{PG} = 1.22$$

Similarly,

$$e_{PS} = \frac{\Delta Q_S}{\Delta P_S} \cdot \frac{P_S}{Q_S}$$

Since,

$$Q_S = 1200 - 100P_S$$

$$\frac{\Delta Q_S}{\Delta P_S} = -100$$

Thus,

$$e_{PS} = -100 \times \frac{7}{500} = -1.4$$

$\therefore$
$$e_{PS} = 1.4$$

Hence, $e_{PS} > e_{PG}$ while $P_S < P_G$.

This proves that under price discrimination price is lower in the more elastic market than in the less elastic market.

 ## PRICING METHODS IN PRACTICE

While the preceding discussions on pricing mechanisms in different market structures will provide you with a sound theoretical base to understand how price and output decisions are made. There are several other common pricing practices that exist in real marketplaces. Some of them are as follows:

1. Going rate pricing
2. Full cost pricing
3. Marginal cost pricing
4. Differential pricing
5. Trade association pricing
6. Loss leadership pricing
7. Administered pricing.

There are some products where firms have very little leeway to decide on pricing.

of their products. Such products are homogenous in nature and are produced using easily available technology and resources. There are a large number of sellers and the industry has free entry and exit conditions. For such products, firms have no choice but to sell their product at the rate at which the same product is being sold by other firms. It will be able to make profits by being cost-competitive. Such pricing, which is guided by the going rate of that product in the market, is known as *going rate pricing*.

Full cost pricing, as the name indicates, is a pricing practice in which the product is priced by adding the desired margin to the full cost of the product. This generally happens in the case of monopoly or oligopoly firms. The product belongs to a sellers market. The consumer is at the receiving end. The process involves listing out all the costs related to the product, be the manufacturing, packing, marketing and other overheads; adding all the costs and finally adding to this cost the desired profit margin. When it is not possible for the firm to price the product comfortably, firms which have been operating for quite some time and have already covered their fixed costs, sell their product at a lower price, which just covers the variable or the marginal cost. Such a pricing mechanism is known as *marginal cost pricing*.

Differential pricing involves pricing the product in such a manner that the same product is available at different prices under different circumstances. This differential treatment may be based on time, place or use. Different charges for STD calls during different hours of the day, is an example of a time-price differential. Use price differential is seen in case of pricing of electricity where different prices are charged for home and industrial use.

In the case of oligopoly markets, there exist trade associations. These come into being to take care of the interests of member firms. When the pricing decision for a product is taken by an association and the member firms only follow this decision, it is known as *trade association pricing*.

When the products are priced low, not with a view to maintain their own demand but to take care of the demand of some other products of the firm, we have a case of *loss leadership pricing*. In this method, the product under consideration happens to have a good brand image in the minds of the consumer. It is priced so low that it is sold at a loss. But this acts as a bait for the customers to come and see other products of the firm and buy them under a package deal.

The last pricing method in practice is *administered pricing*. There are some products that are essential commodities. The government ensures that such products are available to citizens at a reasonable price. The firm is bound to sell its product at a subsidized rate. The negative difference between the cost price and selling price is given to the firm by the government as a subsidy. Sugar, fertilizers, etc. are prominent illustrations of this kind of pricing.

QUESTIONS

1. Discuss the significance of pricing decisions in practice.
2. Several factors affect the pricing of a product. Briefly discuss some of the important ones.

3. Explain pricing decisions under the conditions of perfect competition. Can a firm make profits in both the short-run and the long-run?

4. 'The monopolistic competition is a special case of imperfect competition. It stands between monopoly and perfect competition and accordingly the pricing decisions are determined by the characteristics of both these market forms.' Discuss.

5. Pricing in an oligopoly market requires forming some assumptions about the behaviour of rival firms. Several models have been put forward for this purpose. Discuss the three most prominent models explaining the behaviour of rival firms in an oligopoly market.

6. What is a kinked demand curve? Explain the price-output behaviour in an oligopoly market.

7. 'Firms in a monopoly market tend to sell lesser output at a higher-than-equilibrium price. This forms the basis for the existence of the Monopolistic Restrictive Trade Practices (MRTP) Act.' Explain the pricing mechanism in a monopoly market in the light of this statement.

8. The demand and supply functions for a firm's product are given as $Q = 15 - P$ and $Q = 5 + P$, respectively. Find out the price and quantity sold of that product under equilibrium conditions. How will the price be affected if the product attracts a customs duty of Rs. 2 per unit?

9. Accurate Calculators Limited manufactures calculators. Its demand function is $Q = 25 - 3P$ as against the industry demand function of $Q = 20 - P$. The cost of the firm's products varies with its quantity supplied as $C_1 = Q_1^2 - 11Q_1 + 24$. Find out:

   a. equilibrium price and quantity of calculators
   b. profit maximizing output of Accurate Calculators.

   Given that the calculators are sold in a perfectly competitive industry with a supply equation of $Q = 2P + 5$.

10. Find out the price and quantity for a monopolist firm which has a cost equation of $C = 2Q^3 + 8Q^2 - 12Q + 25$. The demand for the firm's product is a function of the price of the product, the function being $Q = 8 - P$.

11. A firm is able to discriminate its market. It has a constant marginal cost of production equal to Rs. 10. The demand function for the two markets are: $Q_1 = 14 - P_1$ and $Q_2 = 10 - 3P_2$. The marginal revenue equations for these markets are $MR_1 = 14 - 2P_1$ and $MR_2 = 10 - 4P_2$. Compute the profit maximizing price and output in each market.

CASE STUDIES

Case 9.1   Gail to Sail Low

The public sector giant Gail is likely to be dropped as the only builder of trunk gas pipelines in the country and as part of opening up the sector, Reliance Industries might be allowed to lay a line from Andhra Pradesh to Gujarat. Reliance will get the rights to lay the 1,400-km pipeline from Kakinada in Andhra Pradesh to Ahmedabad in Gujarat to transport natural gas from its gigantic gas field in Bay of Bengal to NTPC's Kawas and Gandhar power projects in Gujarat.

The new gas pipeline policy could make laying inter-state pipeline open for competition and anyone offering "the least terms of transportation tariff" and "most efficient means of operations" would get the contract. All pipelines, laid on common carrier principle, should have at least 25 per cent more capacity than what is required by the owner for leasing to the third party users.

Earlier, a draft gas pipeline policy nominated Gail as the sole transporter, but the industry saw it as a conflict of interest with Gail also involved in gas production and trading. They feared that this would give Gail the power to arbitrarily fix tariffs, although a regulatory body would monitor price movements.

Basing its arguments on the draft policy, Gail had claimed the right to lay the Kakinada-Ahmedabad pipeline. However, the government was contractually bound to allow Reliance to lay a pipeline to market produce from the D6 block it won through the competitive bidding. According to the revised gas pipeline policy—drafted after eliciting suggestions from 38 stakeholders, including state governments, companies and chambers of commerce—a pipeline network will only be handed over to Gail, if the government feels necessary to do so to ensure appropriate grid connectivity.

Reliance had impressed upon the fact that Kakinada-Ahmedabad pipeline was crucial for the company to fulfill the contract it had won from NTPC for supply of gas for 17 years at a delivered price of $2.97 per million British thermal unit (MBTU). It said that they have proposed to lay this pipeline in a separate subsidiary to comply with all the norms laid down by the proposed regulatory authority and abide by common carrier principles. Gas Transportation and Infrastructure Company Ltd (GTCL), a subsidiary of Reliance, was the first company to have sought approval for the pipeline project in 2001–02, much prior to the announcement of the draft pipeline policy. And GTICL wanted to build Kakinada-Ahmedabad gas pipeline.

To checkmate Reliance, Gail had offered NTPC to transport D6 gas at $0.39 per MBTU, lower than $0.48 per MBTU tariff quoted by Reliance in its winning bid for Kawas and Gandhar gas contract. NTPC, however, ignored Gail's offer as Reliance quotation met its condition of securing supplies at the plant at less than $3 per MBTU.

What type of market structure existed for gas transportation? With the proposed change being mulled by the petroleum ministry, what change will come to the market structure and whether that will bring any advantage to the gas consumer units downstream?

(*Source:* Business Standard, August 05, 2004)

Case 9.2   HLL Basket

Call it the mega *mahine ka* deal or extreme measures to check the dripping topline. Hindustan Lever Limited (HLL) has devised a marketing initiative to push the concept of 'monthly household basket' at superstores and convenience outlets in malls across the country. The move, being tried out for the first time, is likely to trigger off similar schemes by other fast moving consumer goods companies too.

The consumer can take his pick from HLL's 20-odd FMCG product baskets and at a sizeable discount. Say, a sample basket would contain a bar of soap, a pack of shampoo, a toothpaste, a pack of tea, a pack of atta and a pack of detergent, all based on specific gramages-typically items that would find a place in the shopping basket of an average household. The value of the two baskets need to be Rs. 560 and Rs. 250, for which HLL is offering discount of Rs. 60 and Rs. 50 respectively.

The idea takes birth from the realization that companies need to increase family share instead of market share alone. This was probably being overlooked by most of the fast moving consumer goods companies. The family of brands and the brand family complement each other. Any company having a set of complementary products should target not the individual but the family as its unit consumer. For multinational as well as domestic fast moving consumer goods majors alike, the concept promises to work well across countries in Asia, where the family is at the heart of household consumption. For example, Reckitt & Coleman, Pidilite, Dabur and telecom service providers stand to gain from a similar offering.

Perhaps, it as boils down to ensuring consumer loyalty across a product range. Apart from a specified discount, the companies would also like to reward a regular customer to build on the value of relationship over time. To hard sell the concept, HLL is mainly targeting modern trade like superstores and malls, where its products are ensured higher visibility and thus promise better activation. For the retail stores, this perhaps could not have been better. Each store can use the local context to promote the offer.

For the market structure that the aforesaid products of HLL have, comment on the type of pricing policy that the company is now trying to bring in with the monthly household basket scheme. How is this strategy going to save the dripping top line?

(*Source*: The Economic Times, October 06, 2004)

CHAPTER TEN

Linear Programming

LEARNING OBJECTIVES

* the linear programming technique
* applications of linear programming
* how to solve the LPP

 WHY LINEAR PROGRAMMING?

Managerial economics as a subject concerns finding solutions to practical business problems. It provides the concepts and methodologies that help in the same. The application of these concepts, however, requires that these problems be structured in some mathematical form. *Linear programming* is a mathematical technique that can be used to obtain optimal solutions to problems. Managerial economics thus makes generous use of the linear programming technique to provide solutions to managerial problems.

If the problems were simple, any other mathematical technique would have provided solutions to it. But business problems are complex. They always need to be worked out under some constraints. Further, the variables in business problems are related by inequalities rather than equations. This is because the specifications are seldom precise. In most cases, they require some minimum or maximum requirements to be met. This programming model is termed *linear* because both the function to be maximized and the inequalities involve only the variable multiplied by constants and then added together. The power of the variables is only one. Linear programming is the best way to solve multivariate problems under constraints.

Thus, linear programming is an analytical technique for finding out optimal solutions to managerial problems characterized by constraints. The technique is used to solve problems where the course of action available to the decision-making phenomenon is restricted by some constraints. The problem may be that of maximization or minimization. The decision problems under constraints are the ones which involve the allocation of scarce resources to achieve some specific goal. The linear programming technique is the most important mathematical programming technique available to managers.

 ## APPLICATIONS OF LINEAR PROGRAMMING

Linear programming finds application in a wide range of managerial problems. Whether it be allocation of inputs, distribution of products, product/promotional mix, inventory management or capital budgeting decisions, all decisions involve the allocation of scarce resources under a given set of constraints. Optimum utilization of these resources is the goal pursued by managers. All these decisions involve many inter-related aspects. Normally there are several feasible alternatives available and choosing the best alternative is a complex job.

Some of the important applications of linear programming are:

1. **Production decisions:** A given set of inputs can produce more than one type of output. In such a situation the manager would like to decide which combination of output should be produced to maximize the firm's profits. For example, a dairy product manufacturing company has to decide how much butter, *ghee* and cheese to produce from a given quantity of milk.

2. **Advertising decisions:** Different advertising media like television, newspaper, magazines, radio, hoardings, pamphlets, etc. involve different costs and have varying levels of effectiveness. The frequency of advertising is another variable. These variables have to be addressed under the resource constraint of the money that can be spent on advertising.

3. **Distribution decisions:** An illustration of the complex multivariate problems is the case of a firm having its production units located at three different places *A*, *B* and *C*. Its distribution units are also spread over three other places *X*, *Y* and *Z*. Linear programming can be applied to decide the transportation schedule for the firm's product from the production units to the distribution units. This schedule has to worked out under some inequality constraints. For instance, the total cost of transportation has to be minimized, the total quantity to be sent from any production unit should not exceed the quantity available at that unit and the total quantity received at any distribution unit should meet the demand for the product at that unit.

4. **Investment decisions:** When a firm has some investible resources but is faced with a choice of available alternatives/sets of alternatives, linear programming techniques help in making the optimal decision. For example, suppose a firm has Rs. 20 crore to invest and has three available alternatives *A*, *B* and *C*. Alternative *A* is to expand the existing production capacity, alternative *B* is to start manufacturing a new related product and alternative *C* is to diversify into an altogether unrelated product line. All the three alternatives involve a cash outlay of Rs. 10 crore each. The firm has to decide which of the alternatives has to be chosen.

5. **Inventory decisions:** What to order and how much to order are the two basic questions faced by a person managing a firm's inventory. These problems can be effectively handled using linear programming techniques.

Most managerial problems, like the ones described aforementioned, are constrained through inequalities rather than equalities. The constraints sometimes limit the use of available resources to less than or equal to some fixed availability while at other times limit the quantity or quality of the output to greater than or equal to some minimum requirement. Since constraint inequalities can be easily dealt with in linear programming, it has established itself as a very useful technique for managerial decision-making.

 ## ASSUMPTIONS OF LINEAR PROGRAMMING

Linear programming assumes all relationships to be linear. Although the assumption may not hold good in all cases, it remains valid in quite a few situations and does not distort the analysis in the remaining cases.

The major assumptions underlying linear programming are:

1. **The revenue function is linear:** This means revenue increases linearly with the output. For this to happen it is obvious that the price of the product should remain constant, which happens only in the case of a perfectly competitive market.
2. **The cost function is linear:** The cost will increase or decrease in a constant manner with the output when the returns to scale and the factor input prices are constant and the firm can buy any quantity of inputs at the same price.
3. **The profit function is linear:** With both revenue and cost behaving linearly with output, the profit function is also linear. This holds true over limited output ranges.

 ## LINEAR PROGRAMMING PROBLEM

A typical linear programming problem (LPP) has an objective function, which is governed by a set of constraints and all the variables in the problem must be equal to or greater than zero. *Objective function* is the equation that expresses the goal of the linear programming problem. There can be two kinds of solutions to linear programming problem.

1. Graphical solution
2. Algebraic solution.

We will now explain these two methods. Consider a hypothetical example. Let an objective function be

$$\text{Maximize} \quad P = aX + bY \tag{10.1}$$

Where P, X and Y are all variables. X and Y are independent and P is a dependent variable. We wish to maximize P. Also, we are constrained for our independent variables. Thus,

$$cX + dY \leq l \tag{10.2}$$

$$eX + fY \leq m \qquad (10.3)$$

$$gX + hY \leq n \qquad (10.4)$$

The non-negativity requirement, which is a must for avoiding nonsensical solutions lays down that :

$$X \geq 0, \ Y \geq 0 \qquad (10.5)$$

Graphical Solution

Let us consider the above problem. The graphical method first prescribes the determination of a feasible space. *Feasible space* is the area, which satisfies all the constraints. This space is found by considering one constraint equation at a time.

Let us begin with the first constraint Equation (10.2). We plot the equality relationship and then shade the inequality representing side of the line.

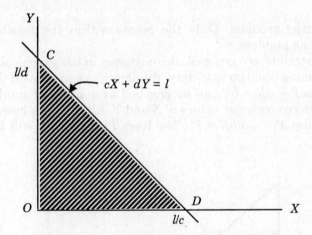

FIGURE 10.1   Graphical Solution to LPP

The straight line is drawn by joining the intercepts on the x- and y-axis. Here the intercepts on the two axes are l/c and l/d respectively. The area on the left of the line $cX + dY = l$ will naturally represent the inequality. Anywhere on this side, the sum of the two independent variables and their product coefficients will be less than l. The shaded triangle OCD represents the area that satisfies the constraints. Due to the non-negativity requirement, we are only considering the positive values of X and Y.

Similarly, we plot the other two inequality constraints. The satisfying area will decrease with every increase in the constraining equation. The final graph will be as shown in Figure 10.2.

The satisfying area for the first constraint as marked by the triangle OCD gets reduced to the area $OGID$ for all the three constraints. This area $OGID$, which satisfies all the three inequality constraints, is known as the feasible area. The three inequality constraints and the non-negativity requirement thus define the feasible space of our

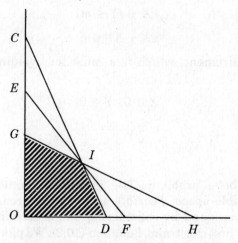

FIGURE 10.2   Graphical Solution to LPP

linear programming problem. Only the points within the feasible space meet the requirements of the problem.

Once the constraints are grouped, the next step in the graphical method for solving a linear programming problem is to draw the objective equation on the same graph. The objective function $P = aX + bY$ can be graphed as a series of similar lines P_1, P_2, P_3, ..., P_n for different symmetrical values of X and Y. All the lines however have the same slope $-a/b$ (because $Y = -a/bX + P$). The lines P_1, P_2, ..., P_n will be drawn as shown in Figure 10.3.

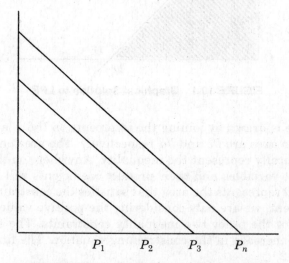

FIGURE 10.3   Objective Equation of LPP

Now we need to find out that objective function which would be the maximum subject to the constraints as laid down earlier. In other words, the highest objective function in the feasible space has to be found out.

For this we superimpose the objective function curves on the feasible space graph as shown in Figure 10.4. The optimal solution to the linear programming problem occurs either at the corner or the boundary of the feasible space. This corner or boundary would be the one, which is farthest from the origin. The optimal solution always lies on the corner or the boundary because of the linearity assumptions of the constraints and the objective functions. In case where the highest objective function is touching a boundary and not the corner of the feasible space, either of the two corners of the concerned boundary line provide the optimal solution to the linear programming problem.

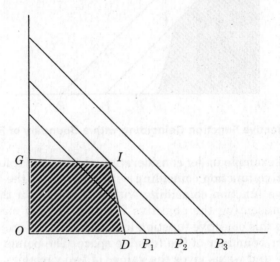

FIGURE 10.4   Highest Objective Function

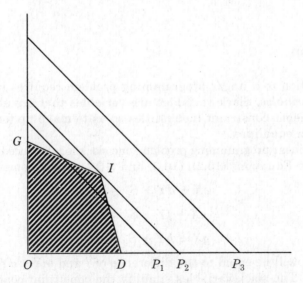

FIGURE 10.5   Objective Function Coinciding with a Corner of Feasible Space

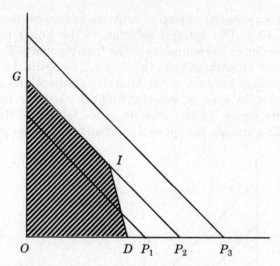

FIGURE 10.6   Objective Function Coinciding with a Boundary of Feasible Space

In the hypothetical example under consideration, the optimal solution to the problem will be I for the objective function coinciding with a corner of the feasible space, and G or I for the objective function coinciding with a boundary of the feasible space.

Draw the line representing the objective function for any one value of P. Then project lines parallel to this objective function line such that the projected lines coincide with only one corner or boundary of the feasible space. The points of intercept of this projected line on the x- and y-axis gives the values of two variables. Substituting these values in the objective function equation we get the maximum value of the objective function.

Algebraic Solution

The algebraic solution to a linear programming problem requires introduction of the concept of *slack variables*. Slack variables are variables that are added to the linear programming problem's constraint inequalities so as to make up for the difference in order to make them equalities.

For solving the linear programming problem, one slack is introduced for each constraint in the problem. The Equations (10.2), (10.3) and (10.4) now become

$$cX + dY + S_1 = l \tag{10.6}$$

$$eX + fY + S_2 = m \tag{10.7}$$

$$gX + hY + S_3 = n \tag{10.8}$$

The value of S_1 will be equal to the difference of l and $(cX + dY)$. The same holds good for S_2 and S_3. The slack variables simplify the constraint condition by bringing them in equation form. They can be either zero or positive. Slack variables, for obvious reasons, can never be negative because this signifies an absurd situation where the amount of a resource employed exceeds the amount available. Slack variables measure the excess capacity in the related factor. A zero slack variable indicates that there is no scope of variation in the constrained inputs.

The complete linear programming problem can now be stated as under:

Objective Function: Maximize

$$P = aX + bY \qquad (10.9)$$

$$cX + dY + S_1 = l \qquad (10.10)$$

$$eX + fY + S_2 = m \qquad (10.11)$$

$$gX + hY + S_3 = n \qquad (10.12)$$

where

$$X \geq 0, \ Y \geq 0, \ S_1 \geq 0, \ S_2 \geq 0 \text{ and } S_3 \geq 0 \qquad (10.13)$$

The algebraic solution will aim at finding the values of X, Y, S_1, S_2 and S_3 which will satisfy all the constraining conditions and at the same time maximize the Equation (10.9). The constraint equations need to be solved simultaneously. This however requires that the number of equations be equal to the number of unknowns. When this is not the case, the simultaneous solution is not possible. In such cases, solution of the linear programming problem can be obtained by working on the fact that the solution occurs only at a corner of the feasible space. We therefore need to examine only the corners and not the entire feasible space.

At every corner, two variables of the entire set of variables will have zero values. Also, the number of non-zero variables equals the number of constraint equations. The equations can then be solved algebraically. The corner solution that produces the maximum profit is the solution to the linear programming problem.

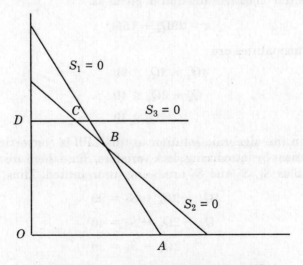

FIGURE 10.7 Algebraic Solution to LPP

From Figure 10.7, we have a given set of equations. The variables assuming zero values at different corners are as follows:

At

$$O : \quad X = 0, \qquad Y = 0$$
$$A : \quad S_1 = 0, \qquad Y = 0$$
$$B : \quad S_1 = 0, \qquad S_2 = 0$$
$$C : \quad S_2 = 0, \qquad S_3 = 0$$
$$D : \quad X = 0, \qquad S_4 = 0$$

Solving the constraint equations at each corner point provides values for X and Y as also for S_1, S_2, S_3 and S_4. The profit contribution at each corner can then be found by substituting the values of variables X and Y into the objective function as shown in Equation (10.2). The corner solution that produces the maximum profit is the solution to the linear programming problem.

ILLUSTRATION 10.1   A firm wishes to maximize its profit given by

$$\pi = 20Q_x + 15Q_y$$

Subject to the constraints imposed by the following limitations on its resources:

Input A : $4Q_x + 3Q_y \leq 90$

Input B : $Q_x + 2Q_y \leq 40$

Input C : $2Q_y \leq 30$

where,

$$Q_x \geq 0 \text{ and } Q_y \geq 0$$

Solution   Here the objective function is given as

$$\pi = 20Q_x + 15Q_y \tag{i}$$

and the constraint inequalities are

$$4Q_x + 3Q_y \leq 90 \tag{ii}$$

$$Q_x + 2Q_y \leq 40 \tag{iii}$$

$$2Q_y \leq 30 \tag{iv}$$

The first stage in the algebraic solution to this LPP is converting the constraint inequalities into equations by introducing slack variables. Since there are three inequalities, so three slack variables S_1, S_2 and S_3 are being incorporated. Thus,

$$4Q_x + 3Q_y + S_1 = 90 \tag{v}$$

$$Q_x + 2Q_y + S_2 = 40 \tag{vi}$$

$$2Q_y + S_3 = 30 \tag{vii}$$

where, Q_x, Q_y, S_1, S_2 and S_3 are all greater than zero, that is, they are positive values.

$$Q_x \geq 0, \ Q_y \geq 0, \ S_1 \geq 0, \ S_2 \geq 0, \ S_3 \geq 0 \tag{viii}$$

We now have to find those values of Q_x, Q_y, S_1, S_2 and S_3 that will maximize the objective Equation (xiv) and at the same time satisfy the constraint Equations (xv), (xvi) and (xvii).

It is known to us that the optimal solution occurs at a corner point and at each corner the number of non-zero variables exactly equals the number of constraint equations. We will proceed to solve the constraint equations keeping at a time, two variables as zero.

Although we can begin with any two variables but it is convenient to begin from the origin, i.e. $Q_x = 0$ and $Q_y = 0$.

(i) Corner O:

Substituting $Q_x = 0$ and $Q_y = 0$ in the constraint and objective equations, we get

$$4 \times 0 + 3 \times 0 + S_1 = 90 \tag{ix}$$
$$1 \times 0 + 2 \times 0 + S_2 = 40 \tag{x}$$
$$2 \times 0 + S_3 = 30 \tag{xi}$$
$$\pi = 20 \times 0 + 15 \times 0 \tag{xii}$$

Solving these equations, we get

$$S_1 = 90, \; S_2 = 40, \; S_3 = 30 \text{ and } \pi = 0$$

(ii) Corner A:

Substituting $Q_x = 0$ and $S_3 = 0$ in the constraint and objective equations, we get

$$4 \times 0 + 3Q_y + S_1 = 90 \tag{xiii}$$
$$1 \times 0 + 2Q_y + S_2 = 40 \tag{xiv}$$
$$2Q_y + 0 = 30 \tag{xv}$$
$$\pi = 20 \times 0 + 15Q_y \tag{xvi}$$

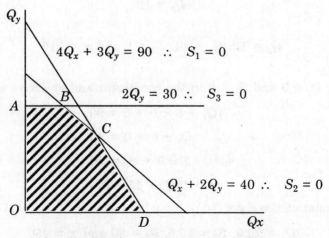

FIGURE 10.8 Algebraic Solution to LPP

Solving these equations, we get

$$S_1 = 45, \ S_2 = 10, \ Q_y = 15 \text{ and } \pi = 225$$

(iii) Corner B:

Substituting $S_2 = 0$ and $S_3 = 0$ in the constraint and objective equations, we get

$$4Q_x + 3Q_y + S_1 = 90 \tag{xvii}$$

$$Q_x + 2Q_y + 0 = 40 \tag{xviii}$$

$$2Q_y + 0 = 30 \tag{xix}$$

$$\pi = 20Q_x + 15Q_y \tag{xx}$$

Solving these equations, we get

$$Q_x = 10, \ Q_y = 15, \ S_1 = 5 \text{ and } \pi = 425$$

(iv) Corner C:

Substituting $S_1 = 0$ and $S_2 = 0$ in the constraint and objective equations, we get

$$4Q_x + 3Q_y + 0 = 90 \tag{xxi}$$

$$Q_x + 2Q_y + 0 = 40 \tag{xxii}$$

$$Q_y + S_3 = 30 \tag{xxiii}$$

$$\pi = 20Q_x + 15Q_y \tag{xxiv}$$

Equations (xxi) and (xxii) have to be solved as simultaneous equations. Multiplying Equation (xxii) by 4 and subtracting Equation (xxi) from it, we have

$$Q_y = 14$$

Putting this value of Q_y in any of these two simultaneous equations,

$$Q_x = 12$$

Thus,

$$Q_x = 12, \ Q_y = 14, \ S_3 = 2 \text{ and } \pi = 510$$

(v) Corner D:

Substituting $Q_y = 0$ and $S_1 = 0$ in the constraint and objective equations, we get

$$4Q_x + 3 \times 0 + 0 = 90 \tag{xxv}$$

$$Q_x + 0 + 0 = 40 \tag{xxvi}$$

$$2 \times 0 + S_3 = 30 \tag{xxvii}$$

$$\pi = 20Q_x + 15 \times 0 \tag{xxviii}$$

Solving these equations, we get

$$Q_x = 22.5, \ S_2 = 17.5, \ S_3 = 30 \text{ and } \pi = 450$$

Comparing the equations, we note that the profit is maximum at corner C. So the solution to the given LPP is that the profit for the firm is maximum when $Q_x = 12$ and $Q_y = 14$ and the profit is equal to 510.

The minimization problem can be solved in the same manner as the maximization problem above. A typical minimization problem will be

$$\text{Minimize } C = a'X + b'Y$$

Subject to the constraints that

$$c'X + d'Y \geq l'$$
$$e'X + f'Y \geq m'$$
$$g'X + h'Y \geq n'$$

and the non-negativity requirement of $X \geq 0$ and $Y \geq 0$.

In the graphical method, the constraints will be plotted in the same manner as we did in the maximization problem. The only difference in the two solutions lies in the feasible region. While in the earlier problem it is extended between the origin and the constraint equation, here due to the nature of resource constraints, the feasible region extends upwards and to the right of the constraints as shown in the Figure 10.9.

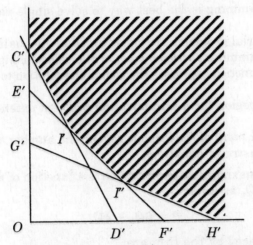

FIGURE 10.9 Graphical Solution to LPP

To find the minimum value of the objective function draw the function and move away from the origin until it just touches the feasible region. This is the point of optimal solution to the minimization problem.

Algebraically also, the solution to a minimization problem is similar to that of the maximization problem. First the values of variables at each corner of the feasible region are found. The one that minimizes the objective function is the solution to the problem. In contrast to the earlier problem, where the positive slack variables were added to the inequalities, here the positive slack variables will be subtracted from the constraint equations for obvious reasons.

Thus, whether the objective of the firm is maximization or minimization of the objective function, the approach to solving the linear programming problem is essentially the same.

QUESTIONS

1. 'Linear programming is an analytical technique for finding out optimal solutions to business problems characterized by constraints.' Discuss.

2. Elucidate the important applications of linear programming in managerial decision-making.

3. 'Linear programming assumes all relationships to be linear.' Comment on the statement.

4. Discuss the different methods for solving a linear programming problem. What are the conditions where the algebraic method provides easier solutions to the linear programming problems?

5. What are the differences in the solving of maximization and minimization problems?

6. State which of the following statements are *true* and which are *false*:

   (a) Linear programming is the best way to solve single variate problems under constraints.

   (b) Most managerial problems are constrained by inequalities.

   (c) Linear programming assumes most of the relationships to be linear.

   (d) An objective function expresses the goal of the solution to a linear programming problem.

   (e) The feasible region for a minimization problem extends to the right of the constraints.

   (f) At each corner point of the feasible region, the number of variables equals the number of constraint equations.

7. A firm wishes to maximize its profit which is a function of the quantity of its two products Q_x and Q_y as under:

$$P = 6Q_x + 4Q_y$$

The constraints faced by the firm are:

$$Q_x + Q_y \leq 40$$
$$2Q_x + 2Q_y \leq 100$$
$$3Q_y \leq 60$$

With the non-negativity requirement holding good, find out what quantities of the two products will maximize the profits of the firm? Support your views both graphically and algebraically.

8. The patients of a hospital have to be provided with a balanced diet having 300 calories, 250 proteins and 100 vitamins. The patients can only be given milk and

cereals. The per unit calorie, protein and vitamin possessed by milk and cereals are given below:

	Calories	Proteins	Vitamins
Milk	20	10	10
Cereal	15	25	4

The price of each unit of milk and cereal is Rs. 12 and Rs. 15 respectively. Find out the lowest cost for a balanced diet composition and the cost of that meal.

CASE STUDY

Case 10.1   Accura Factor

With sales of over 1-million wristwatches, Accura claims to be the number three brand in India. It is now looking at the world as its market. A deal with Wal-mart as a supplier is in the offing and it is talking to several European giants too. The promoters of the company are confident that they can give Chinese manufacturers, known to have cracked the low-cost timepiece game, a run for their money. They might also be talking to a few designers to put out an array of watches and clocks.

The company manufactures only wristwatches. It has an export market for its wristwatches spread over the different parts of United States of America, United Kingdom and Europe, besides being present in some parts of Brazil and Japan. Quality was probably the most important factor in making the company's product well accepted in the overseas market in a short span of less than five years. The wristwatches that are exported are of superior quality and each requires 2 labour hours and 4 machine hours for its manufacturing.

Even in the domestic market, the company has done remarkably well by reaching up to the number three position. Accura has already captured a big slice of the Indian market with a market share of 20 per cent. The resource requirement for the domestic product is different from the export quality wristwatches, the labour and machine hours being 3 each. The growing market share is already creating expansion possibilities in the minds of the promoters as it will not be far when the company will find it difficult to keep up pace with its existing manufacturing capacity of 1,00,000 wristwatches. At this capacity the company has a maximum of 60 labour hours and 96 machine hours available for the manufacturing of wristwatches.

With the given set up the company wishes to maximize its profits, while maintaining the best possible market mix. It has a pricing policy, which keeps a constant mark-up for its wristwatches in the two different markets that it operates in. If the per unit profit in the export and domestic market is Rs. 40 and Rs. 35 respectively, suggest the profit maximizing market mix for the company.

CHAPTER | ELEVEN

Introductory Macroeconomics

LEARNING OBJECTIVES

* the basic concept of national income/gross domestic product
* the interplay of consumption, savings, and investment
* the dynamics of money and money supply
* the concepts of inflation, business cycle, and unemployment
* the importance of monetary and fiscal policies
* the balance of payments and exchange rates
* the issues relating to globalization

While we were discussing the nature of managerial economics in the third chapter of this book, it was stated that managerial economics utilizes some concepts of macroeconomics. It would therefore be worthwhile if, before closing down, we make ourselves aware of some basic concepts of macroeconomics that are extremely important for solving the managerial problems effectively.

 THE CONCEPT

Macroeconomics is that branch of economics, which studies the aggregate behaviour of economic system. As against microeconomics, which was concerned with an individual unit, macroeconomics deals with the analysis of economic factors on the national level. Say for example, microeconomics deals with the division of total output among individual units, allocation of scarce resources, and pricing of particular products while macroeconomics studies the gross or total national product, aggregate national income, and general price level.

Macroeconomics thus determines the level of total economic activity in any nation. Through its explanation, measurement and determination of aggregates such as national income, employment and output, it helps us in understanding the causes of rise in general price level in an economy and determine the inflation rate. It also analyzes the economic growth of an economy. Growth is a function of investment, which in turn is dependent upon savings or consumption. The market economies never always perform at the same level. They are marked with boom and recession periods in alternate cycles. Macroeconomics provides us with concepts that explain the causes of these business cycles. It aims at achieving economic stability by controlling these ups and downs in the market economies.

Yet another parameter, which is considered very important in adjudging the economic health of any nation, is the balance of payments and exchange rate. Nations make payments for goods and services imported while receive payments for goods and services exported. The net payments received and payments made is known as *balance of payments*. The rate at which a nation's currency is exchanged for currencies of other nations, that is, the exchange rate, also influences the balance of payments. For any economy to be stable, the balance of payments should neither be in surplus nor in deficit and the exchange rate should not be fluctuating briskly.

We begin our discussion on the major macroeconomic concepts with an introductory explanation of the basic working platform in any economy, that is, the constituent players and the markets therein.

CONSTITUENT GROUPS OF AN ECONOMY

The constituents of any economy can be grouped under four heads, namely, *the households, the firms, the government,* and *the rest of the world*. These four groups interact in a variety of ways, many involving either the receipt or payment of income.

Figure 11.1 attempts to present a simple view of how these groups interact, as to how they receive income and make payments, and to whom.

As seen in the figure, the households receive income from firms and the government, purchase goods and services from firms, and pay taxes to the government. They also purchase foreign-made goods and services (imports). The firms receive payments from households and the government for goods and services; they pay wages, dividends, interest and rents to households, and taxes to the government. The government receives taxes from both, the firms and households, pays both firms and households for goods and services, including wages to government workers. It also pays interest and makes transfer payments to households. Finally, the domestically made goods and services are purchased by people residing in other nations (exports).

Households work for firms and the government, and they receive wages for their work. The figure shows a flow of wages into the household sector as payment for those services. Households also receive interest on corporate and government bonds and dividends from firms. Many households receive other payments from the government for which they do not supply goods, services, or labour. Such payments are called *transfer payments*. Together, all these receipts make up the total income received by the households.

Households spend by buying goods and services from firms and by paying taxes to

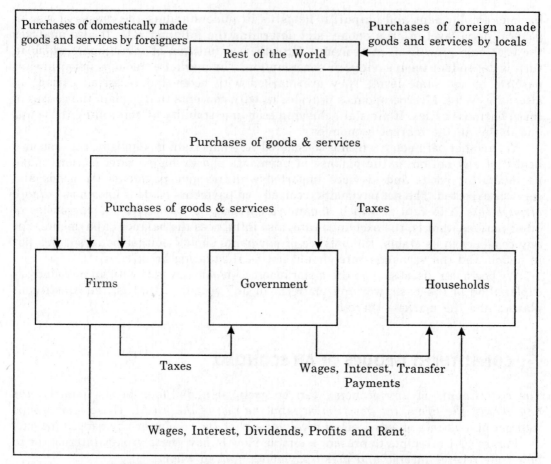

FIGURE 11.1   Flow of Payments among the Constituents

the government. These items make up the total amount paid out by the households. The difference between the total receipts and the total payments of the households is the amount that the households save or dissave. If households receive more than they spend, they save during a period of time. If they receive less than they spend, they dissave. Dissaving, in other words, is negative saving. A household can dissave by using up some of its previous savings or by borrowing. In the figure, household spending is shown as a flow out of the household sector. Saving by households is sometimes termed as a leakage from the flow because it withdraws income or current purchasing power from the system.

Firms sell goods and services to households and the government. These sales earn revenue, which shows up in the figure as a flow into the firms sector. Firms pay wages, interest, and dividends to households, and they pay taxes to the government. These payments are shown flowing out of the firms sector.

Government collects taxes from households and firms. The government also makes payments. It buys goods and services from firms, pay wages and interest to households, and makes transfer payments to households. If the government's revenue is less than its payments, the government is said to be dissaving.

Finally, households spend some of their income on import of goods and services produced in the rest of the world. Similarly, people in foreign nations purchase exports, that is, goods and services produced by domestic firms and sold to other nations.

Another way of looking at the ways in which the constituents of economy—households, firms, the government and the rest of the world—relate to each other is to consider the markets within which they interact.

 MARKETS IN AN ECONOMY

Economies are generally characterized by the following three markets:

1. Goods and Services market
2. Labour market
3. Money market

Let us discuss these markets, as depicted in Figure 11.2, in a little detail.

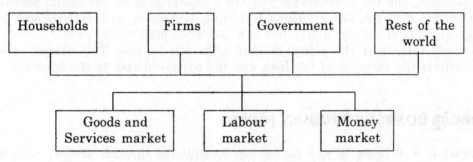

FIGURE 11.2 Markets in an Economy

Goods and Services market. Households and the government purchase goods and services from firms in the goods and services market. In this market, firms also purchase goods and services from each other. Firms supply to the goods and services market. On the other hand, households, the government, as also firms demand from this market. Finally, the rest of the world both buys from and sells to the goods and services market.

Labour market. Interaction in the labour market takes place when firms and the government purchase labour from households. In this market, households supply labour, and firms and the government demand labour. The total supply of the labour in the economy depends on the sum of decisions made by households. Individuals must decide whether to enter the labour force and how many hours to work. Labour is also supplied to and demanded from the rest of the world. In recent years, the labour market has become an international market.

Money market. In the money market, households purchase stocks and bonds from firms. It is also known as financial market. Households supply funds to this market in the expectation of earning income in the form of dividends on stocks and interest on bonds. Households also demand (borrow) funds from this market to finance various purchases. Firms borrow to build new facilities in the hope of earning more in the future. The government borrows by issuing bonds. The rest of the world both borrows from and lends to the money market. Much of the borrowing and lending of households, firms, the government and the rest of the world is coordinated by financial institutions such as commercial banks, development finance institutions, non-banking finance companies, savings and loan associations and insurance companies. These institutions take deposits from one group and lend them to others.

When a firm, household, or the government borrows to finance a purchase, it has an obligation to pay that loan back, usually at some specified time in the future. Most loans also involve payment of interest as a fee for the use of the borrowed funds. When a loan is taken, the borrower nearly always signs a promise, a promissory note, to repay to the lender.

Instead of issuing bonds to raise funds, firms can also issue shares. A share is a financial instrument that gives the holder a share in the firm's ownership and therefore the right to have a share in the firm's profits. If the firm does well, the value of the stock increases, and the shareholder receives a capital gain on the initial purchase. In addition, the stock may pay dividends. If the firm does poorly, so does the shareholder. The capital value of the stock may fall and dividends may not be paid.

A critical variable in the money market is the *interest rate*. The interest rate on a loan reflects the duration of the loan and the perceived risk to the lender.

GROSS DOMESTIC PRODUCT (GDP)

The economic well being of any nation can be depicted through several measures. However, the annual total output of goods and services stands out as the best available measure. The most commonly used measure of the aggregate output of any economy is the Gross Domestic Product or GDP.

Gross Domestic Product (GDP) is the total market value of a nation's output. It is the market value of all final goods and services produced within a given period of time by factors of production located within a nation. It is a key concept in the national income and product accounts. GDP, as a measure of the total production of an economy, acts as an economic barometer of a nation.

GDP measures the market value of the output of a nation and not just the quantity of goods and services produced. It is a monetary measure arrived at by finding the sum total of the products of quantity produced and price of all goods and services produced in any specific year. An accurate measurement of the aggregate output requires that a particular good or service must be counted only once. This means that they are final goods, also known as consumer goods. *Final goods* are the goods and services that are purchased by the consumer for final use and not for any further processing, manufacturing or resale. Most products and services go through a series of production stages before finally getting consumed. Such goods and services that are purchased by an intermediary for further processing, manufacturing or resale are called *intermediate goods*.

For example, tyres sold to automobile manufacturers are intermediate goods. GDP considers only the market value of final goods and ignores the transactions involving intermediate or producer goods. This is because to count intermediate transactions separately would lead to double counting and hence blowing up the value of GDP. The value of intermediate goods is already incorporated in the value of final goods. To count in GDP, both the value of the tyres sold to the automobile manufacturers and the value of the automobiles sold to the consumers, would result in double counting.

A very simple approach to understanding this otherwise complex macroeconomic indicator is as follows. Consider that a nation produces only three goods, namely, pens, paper, and notebooks. All the paper produced is used in the manufacturing of notebooks. Let the quantity of these three goods produced and the price at which they are sold in the market is depicted in Table 11.1.

TABLE 11.1 GDP Calculation

	Quantity	Price (Rs./unit)	Market value (Rs.)	Value added
Pen	10 Nos.	7	70	70
Paper	5 kg	30	150	150
Notebook	20 Nos.	12	240	90
	Total		310	310

Thus the GDP in this case is Rs. 310. It may be noted here that both pen and notebook are final goods. So only their market values are added up to arrive at the GDP. The market value of paper is not considered in the calculation of GDP as it is an intermediate good and its value is already included in the market value of notebooks.

Yet another way to avoid double counting is to calculate the aggregate value added by all firms/sectors of the economy. The value added during some stage of production is the difference between the value of goods as they leave a stage of production and the cost of the goods as they entered that stage, that is, the market value of a firm's output less the value of inputs that it purchases from others. Thus in calculating GDP, we can either sum up the value added at each stage of production or can take the value of final sales.

In our example, the value added in case of notebook production is 240 – 150 = Rs. 90, while that for pen and paper is Rs. 70 and Rs. 150 respectively since the cost of their inputs is not considered here. Adding up the three values gives us the GDP as Rs. 310 which, can be noted, as the same as calculated earlier.

Double counting may also arise if old production is included in the GDP. As a concept, GDP is concerned only with new or current production. Old output is not counted in current GDP because it was already counted back at the time it was produced. GDP ignores all transactions in which money or goods change hands but in which no new goods and services are produced. Sales of stocks and bonds are not counted in GDP. These sales are exchanges of paper assets and do not correspond to current production. However, brokerage is included in GDP as it is a service. This service is a part of current production.

GDP is the value of output produced by factors of production located within a nation. The three basic factors of production are land, labour, and capital. The labour of a nation's citizens counts as a domestically owned factor of production for that nation. The output produced by its citizens abroad is not counted in its GDP because the output is not produced within the nation. Likewise, profits earned abroad by the nation's companies are not counted in its GDP. However, the output produced by foreigners working in the nation is counted in its GDP because the output is produced within the nation. Also, profits earned in the nation by foreign-owned companies are counted in the GDP of that nation.

Care has to be taken since GDP measures the annual production of any nation, so all the non-production transactions must be excluded. Non-production transactions include purely financial transactions and second hand sales. Purely financial transactions include public transfer payments, private transfer payments, and stock market transactions.

It is sometimes useful to have a measure of the output produced by factors of production owned by a nation's citizens regardless of where the output is produced. This measure is called *Gross National Product* (GNP). For most nations, the difference between GDP and GNP is small.

Both GNP and GDP are closely related in the sense that both measure the total market value of all the final goods and services produced in an economy in one year. The difference between them is only in how the economy is defined. While GNP comprises the total output produced with the resources of a nation regardless of whether these resources are located in that nation or abroad, GDP relates to the value of total output produced within the boundaries of a nation whether by resources of the nation or foreign nations.

Calculating GDP

GDP can be computed in two ways. One is to add up the amount spent on all final goods during a given period. This is the *expenditure approach* to calculating GDP. The other is to add up the income i.e. wages, rents, interest and profits, received by all factors of production in producing final goods. This is the *income approach* to calculating GDP. These two methods lead to the same value for GDP because every payment (expenditure) by a buyer is at the same time a receipt (income) for the seller.

The expenditure approach. Corresponding to the four main constituent groups in an economy—households, firms, the government, and the rest of the world—there are four main categories of expenditure, namely,

    (i) Personal consumption expenditures (C)
    (ii) Gross private domestic investment (I)
    (iii) Government purchases (G)
    (iv) Net exports (X)

The expenditure approach calculates GDP by adding together these four components of spending. In equation form, this can be written as

$$GDP = C + I + G + X$$

Personal consumption expenditures (C). A large part of GDP consists of *personal consumption expenditures*. These are expenditures by consumers on goods and services.

There are three main categories of consumer expenditures: durable goods, non-durable goods, and services. Durable goods, such as automobiles, furniture, and household appliances, last a relatively longer time. Nondurable goods, such as food, clothing, and cigarettes are used up fairly quickly. Payments for services, the things we buy that do not involve the production of physical items, include expenditures for doctors, lawyers, and educational institutions.

Gross private domestic investment (I). *Investment* refers to the purchase of new capital such as housing, plants and equipment, and inventory.

Investment can be made both by the private sector as well as public sector. Total investment in capital by the private sector is called *gross private domestic investment.* Private sector investment is generally categorized into residential and non-residential investment. Expenditures by firms for machines, tools, plants, etc. constitute the non-residential investment. Because these are goods that firms buy for their own final use. These form a part of the final sales and are counted in the GDP.

Expenditures for new houses and apartment buildings constitute residential investment. The third component of gross private domestic investment, the change in business inventories, is the amount by which firm's inventories change during a period. Business inventories can be looked at as the goods that firms produce now but intend to sell later.

GDP includes gross investment, which is the total value of all newly produced capital goods in a given period. It takes no account of the fact that some capital wears out and must be replaced. Net investment is equal to gross investment minus depreciation. Net investment is a measure of the change in the stock of capital during a period.

Government purchases (G). *Government purchases* are the purchases of newly produced goods and services by central, state, and local governments. They include any goods that the government purchases plus the wages and salaries of all government workers. The wages and salaries are included here because in a way it is a payment that the government makes to the employees when it purchases their services as employees. This category does not include all the spending by governments. It excludes transfer payments, that is, funds that are paid to individuals but are not associated with the production of goods and services.

Net exports (X). An open economy trades with other economies. Imports are goods bought by a nation from other nations and exports are goods made in a nation and sold to other nations. *Net exports* are total exports minus total imports. Net exports can be positive or negative.

GDP measures the goods produced in a nation. Consumption, investment and government purchases include all purchases by consumers, firms, and the government, whether or not the goods were produced in that nation. But purchases of foreign goods by households, firms, or the government should be subtracted from GDP because these goods were not produced in that nation. At the same time, any goods produced in the nation and sold abroad need to be added to GDP.

When a nation buys more goods from abroad than it sells, it is said to have a *trade deficit*. A *trade surplus* occurs when exports exceed imports. When a nation runs a trade deficit, it means its residents are spending more on goods and services than they are currently producing. Although the nation does sell many goods abroad, it buys even more goods and services from abroad. The result is that such a nation is forced to sell some of its assets to individuals or governments in foreign nations. When residents buy more goods abroad than they sell, they give up more local currency for imports than they receive from exports. This currency given up to purchase imports ends up in the hands of foreigners, who can use them to purchase assets such as stocks, bonds, or real estate.

It is the total trade surplus with all the other nations that determines the amount of foreign assets that a nation will acquire. A trade surplus with one nation and an equally large trade deficit with another, would not add to the foreign assets of a nation.

The income approach. The income approach to calculating GDP looks at GDP in terms of who receives it as income and not who purchases it. The income approach breaks down GDP into four components, namely

    (i) National income (N)
    (ii) Depreciation (D)
    (iii) Indirect taxes minus subsidies (T)
    (iv) Net factor payments to the rest of the world (F)

GDP is then arrived at, by adding together these four components of earnings. In equation form:

$$GDP = N + D + T + F$$

National income (N).   *National income* is the total income earned by factors of production owned by a nation's citizens. When output is produced, income is created. The income that flows to the private sector is called *national income*. It is the sum of five items, namely compensation of employees, proprietor's income, corporate profits, net interest, and rental income. Compensation of employees, the largest of the five items by far, includes wages and salaries paid to households by firms and by the government. Proprietor's income is the income of unincorporated businesses, and corporate profits are the income of corporate businesses. Net interest is the interest paid by business. Rental income, a minor item, is the income received by property owners in the form of rent. In other words, national income is the aggregate factor income that arises from the current production of goods and services by the nation's economy.

Depreciation (D).   Capital assets wear out or become obsolete over time. In the process, they decline in value. The measure of this decrease in values of capital assets is called *depreciation.* Depreciation is a part of GDP in the income approach. Since national income includes corporate profits after the depreciation has been deducted, so depreciation must be added back.

Indirect taxes minus subsidies (T).   In calculating the final sales on the expenditures side, indirect taxes such as sales taxes, customs duties, and license fees are included. Because these taxes are counted on the expenditure side, they must also be counted on the income side.

   Subsidies are payments made by the government for which it receives no goods or services in return. These subsidies are subtracted from national income to get the GDP. For example, farmers receive substantial subsidies from the government. Subsidy payments to farmers are income to farm proprietors and are thus part of national income, but they do not come from the sale of agricultural products, so are not a part of GDP. To balance the expenditure side with the income side, these subsidies need to be subtracted on the income side.

Net factor payments to the rest of the world (F).   Net factor payments to the rest of the world equal the payments of factor income to the rest of the world minus the receipts of factor income from the rest of the world. National income is the income of factors of production owned by a nation. GDP, however, is the output produced by factors of production located within the nation. In other words, national income includes some income that should not be counted in GDP, like the income that a nation's citizens earn abroad. This income must be subtracted. In addition, national income does not include some income that is counted in GDP, like the foreigner's income in the nation whose GDP is being computed. This income must be added.

Other Related Social Accounts

Although Gross Domestic Product (GDP) is the most important item in national income accounting, other concepts are also useful to know. As described earlier, a nation's GDP is total production by factors of production located within that nation, while its *Gross National Product* (GNP) is total production by factors of production owned by that nation.

   For arriving at GNP, we add to the GDP the net income earned by the nation's firms and residents abroad. To make this calculation, we add to GDP any income earned abroad by nation's firms or residents and subtract any income earned in the nation by foreign firms or residents. The result of these adjustments is the total income earned worldwide by the nation's firms and residents. This is called the Gross National Product (GNP).

   Both GDP as well as GNP do not account for the fact that some of the nation's capital stock is used up in the process of producing the nation's product. This wear and tear on plant and equipment that occurs during the year is what we have known as depreciation. In a sense, our income is reduced because our buildings and machines are wearing out. When we subtract depreciation from GNP, we reach Net National Product (NNP), where "net" means after depreciation.

To calculate *National Income* (*N*), the indirect taxes minus subsidies are subtracted from NNP. Indirect taxes are deducted because they are included in NNP but do not represent payments to factors of production and are not a part of national income. If a store sells you a product for Rs. 100 and the sales tax is 4%, your total bill is Rs. 104. However, only Rs. 100 of that purchase goes to the store to pay wages, rent, interest, and maybe even some profit to the owners. The remainder, Rs. 4, goes to the government as it is not part of private-sector income. Subsidies are added because they are payments to factors of production but are not included in the NNP.

Personal income (*PI*) is the total income of households. Personal income can be derived from national income on making some adjustments. All the income, which is earned, is not actually received by the household sector. This difference is accounted for by the corporate income taxes, retained earnings of firms and social security contributions. It also happens that some income that is received is not currently earned, say for example transfer payments.

While corporate profits minus dividends and social insurance payments are subtracted, personal interest income received from the government and consumers and transfer payments to persons are to be added. Some corporate profits are paid to households in the form of dividends, and dividends are a part of personal income. The profits that remain after dividend payments i.e. retained earnings are not paid to households as income. Therefore, corporate profits minus dividends must be subtracted from national income when computing personal income. Social insurance payments are payments made to the government, some by firms and some by employees. Since households do not receive these payments, they must be subtracted from national income when computing personal income.

Interest payments made by the government and households are not counted in GDP and not reflected in national income figures. However, these payments are income received by households, so they must be added to national income when computing personal income. Households can pay and receive interest. As a group, households receive more interest than they pay. Similarly, transfer payments to persons are not counted in GDP because they do not represent the production of any goods or services. However, they must also be added to national income when computing personal income.

Personal income is the income received by households before paying personal income taxes but after paying social insurance contributions. The amount of income that households can spend or save is called *disposable personal income* or simply *disposable income*. It is equal to personal income minus personal taxes. Because disposable personal income is the amount of income that households can spend or save, it is an important income concept. There are three categories of spending, namely, personal consumption expenditures, interest paid by consumers to business and personal transfer payments to foreigners. The amount of disposable personal income left after total personal spending is called *personal saving*.

Personal saving rate is the percentage of disposable personal income saved, an important indicator of household behaviour. A low saving rate means that the households are spending a large amount of their income while high saving rate means households are cautious in their spending. Saving rates tend to rise during recessionary periods when consumers become anxious about their future and fall during boom times.

Another way to look at the GDP is to define it as the money value of all final goods and services produced in domestic territory of a nation during an accounting year. The concept of domestic territory has a special meaning in national income accounting. Domestic territory is defined to include the following:

(a) Territory lying within the political frontiers, including territorial waters of the nation.
(b) Ships and aircrafts operated by the residents of the nation between two or more nations.
(c) Fishing vessels, oil and natural gas rigs, and floating platforms operated by the residents of the nation in the international waters or engaged in extraction in areas in which the nation has exclusive rights of exploitation.
(d) Embassies, consulates, and military establishments of the nations located abroad.

Thus, GDP is the total income generated from production within the territorial boundaries of an economy. It is obtained by adjusting the GNP with the net factor income from outside the nation under concern but within the territorial boundaries of the economy. Net factor income means the net of factor income received and factor income paid.

The GDP measured in current prices we pay for things is known as *Nominal GDP*. It however needs to be adjusted for price changes for a true reflection of the state of affairs. Nominal GDP adjusted for price changes is called *Real GDP*.

GDP can be estimated both at factor cost and at market prices. The contribution of each producing unit to the current flow of goods and services is known as the *Net Value Added* (NVA). GDP at factor cost is estimated as the sum of NVA by the different producing units and the consumption of fixed capital. Since the NVA gets distributed as income to the owners of factors of production, we also estimate GDP as the sum of domestic factor incomes and consumption of fixed capital.

Conceptually, the value of GDP, whether estimated at market price or factor cost, must be identical. This is because, the final value of goods and services (market price) must be equal to the cost involved in their production (factor cost). However, the market value of goods and services is not the same as the earnings of the factors of production. GDP at market prices includes indirect taxes and excludes the subsidies given by the government. Therefore, in order to arrive at GDP at factor cost, we must subtract indirect taxes net of subsidies from the GDP at market prices. Indirect taxes minus subsidies are commonly termed as net taxes (T). The value of any product at market prices can be obtained by adding the net taxes to its value at factor cost. Thus,

$$GDP_{mp} = GDP_{fc} + T$$

Limitations of the GDP Concept

Increasing the GDP (or preventing its decrease) is usually considered one of the chief goals of a government's macroeconomic policy. There are however some limitations of the GDP concept as a measure of welfare.

If crime levels went down, society would be better off, but a decrease in crime is not an increase in output and is not reflected in GDP. Neither is an increase in leisure time. Yet, to the extent that households desire extra leisure is also an increase in social welfare.

Most non-market and domestic activities, such as housework and childcare are not counted in GDP even though they amount to real production. However, if a household decides to send the children to day care or hire someone to clean the house, GDP increases. The salaries of day care staff, cleaning people etc. are counted in GDP, but the time that the household spends doing the same things is not counted. A mere change of institutional arrangements, even though no more output is being produced, can show up as a change in GDP.

Furthermore, GDP seldom reflects losses or social ills. GDP accounting rules do not adjust for production that pollutes the environment. The more is the production, the larger is the GDP, regardless of how much pollution results in the process. GDP says nothing about the distribution of output among individuals in a society. It does not distinguish, for example, between the case in which most output goes to a few people and the case in which output is evenly divided among all people. GDP is also neutral about the kinds of goods an economy produces.

Many transactions are missed in the calculation of GDP, even though they should be counted in principle. Most illegal transactions are missed unless they are laundered into legitimate business. Income that is earned but not reported as income for tax purposes is usually missed, although some adjustments are made in the GDP calculations to take misreported income into account. The part of the economy that should be counted in GDP but is not, is sometimes called the *underground economy*.

In spite of these limitations, GDP is a highly useful measure of economic activity and well being of a nation.

Equilibrium GDP

In order to establish equilibrium GDP, the following assumptions are made:

    (a) GDP is ultimately determined by demand,
    (b) investment spending is constant with respect to changes in income, and
    (c) consumption increases with the level of income.

The equilibrium level of GDP is determined through the equation of aggregate demand and aggregate supply.

Aggregate demand represents the expenditure that the households and the firms are undertaking on consumption and investment. Thus,

Aggregate Demand = Consumption Demand + Investment Demand

The consumption demand depends upon the output (income) and the propensity of the community to consume, while the investment demand is a function of the marginal efficiency of capital and the rate of interest. The marginal efficiency of capital means the expected rate of profit that the firms hope to get from the investment in capital assets.

Aggregate supply means the total money value of goods and services produced in an economy. The aggregate supply comprises of the output of final consumer goods and services and the output of capital or investment or producer goods. The aggregate supply of goods in an economy depends upon the stock of capital, the amount of labour used, and the state of technology. It is same as the gross national product since both represent the value of output of final goods and services produced.

Figure 11.3 shows how GDP is determined. First, the consumption function (*C*) is plotted as a sloping line graphically representing that consumption spending is a function of income. Since investment has been assumed to be constant at all levels of income, the constant level of investment when vertically added to the consumption function, gives us the *C* + *I* line. This line represents the total spending in the economy. The line is upward sloping because consumption spending is assumed to increase with income.

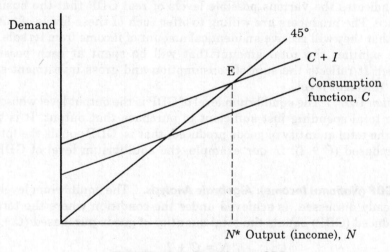

FIGURE 11.3   Equilibrium GDP

The level of equilibrium output (*N**) occurs where the spending line (*C* + *I*) crosses the 45° diagonal line. At this level of output, total spending equals output. At any other level of production, spending will not equal output and the economy will adjust back to *N**.

The aggregate demand and the aggregate supply curves intersect at the point E. Thus at the point E, the entire income is consumed and there is no saving i.e., at this point the aggregate demand equals the aggregate supply. The point corresponds to the equilibrium output (income). The particular aggregate demand, which is equal to aggregate supply and determines the equilibrium level of national income, is called *effective demand*.

A hypothetical example will help to understand the concept of equilibrium GDP better. This approach uses the consumption, saving, and investment schedules to explain the equilibrium level of GDP by combining the income-consumption, income-saving, and income-investment data. The combined tabular representation will be as shown in Table 11.2.

TABLE 11.2   Equilibrium GDP Calculation

Output (Income) GDP	Consumption C	Saving S	Investment I	Aggregate expenditure (C+I)
100	105	−5	10	115
120	120	0	10	130
140	135	5	10	145
160	150	10	10	160
180	165	15	10	175
200	180	20	10	190

Table 11.2 indicates the various possible levels of real GDP that the business sector might produce. The producers are willing to offer each of these levels of output on the expectation that they will receive an identical amount of income from its sale. Aggregate expenditure signifies the total amount that will be spent at each possible output (income) level. It reflects the sum of consumption and gross investment spending at each output (income) level.

Equilibrium GDP: The equilibrium level of GDP is the output level whose production will create a total spending just sufficient to purchase that output. It is the level of GDP where the total quantity of goods produced, that is, GDP equals the total quantity of goods purchased ($C + I$). In our example, the equilibrium level of GDP is 160.

Equilibrium GDP (National Income): Algebraic Analysis. The equilibrium level of GDP, as we have already discussed, is achieved under the condition where the total quantity of goods produced (GDP) equals the total quantity of goods purchased ($C + I$). That is,

$$N = C + I$$

The knowledge of consumption function expresses consumption in terms of income as follows:

$$C = a + bN$$

Solving these two equations, we have

$$N = a + bN + I$$

$$(1 - b)\, N = a + I$$

$$N = \frac{1}{(1 - b)}\, (a + I)$$

This is the equilibrium level of national income or GDP. A simpler model to understanding the equilibrium GDP is the Keynesian Cross, described as follows.

Keynesian Cross. Keynesian Cross is perhaps the simplest model explaining how demand determines output in the short run. It is a graph with the demand for goods and services represented on the vertical axis, output (income) represented on the horizontal axis and a 45° diagonal line, representing a key relationship between the demand and output.

The model is based on the following assumptions:

(i) Neither the government nor the foreign sectors exist. Only consumers and firms can demand output, where consumers demand consumption goods and firms demand investment goods.
(ii) Consumers and firms each demand a fixed amount of goods.

Let consumption demand be C and investment demand be I. The total demand will then be $(C + I)$. In the short run, the demand determines output. That is,

$$\text{Output} = \text{Demand}$$

In this case,

$$\text{Output} = \text{Demand} = C + I$$

On the demand-output diagram, we superimpose the line representing demand, that is, $(C + I)$, which is a horizontal line because both C and I are fixed amounts. Since the total demand is fixed at $(C + I)$, it does not depend on output. The plot is shown in Figure 11.4.

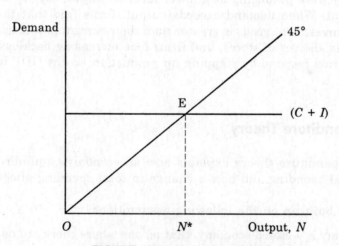

FIGURE 11.4 Keynesian Cross

Equilibrium output is at N^*, the level of output at which the demand line crosses the 45° line. They cross at point E, where output measured on the horizontal axis equals demand by consumers and firms measured on the vertical axis. This is because point E is on the 45° line and therefore, the vertical distance EN^* equals the horizontal distance ON^*. Therefore, at output N^*, total demand equals output.

Economy operations, at any level higher or lower, will eventually strive to attain equilibrium. If the economy were producing at a higher level of output, such as N_1 as in Figure 11.5, more goods and services are being produced than consumers and

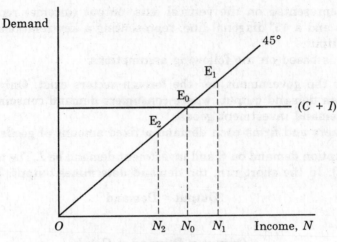

FIGURE 11.5 Equilibrium Output

firms are wanting and buying. Goods that are produced but not purchased pile up on the shelves of stores. Firms react to this by cutting back on production. The level of output will fall until the economy reaches N^*.

If the economy were producing at a lower level of output, say N_2, demand would exceed total output. When demand exceeds output, firms find that the demand for consumption and investment goods is greater than their current production. Inventories disappear from the shelves of stores, and firms face increasing backlogs of orders for their products. Firms respond by stepping up production, so the GDP increases back to N^*.

Aggregate Expenditure Theory

The aggregate expenditure theory explains how an economy's equilibrium real GDP relates to the total spending and how a change in total spending affects the level of real GDP.

The theory is built up on the following assumptions:

1. The economy is a closed economy, that is, one where there are no international trade transactions.
2. The economy is a private economy, that is, the government does not exist.
3. All the savings are personal savings.
4. Depreciation and net foreign factor income are zero.

A careful look at the assumptions would help the reader in understanding two things. While the assumptions 1 and 2 mean that for now we are concerned only with investment and savings, assumptions 2, 3, and 4 signify that the gross domestic product, national income, personal income and disposable income are all equal.

The aggregate expenditure theory or model propounds that the amount of goods and services produced and thus the level of employment in an economy depends directly on the level of aggregate expenditure. The businesses will produce a level of output that they can profitably sell. Workers and machinery are idle when there are no markets for the goods and services that they can produce. Thus, the aggregate expenditures determine the amount of output produced which in turn establishes the level of employment in an economy.

A better appreciation of the model requires us to understand the components of aggregate expenditure in depth. In terms of absolute size, consumption is the largest component of aggregate expenditure. And the part of the income that is not consumed is saving. In other words, the income equals consumption plus savings. Thus when we are studying consumption, we are also simultaneously studying savings. The second component of aggregate expenditure is investment. In order to understand them better, we take them one by one.

Consumption and saving. Of all the determinants of consumption, income and in particular disposable income, is the most significant one. Since consumption is the largest component of aggregate expenditure, it is important to understand the factors that determine consumption spending. And it is evident that while doing so, the determinants of saving are explored simultaneously.

With the assumptions equating the gross domestic product, national income, personal income and disposable income to each other, it can be interpreted that the output always generates an equal level of income. However, all output levels do not give rise to a level of spending sufficient to purchase all the goods and services produced. This is because households may choose to save some income rather than spend the whole of it. Since income is the sum of consumption and saving, that is,

$$N = C + S$$

So, any saving is done at the cost of additional spending. Of course, the saving of households may eventually be utilized by businesses for investment purpose. But that is not essential. Saving and investment are two different things. And there is no reason for us to assume that the amount that households wish to save will equal the amount that businesses wish to invest. In context of income analysis, saving refers only to that portion of income, which is left over after current expenditures.

Many factors influence the level of consumption spending of households. But the most significant among them is the size of its income. A household may save more or it may save less, but its spending will always be closely linked to the income and the amount of saving is usually only a small part of the income. Since saving is that part of the income, which is not consumed, the income is also the basic determinant of personal saving. The historical data for last several decades have shown that consumption is directly related to income and that the households spend most of their income. Their relationship is as shown in the Figure 11.6.

The 45° line is added to the diagram for reference purpose. Each point on this line is equidistant from both the *x*-axis as well as the *y*-axis. Therefore, the vertical distance from any point on the horizontal *x*-axis to this line is either consumption or income. The amount by which the actual consumption falls short of the 45° line

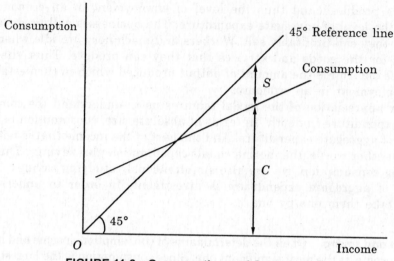

FIGURE 11.6   Consumption and Savings Plot

indicates the amount of savings in that year. The figure suggests that households consume most of their income and that both consumption and saving are directly related to the income level.

The data on relationship between consumption and income gives us a consumption schedule. Before we proceed further with the explanation of the consumption and saving schedules, it would be worthwhile to introduce the relationship between consumption and income mathematically through the concept of consumption function to be followed by that of savings.

Consumption function. The level of income in an economy is perhaps the most important determinant of the consumer spending therein. More is the income, higher is the consumption and vice versa. In other words, the amount of consumption is directly proportional to the level of income. When income of a community rises, its consumption also rises. Consumers want to purchase more goods and services when they have more income than they do when the income levels are low. The mathematical relationship between the amount of consumption and the level of income is known as *consumption function*.

$$C = a + bN$$

As shown in the equation above, the consumption spending C is a function of the income N. The other two terms 'a' and 'b' are constants. The relationship between consumer spending/consumption and income is thus a linear and directly proportional. In a simple economy where the output or the real GDP equals the income that flows to the households, the symbol N can be used to represent both output as well as income. 'a' is a constant and is independent of income. It denotes that part of consumption spending which does not depend on the level of income. Examples of such consumption spending include necessities such as essential food, clothing etc. Such consumption, which exists regardless of the level of income, is also known as *autonomous consumption*.

Another constant '*b*' indicates how much will the consumption spending change for every rupee change in the income. For example, if $b = 0.75$, then for every rupee rise in the level of income, the consumption in the economy increases by 75 paise. This component of consumption, '*b*' is known as *marginal propensity to consume.*

The consumption function when plotted on a graph would look like Figure 11.7 as follows. As seen in the figure, the consumption function is a line that intersects the vertical axis at '*a*', the level of autonomous consumption spending. Since in any logical case, the autonomous consumption must be greater than zero, so the line does not pass through the origin. It has a positive slope, which equals '*b*', the marginal propensity to consume. In the figure, while the consumption is plotted on the vertical axis, the output (income) is plotted on the horizontal axis.

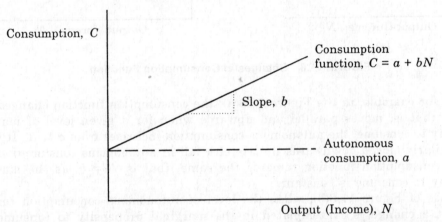

FIGURE 11.7 Consumption versus Income Plot to Depict Consumption Function

The marginal propensity to consume, which is the slope of the line, is always less than one. A consumer who receives a rupee of income will spend a part of it and save the rest. In an eventuality, when a consumer does not or is unable to save anything from the income and consumes all, the marginal propensity to consume will be one.

The fraction that the consumer spends is given by the marginal propensity to consume. It is thus evident that the sum of marginal propensity to consume and the marginal propensity to save is always equal to one.

Changes in consumption function. The aforesaid discussion has made it clear that the level of autonomous consumption and the marginal propensity to consume determine the consumption function. Both of these quantities are constant for a given situation but vary from situation to situation. And when they change, the consumption also changes. Any change in either one or both quantities shifts the consumption function to another position on the graph.

While a change only in autonomous consumption will shift the entire consumption function parallel to its original position, a change in marginal propensity to consume with no change in autonomous consumption will change the slope of the consumption function. Both the cases are clearly shown in the Figure 11.8 as follows:

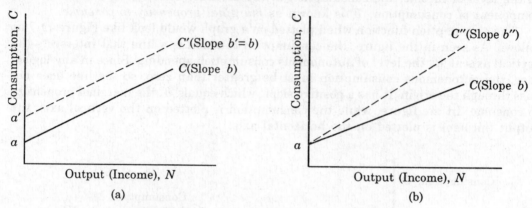

FIGURE 11.8   **Changes in Consumption Function**

Here for example, in the Figure 11.8(a), the consumption function changes from C to C', that is, moves parallel and upwards when for a given level of marginal propensity to consume, the autonomous consumption increases from a to a'. It would have similarly moved downwards in case of a fall in autonomous consumption. The slope of consumption function remains the same, that is, $b = b'$ as the marginal propensity to consume is constant.

In case of Figure 11.8(b), when the level of autonomous consumption remains same but a change is contemplated in the marginal propensity to consume, the consumption function originates from the same point but its slope changes. An increase in marginal propensity to consume for the same level of autonomous consumption, a, has increased the slope of the consumption function from b to b'' as the function changes from C to C''.

Autonomous consumption may change due to several reasons such as a change in consumer wealth, a change in consumer confidence etc. Similarly, the marginal propensity to consume may change due to consumers' perceptions of changes in their income and changes in tax rates, among others.

Savings.   Savings, in its most simple terms, is defined as an excess of income over expenditure. Be it an individual or a nation as a whole, income is earned to meet the expenditure on consumption. When all that is earned is not spent, an economic surplus results. This is known as *savings*.

$$S = N - C$$

where S = Savings

       N = Income

       C = Consumption

Savings is a function of income. All other things remaining same, savings increase with an increase in the income and vice versa. The aggregate amount of savings depends upon the propensity to save, which in turn is dependent on the propensity to consume. And only two ends are possible for income. It can either be saved or consumed or both. The sum total of saving and consumption, in other words, is the income. We also know that the propensity to save and the propensity to consume are the ratios of savings to income and consumption to income respectively. The propensity to save and the propensity to consume thus add up to unity.

$$PS + PC = 1$$

Where *PS* = propensity to save = *S/N*
      PC = propensity to consume = *C/N*

We have already discussed that an economy in general is composed of households, firms, and government. Its *Aggregate Domestic Savings* (ADS) are therefore, the sum of the savings made by all these three components, that is, the households, firms and government. While the households and firms fall under the private category, government savings are public savings. Savings mean different for each one of these. For households, saving is the excess of disposable personal income over the consumption expenditure. A firm's saving is obtained by deducting the dividend from the net profit. Similarly government savings are the positive difference of the public revenue and expenditure. In developing economies like India, household sector contributes the maximum to the aggregate domestic savings accounting for more than three-fourth of the total savings.

There are a number of factors that affect savings. Some important determinants of savings are: level of income, distribution of income, consumption pattern, level of consumption, population, rate of interest on savings and political stability. A high level of income automatically translates into higher savings, *ceteris paribus*. High-income group sectors of the community have a greater marginal propensity to save. Besides income level, the distribution of income also plays an important role in determining savings. Unequal distribution of income in the economy leads to higher savings. The level and pattern of consumption also affects savings. These in turn depend upon the types of consumption habits, desire to accumulate wealth, urgency of present needs, and fear of inability to enjoy future consumption. Savings have an inverse relationship with population. If population is more, per capita income is low. A lot depends upon the prevailing interest rates also. Higher interest rates will attract higher savings. To a person who doesn't have any investment opportunity, it makes no sense to save. Similarly, political stability and security of life and property encourage people/firms to save more.

Consumption and saving schedules. *Consumption schedule* is a set of data depicting the relationship between consumption and income. This is simply an income-consumption relationship. The schedule indicates the various amounts that the households plan to consume at various levels of income which might prevail at some specific point in time. The relationship is direct, as the commonsense would suggest, and the households will spend a larger proportion of a low income than of a high income. Figure 11.9 depicts the consumption schedule plot.

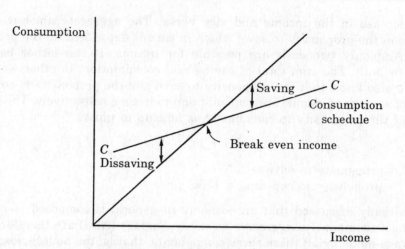

FIGURE 11.9 Consumption Schedule

Although there are many factors influencing how much of its income a given household will actually decide to spend, a consumption schedule assumes that all these other determinants of consumption remain unchanged, that is, *ceteris paribus* and the only change is in the level of income.

The amount saved at each level of the income can then be simply arrived at by deducting the consumption from the income. This relationship between saving and income is known as the *saving schedule* (shown in Figure 11.10). Just as the consumption schedule, there is a direct relationship between saving and income but saving is a smaller proportion of a low income than of a high income. This implies that if households consume a smaller proportion of the income as the income goes up, they must save a larger proportion.

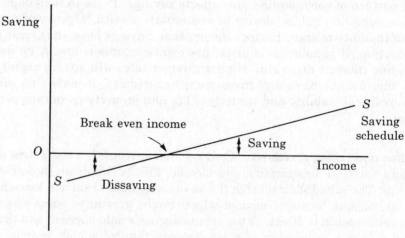

FIGURE 11.10 Saving Schedule

It can be observed that dissaving would occur at a relatively low level of income. Households will consume more than their current incomes by liquidating accumulated wealth or by borrowing. The point where the households consume their entire income is known as the *break even income*. Graphically, it is the point where the consumption schedule cuts the 45° line or where the saving schedule cuts the horizontal *x*-axis. At higher income, the households save a larger part of their income.

Average and marginal propensities. The fraction of total income that is consumed is called the *Average Propensity to Consume (APC)*. It is arrived at by dividing the consumption by income. Thus,

$$APC = \frac{\text{Consumption}}{\text{Income}} = \frac{C}{N}$$

The remaining fraction of total income, which is saved, is called the *Average Propensity to Save* (APS). That is,

$$APS = \frac{\text{Saving}}{\text{Income}} = \frac{S}{N}$$

It may be noted that *APC* falls and *APS* rises as the income increases (refer Table 11.3). The fraction of total income that is consumed, declines as the income rises and the fraction of income that is saved rises as the income increases. Since the income is either consumed or saved, the sum total of the fraction of income consumed

TABLE 11.3   Consumption and Saving Schedules

Output (Income) GDP=N	Consumption C	Saving S(N – C)	APC C/N	APS S/N	MPC ΔC/ΔN	MPS ΔS/ΔN
100	105	−5	1.0500	−0.0500	—	—
120	120	0	1.0000	0.0000	0.75	0.25
140	135	5	0.9643	0.0357	0.75	0.25
160	150	10	0.9375	0.0625	0.75	0.25
180	165	15	0.9167	0.0833	0.75	0.25
200	180	20	0.9000	0.1000	0.75	0.25

or saved must exhaust that level of income. In other words, the sum of the average propensity to consume and save is always one.

$$APC + APS = 1$$

Although the average household consumes a certain percentage of income at any given point in time, it will not necessarily spend that same percentage of any future income. The proportion of extra income devoted to consumption is called the *Marginal Propensity to Consume (MPC)*.

It is mathematically expressed as,

$$MPC = \frac{\text{Change in consumption}}{\text{Change in income}}$$

Marginal propensity to consume, in other words, is the change in consumption to a unit additional change in income.

Similarly, the ratio of change in saving to the change in income is called the *Marginal Propensity to Save (MPS)*.

$$MPS = \frac{\text{Change in saving}}{\text{Change in income}}$$

Since any increase in income must go either to consumption or saving, we get

$$MPC + MPS = 1$$

Consuming or saving out of extra income is thus an either-or proposition. The fraction of any additional unit of income that is not consumed is, by its very definition, saved. In our example, $0.75 + 0.25 = 1$. That is, the consumer in this case is spending three-fourth of the income and saving one-fourth of it. The graphical interpretation of *MPC* and *MPS* treats them to be the slope of the consumption schedule and saving schedule respectively. Figure 11.11 depicts the marginal propensities.

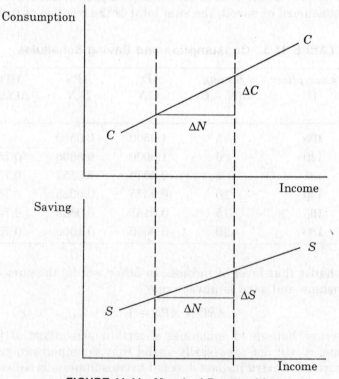

FIGURE 11.11   Marginal Propensities

We have said that income is the most significant determinant of consumption and saving. While the relationship between the changes in consumption/saving and the change in income has already been discussed in detail, it would be pertinent to end this particular topic with a brief description of some other remaining factors besides income, which have a bearing on the amount of consumption and saving.

Some such determinants of consumption and saving are:

   (i) Wealth,
  (ii) Expectations,
 (iii) Indebtedness,
  (iv) Taxation, and
   (v) Average size and age of households.

Generally it has been found that the amount of consumption increases with the increase in wealth accumulated by the households. For obvious reasons, the amount of saving will decrease in such a case. The converse also holds true. Wealth here means both the real assets as well as the financial assets that the households own. Table 11.4 enlists some real and financial assets.

TABLE 11.4   Real and Financial Assets

Real Assets	Financial Assets
House	Cash
Car	Shares
Television	Bonds
Fridge	Bank deposits
Computer	Government securities

Households save to accumulate wealth. The desire to save decreases as this accumulation increases. An increase in wealth shifts the consumption schedule upward and the saving schedule downward. However, wealth may not cause large shifts in consumption and saving schedules because most often it only changes modestly from year to year.

Expectations of the households about the future income, prices of commodities and their quantities available, significantly affect the current consumption and saving. Say for example, a household expects that the prices of goods and services will rise in future. Such an expectation will trigger more consumption and expenditure, and less saving. This will shift the consumption schedule upward and the saving schedule downward. Similarly an expected shortage of a good or service will induce people to buy more today and vice versa. At times, expectations can play a greater role in the sense that households may not only buy for their current consumption but also stock the commodities for times to come.

Consumer indebtedness is yet another factor that affects consumption and hence saving. When the overall debt burden on the households is high, they may not be willing to consume freely. They will look to saving some income in order to honour the payment obligations of the existing debt. Conversely, if the consumer indebtedness is relatively low, households may consume at a high rate and in turn increase the indebtedness.

Taxation also affects the consumption of households. Higher tax rates and stringent tax policies will shift both the consumption and the saving schedules downward because taxes may be paid partly at the expense of consumption and partly at the expense of saving. Consumption also depends on the average size and age of households. A large household or that having more of young members would be more into consumption spending as also more of saving. Thus both the consumption and saving schedules will shift upward. Similar reasoning applies in the converse case. It may be noted that the movement from one point to another on a stable consumption schedule is called a change in amount consumed. Such a change in amount of consumption is only brought about by a change in income. As against this, a change in the consumption schedule refers to the upward or downward shift of the entire consumption schedule. This is caused by changes in any one or more of the non-income determinants. This is explained in the Figure 11.12 that follows:

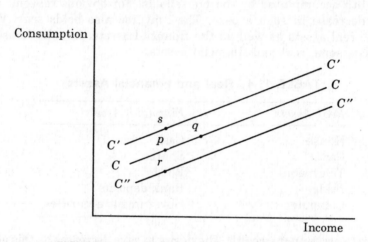

FIGURE 11.12   **Shift in Consumption Schedule**

While the change from *p* to *q* is a change in the amount of consumption from *p* to *r* or from *p* to *s* is a change (shift) in the consumption schedule. Similar reasoning applies to the saving schedule. Although we have discussed determinants that cause a change in consumption amount or schedule, it is generally agreed upon by economists that the consumption and saving schedules are generally stable. This may be because consumption-saving decisions are strongly influenced by habits or because the non-income determinants are diverse and changes in them frequently work in opposite directions and may thus cancel out each other ultimately ending into a null effect.

Investment.   The second major component of private spending is investment. *Investment,* as defined in the beginning of this book, is the addition to the total physical stock of capital. The buying of securities, such as shares, bonds or mutual funds units, which is commonly referred to as investment, is not really investment, in that sense. It is merely a change in the ownership of assets that already exist. No new capital assets are created in the economy. In economics, *investment* signifies the new expenditure on addition of capital goods and inventories. Investment raises the level of aggregate demand, which in turn increases the level of income and employment in the economy.

The volume of investment undertaken by the private entrepreneurs in an economy depends upon the Marginal Efficiency of Capital (MEC) and the Available Rate of Interest (ARI). Investments will be made only when the MEC is greater than the ARI. It is only when the households or the firms get more returns than what they incur, that they will be motivated to invest. Say for example, a person has an economic surplus of Rs. 50,000, which has an opportunity cost of 12% p.a. He will invest that amount of savings only if he expects to earn on his investment, a return of more than 12% p.a. The same logic applies to the other constituents of the economy.

It may be noted that here *marginal efficiency of capital* is the discounting rate that equates the present value of the cash flows generated by an investment project to the present value of cash outflows, that is, the cost of that investment project. The equilibrium volume of investment can be found out by relating the rate of interest to the marginal efficiency of capital.

Equality between savings and investment. By definition, in the actual sense, savings and investment are always equal. However, in the desired, planned sense they are generally not equal. In that case, they are equal only in equilibrium.

This can be understood in the following manner. Consider a situation where the savings increase. With an increase in the savings, the consumption decreases because we know that income can either be consumed or saved. The decline in consumption in the economy will cause the inventories with the manufacturers and/or traders to rise. This addition to the inventories, though not planned, will raise the level of investment. Thus, the investment will become equal to the increased savings and vice versa. In the planned sense, however, savings and investment are not equal because those who save are different from those who invest. The households save while the firms invest.

An economy will be in equilibrium when the aggregate level of investment equals the aggregate domestic savings. All views, whether they originate with the classical economists or in Keynesian theory, are consonant on this. However, the equilibrating variables may be different. While the classical theory on savings-investment equality regarded the rate of interest as the strategic variable bringing about equilibrium, Keynes established variation in income level as the equilibrium variable. There can be divergence between savings and investment only when the economy is not in equilibrium.

According to the classical view, an economy is in equilibrium at the full employment level. The saving-investment equality is brought about by the variations in the rate of interest. Equating saving and investment will bring the economy into equilibrium through automatic changes in the rate of interest. Keynes, however, suggested that an economy achieves the state of equilibrium at a less than full employment level and that the savings and investment are equated by the variations in the level of income. With the fall in rate of interest or rise in the level of income, the investment demand will increase. But the fall in the rate of interest or the rise in the level of income will adversely affect the volume of savings. Thus, equality between savings and investment will be brought about through an expansion in investment and contraction in savings.

Thus while the classical economists believed saving and investment to be equal, thinkers led by Keynes thought of savers and investors as essentially two different groups, motivated by different set of factors. Things could perhaps become simpler when we discuss some important determinants of investment spending. The investment decision is a marginal analysis decision. Ideally an investment decision should be taken if the marginal benefit arising out of it is greater than the marginal cost of the decision. While marginal benefit from investment is the expected rate of net profit, the marginal cost is the interest rate, that is, the cost of capital. These two are therefore the two basic determinants of investment spending.

Expected rate of net profit. Businesses are not for charity. Businessmen invest only when they expect certain options to be profitable. Also called as return on investment, the expected rate of net profit is simply the net profit in percentage terms that one expects to earn out of the business.

ILLUSTRATION 11.1 A firm Exact Photocopiers operates a photocopying shop. It is considering an investment into a new photocopier of Modi Xerox make, costing Rs. 1 lakh and having a useful life of 1 year. The new machine would obviously add to the revenue of the firm. The net revenue after the installation of the new machine is expected to be Rs. 1.15 lakh. Find out the expected rate of net profit.

Solution   Cost of machine   = Rs. 1.00 lakh
Expected Net Revenue   = Rs. 1.15 lakh
Expected Net Profit   = Expected Net Revenue − Cost
= Rs. 1,15,000 − Rs. 1,00,000
= Rs. 15,000

$$\text{Expected Rate of Net Profit} = \frac{\text{Expected Net Profit}}{\text{Original Investment}} \times 100$$

$$= \frac{15,000}{1,00,000} \times 100$$

$$= 15\%$$

Thus, the expected rate of the net profit on the investment on new machine is 15%.

Real interest rate. Whether this investment of Rs. 1 lakh has come from the firm's own funds or from borrowed funds, there is always some interest. If borrowed then it will bear a rate of interest and if own then the opportunity cost. Either way there will be a financial cost to the investment. Our above example was missing this interest cost. If the expected rate of net profit exceeds the real interest rate, only then the investment is profitable, otherwise not.

We have used the term real interest rate. It is worthwhile to mention here that real interest rate is the nominal interest rate less than the rate of inflation. The real rate of interest, rather than the nominal rate of interest, is crucial in making investment decisions.

ILLUSTRATION 11.2 In the Illustration 11.1, state whether the firm should invest in the new machine if the cost of borrowing is 18% and the prevailing rate of inflation is 4.5%.

Solution Here, the nominal interest rate = 18%

$$\text{Rate of inflation} = 4.5\%$$
$$\text{Real interest rate} = (18 - 4.5)\%$$
$$= 13.5\%$$

Since the expected rate of net profit (15%) is greater than the real interest rate (13.5%), the firm may invest in the new machine.

Investment demand curve. The illustrations as above were the case of a single firm. If we aggregate the investment spending decisions of all the firms, we get the cumulative investment data for the economy as a whole. Such a graphical representation is known as *investment demand curve* (refer Figure 11.13). It is derived by arraying all relevant investment projects in descending order of their expected rate of net profitability and applying the rule that investment should be undertaken to the point at which the real interest rate is equal to the expected rate of net profit.

As seen in the Figure 11.13, the investment demand curve is downward sloping, reflecting an inverse relationship between the real interest rate and the quantity of capital goods demanded.

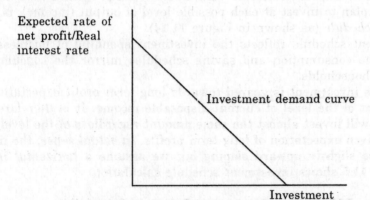

FIGURE 11.13   Investment Demand Curve

Besides these two major determinants, there are some other factors, which affect the investment spending. They are as follows:

   (i) Acquisition and operating costs
  (ii) Corporate taxes
 (iii) Technological change
 (iv) Expectations

As the acquisition and operating costs for the machines rise, the expected rate of net profitability will fall, shifting the investment demand curve to the left and vice versa. Higher wages or electricity bills would thus shift the investment demand curve to the left.

Corporate taxes also affect the investment decisions in any economy. This is because businesses look to the expected net profits in making their investment decisions. An increase in business taxes would lower the net profits thus shifting the investment demand curve to the left. Similarly, a tax reduction would shift the curve to the right.

Technological developments, in general, stimulate investments. Better technology leads to better quality and reduced costs. This improves the profit margins for the businesses. Profitable new products induce a flurry of investment, as firms gear up for the expanded production. A rapid rate of technological progress will shift the investment demand curve to the right.

Investment involves expectations about the future. The businesses make investment because they believe that the venture will be profitable. The profitability of any investment depends upon the expectations of the future sales and profitability, which the investment will help produce. If businesses become more optimistic about the future business conditions, the investment demand curve will shift to the right. A pessimistic outlook, on the other hand, will shift it to the left.

Investment and income. The investment decisions of business can be linked to the consumption plans of the households if the investment plans can be expressed in terms of the level of disposable income. Such a relationship, which shows the amounts that businesses plan to invest at each possible level of output (income), is known as an *investment schedule* (as shown in Figure 11.14).

An investment schedule reflects the investment spending of businesses in the same way as the consumption and saving schedules mirror the consumption and saving plans of households.

The business investment is geared towards long-term profit expectations and is thus independent of the level of current disposable income. It is therefore assumed that businesses will invest almost the same amount regardless of the level of output (income) for a given expectation of long-term profits. In actual sense, the investment schedule may be slightly upward sloping but we assume a horizontal investment schedule. Table 11.5 shows investment schedule calculation.

TABLE 11.5 Investment Schedule Calculation

Level of Output (Income), GDP = N	100	120	140	160	180	200
Investment, I		10	10	10	10	10	10

In contrast to the consumption schedule, the investment schedule is quite unstable. It shifts significantly upward or downward quite often. Proportionately, investment is the most volatile component of total spending. Some factors that cause the variability of investment are durability of capital goods, irregularity of innovation, variability of profits, and variability of expectations.

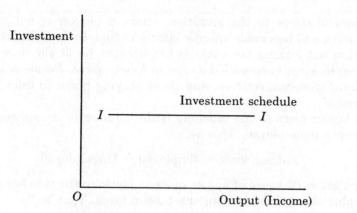

FIGURE 11.14   Investment Schedule

UNEMPLOYMENT

All economies seek to achieve full employment and eliminate unemployment. The understanding of unemployment will be rendered easy if we can first define 'full employment'. *Employment* refers to the condition where large number of able-bodied persons of working age, who are willing to work, can get work at current wage levels. When such persons cannot find such work, it is considered to be a case of unemployment. When persons are only partially employed or are employed in inferior jobs though they can do better ones, underemployment is said to exist. *Full employment* may be defined as a situation wherein all those who are willing and able to work at the prevailing wage rate are in fact employed for the work in which they are trained. Thus in case of full employment, every available resource in the economy is being fully used in the production of goods and services. When all existing resources are fully and efficiently employed, output will be maximum.

Unemployment refers to any unused resource, whether land, labour, or capital. In each case, a cost to the economy is involved. In the production side of the national accounts, the cost is the value of commodities that could not be produced, while on the income side of the account, the cost is the loss of wages and salaries, rent and interest for labour, land, and capital respectively.

Of all the resources, labour is the one on which most attention is concentrated. There are several reasons for doing so. Some of them are as follows:

1. Statistics on unemployed labour serves as a fairly reliable indicator of total unemployment.
2. Costs of human unemployment are usually more obvious and dramatic than the costs of other kinds of unemployment.
3. Labour is usually the sole productive resource that a household has to sell.
4. When labour resources are unemployed, there is a loss of total future output.
5. Human resource depreciates more quickly than other kinds of resources.

We will therefore refer to labour in all our discussions relating to unemployment.

Unemployment refers to the situation where a person is not employed but is available for work and has made specific efforts to find work during the previous four weeks. A person not looking for work, either because he or she does not want a job or has given up looking, is classified as *not in labour force*. People not in labour force include full-time students, retirees, and those staying home to take care of children or elderly parents.

The total labour force in the economy is the number of people employed plus the number of people unemployed. That is,

$$\text{Labour force} = \text{Employed} + \text{Unemployed}$$

The total population 16 years of age or older is equal to the number of people in the labour force plus the number not in the labour force. That is,

$$\text{Population} = \text{Labour force} + \text{Not in labour force}$$

With these numbers, several ratios can be calculated. The *unemployment rate* is the ratio of the number of people unemployed to the total number of people in the labour force. That is,

$$\text{Unemployment rate} = \frac{\text{Unemployed}}{\text{Employed} + \text{Unemployed}}$$

The ratio of the labour force to the population 16 years old or over is called the *Labour force participation rate*.

$$\text{Labour force participation rate} = \frac{\text{Labour force}}{\text{Population}}$$

Types of Unemployment

Unemployment is of three main types, namely, frictional unemployment, structural unemployment and cyclical unemployment. We now discuss all these types in brief.

Frictional unemployment.   *Frictional unemployment* is the unemployment that occurs naturally during the normal working of an economy. At any point in time, some workers will be midway on the jobs. It is not possible for every worker to be employed every single working day of his life. While some will be voluntary switching jobs, others will have been fired and are seeking re-employment. Still others will be temporarily laid off from their jobs due to other factors. For instance, rainy season has got lot to do in the construction industry. And there are some young workers searching their first jobs. All such people lead to frictional unemployment.

In other words, frictional unemployment consists of search unemployment and wait unemployment for workers who are either searching for jobs or waiting to take up jobs in near future. 'Frictional' correctly implies that the labour market is not perfect or instantaneous, that is, it is not without friction in matching workers and the job.

Frictional unemployment can occur for a variety of reasons. People change jobs, move across the nation, get laid off from their current jobs, and search for new opportunities, or take their time after they enter the labour force to find an appropriate job. As jobs become more and more differentiated and the number of required skills increases, matching skills and jobs becomes more complex, and the frictional unemployment rate may rise. For example, frictional unemployment occurs when due to technological progress, some persons presently fully employed are likely to loose jobs.

On the other hand, when a particular productive activity is seasonal in nature and the persons employed in it become unemployed during the slack season, the type of unemployment is called *seasonal unemployment.*

Frictional unemployment is inevitable and sometimes, desirable. While the frictional unemployment rate can never be zero, it may change over time. Many workers are searching or waiting for higher paying and higher productivity positions. This means more income for the workers and a better allocation of labour and therefore a larger real output for the economy as a whole. Thus, this unemployment is both natural and beneficial for the economy.

Structural unemployment. The industrial structure of economies keeps changing continuously over time. Changes also occur over time in the structure of consumer demand and in technology, which alter the structure of total demand for labour. Because of such changes, there is less demand for some skills or they may even become obsolete. The demand for other skills therefore expands, including skills that never exist. Unemployment results because the composition of labour force does not respond quickly or completely to the new structure of job opportunities. Some workers thus find that they have no readily marketable talents. The skills and experience of these workers become obsolete and unwanted by the changes in technology and consumer demand. Unemployment may also result when workers are looking for work in a location that has no industry that can use their skills. Such workers are also reluctant to move to new locations. These workers are potentially employable but no firm in their area is willing to pay the salaries they demand for the skills that they possessed.

Although the unemployment that arises from such structural shifts could also be classified as frictional, it is usually called *structural unemployment.* The distinction between frictional and structural unemployment is hazy. However, the main difference is that frictionally unemployed workers have saleable skills, while the structurally unemployed workers are not readily re-employable without re-training, additional education, and possibly geographic relocation. The term frictional unemployment is used to denote short run job/skill matching problems, that last a few weeks. Structural unemployment, on the other hand, denotes long run adjustment problems that tend to last for years.

Structural unemployment occurs because of a mismatch between the jobs that are available and the skills of workers who are seeking jobs. Workers with low skills may not find opportunities for employment. If the government requires employers to pay wages, taxes, and benefits that exceed the contribution of these workers, firms will not be likely to hire them. Similarly, workers whose skills do not match the employment opportunities in their area may be unemployed.

Although structural unemployment is expected in a dynamic economy, it is painful to the workers who experience it. In some ways, those who lose their jobs because their skills are obsolete are the ones who experience the greatest pain. The fact that structural unemployment is natural and inevitable does not mean it costs society nothing.

Cyclical unemployment. Although unemployment is natural, there are times when the unemployment rate seems to be beyond the natural rate. The unemployment rate is closely tied to the overall fortunes of the economy. Unemployment rises sharply during periods when real GDP falls and decreases when real GDP grows rapidly. The increase in unemployment that occurs during economic recessions and depressions is called *cyclical unemployment.*

All business cycles undergo booms and recessions. During recession the effective demand decreases. As a result, in order to survive, the businesses reduce their production. Some factors of production thus become unemployed causing the cyclical or Keynesian unemployment. In one sense, an increase in unemployment during a recession is simply a manifestation of an even more fundamental problem. The basic problem is that firms are producing less. In that case, firms will not want to employ as many workers as they do in good times because they are not producing as many goods and services.

The reasons for a firm producing less can be many. Level of spending perhaps will stand out to be the most important one. The level of employment may be linked directly to the level of total spending. When spending is at a high level, businesses can produce and sell large volumes at profits, so they can buy nearly all of the productive resources available in general and employ more labour in particular. Thus, unemployment is low. When spending decreases, business firms must cut back on production and consequently they are unable to buy as many resources, including labour as are offered for sale. This results in a rise in unemployment.

A recession causes a decline in real GDP, or real output. When firms cut back and produce less, they employ fewer workers and less capital. Thus, the first and most direct cost of a recession is the loss of real goods and services that otherwise would have been produced. Cyclical unemployment rises during periods when real GDP falls or grows at a slower than normal rate and decreases when the economy improves. As the overall demand for goods and services decreases, employment falls and unemployment increases. For this reason, the cyclical unemployment at times is also called *deficient demand unemployment.*

Costs of Unemployment

When there is excess unemployment, that is, actual unemployment is more than the natural rate of unemployment, both society and individuals suffer economic loss. From a social point of view, excess unemployment means that the economy is no longer producing at its potential. The social loss translates into reduced income and lower employment for individuals. When unemployment increases, more workers are fired or laid off from their existing jobs, and individuals seeking employment find fewer opportunities available. To families with fixed obligations, such as mortgage payments, the loss in income can bring immediate hardships.

The costs of unemployment are not simply financial. In our society, a person's status and position are largely associated with the type of job the person holds. Losing a job can impose severe psychological costs. Some studies, have found that increased crime, divorce, and suicide rates are associated with increased unemployment.

Employment Strategies

Developing economies like India suffer from the problem of surplus labour. They have to formulate a developmental strategy for promoting the growth of employment. This requires the correct measurement of the magnitude of surplus labour, which can be done using the time criterion, willingness criterion, income criterion, or the productivity criterion. Some prominent employment strategies are—growth-oriented strategy, wage-goods strategy, labour-intensive technology strategy, and rural public work strategy of employment.

The growth-oriented strategy of employment suggests that unemployment and underemployment exist due to lack of capital relative to the magnitude of labour force. This happens when the growth in stock of capital is not able to keep pace with the growth in population. The strategy aims at expansion in supply of capital to promote the growth of output and employment in the economy. According to the wage-goods strategy, unemployment is caused due to deficiency of the supply of wage goods. Labour-intensive strategy based the unemployment and underemployment on the use of capital-intensive technology. Rural public works strategy advocates the large-scale launch of rural public works for taking care of unemployment.

BUSINESS CYCLE

Change is a universal phenomenon and businesses are no exception to this. Moreover when they are affected by the external environment which itself is highly volatile, they cannot remain constant for all times. Since these businesses add up to the overall economy at the macro level, no nation can have a steady economic growth in the long-run. The economic growth will intermittently be interrupted by periods of economic instability. The periods of rapid economic expansion will sometimes be marred by inflation. At other times, expansion would give way to recession and depression, that is, falling levels of output and employment. The economic activity of any nation thus experiences alternate ups and downs reflecting the periods of growth and recession.

While the period and intensity of growth or recession may vary from time to time and economy to economy, it is certain that they will exist. This phenomenon of recurring ups and downs in the levels of economic activity extending over a period of time is known as *business cycle*. In the simplest of the terms, a business cycle consists of a period of economic expansion followed by a period of economic contraction. A typical business cycle is as illustrated in the Figure 11.15 as follows:

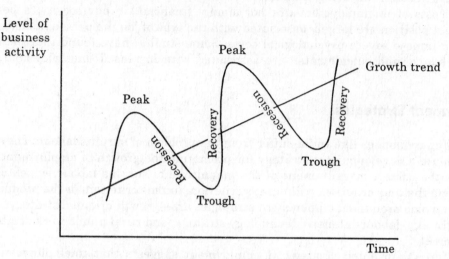

FIGURE 11.15 Business Cycle

Expansion and recession are the two phases of business cycle. A recession is roughly a period in which real GDP declines for at least two consecutive quarters. Real GDP is a measure of the actual output of goods and services in the economy during a given period. An expansion is just the reverse. When recession becomes severe, it is known as depression.

Other economic measures also rise and fall along with real GDP. Both investment spending and consumption spending rise and fall along with increase and decrease in real GDP. The prices of shares of companies also tend to rise and fall as real GDP goes up and down. Economic measures that move in conjunction with real GDP are called pro-cyclical. Thus, investment spending, consumption spending, and share prices are all pro-cyclical. Economic measures that fall as real GDP rises are known as counter-cyclical. Unemployment, for instance, is counter-cyclical.

During the expansionary period, output, income, and employment begin to increase as the business activity increases. Since, the businesses are just coming out of recession, idle resources are available and businesses find it easy to increase production without having to pay more for the inputs. They do not have to raise the prices of their output and so inflation does not generally occur. This continues as the recovery progresses, leading to a peak where the capacity is fully utilized and full employment is achieved. After some time, businesses start feeling shortage of resources to match the increasing business activities. With resources fully employed, any further increase in demand leads to higher prices.

The expansionary period is characterized by high investment spending, high interest rates, and high optimism. But these do not last forever. Eventually the economy witnesses a slowdown in consumption and investment spending. Profits fall as businesses are squeezed between rising costs of production and falling demand. Slowly businesses become unviable leading to unemployment, low output, and low income. A further drag in the contractionary period takes the economy to the trough with heavy unemployment, substantial unused capacity, low income, low profits or even losses, and falling prices. This continues till some positive change lifts up the sentiments.

Several theories have been put forward to suggest the causes of business cycles. Technological change, overproduction and under-consumption, disturbances in available stock of money, and random events such as war are just a few to name. Economists also are of the view that the length of the cycle and even the fluctuations therein may vary in time and severity. Whatever the case may be, every business cycle has four stages, namely peak, recession, trough, and recovery. Let us discuss these in little detail.

Peak

This stage signifies the temporary maximum of the expansionary period. The increased consumption demand is satisfied in the initial stages of the expansionary period by increased production. Eventually, however, the economy will achieve full employment of resources and shortages will begin to develop. This would push up the costs of production and hence the prices. These shortages can be met by additional capital formation only in the short run because soon no more resources will be available. The high level of business activity in this stage ensures that the output is also at full capacity. The prices will rise due to the brisk competition among buyers.

Inflation thus characterizes the peak of a business cycle. Monetary policy tends to be tight in an effort to check inflation. Generally, the central banks use open market operations and higher discount rates to discourage banks from granting new loans. With high level of business activity and lower availability of capital the businesses compete with each other to borrow funds regardless of the cost. There prevails widespread optimism about future.

Recession

The last stages of the boom period set the stage for a recession in the economy. At the peak of business cycle, the consumption demand, though at high level, is no longer growing at the same high rate. This stabilization of the consumption demand starts an *accelerator effect* causing the investment demand to drop sharply. The sharp fall in investment demand, in turn, leads to further decline in consumption. This is called *multiplier effect*. With such a situation, the business activity gets reduced and recession starts. The falling consumption and investment demands necessitate a cut in the capacity utilization and unemployment gets in. This downtrend is marked by a decline in the total output and a widespread contraction of business in several sectors of the economy. The prices however, may not fall during recession, unless the recession is severe and prolonged. The future appears to be dark and tough and the general confidence level in the economy gets affected. People, out of fear, start saving more and consuming less causing further fall in consumption demand, income, and employment. The investment demand will also continue to be low due to the interaction of the accelerator effect and the multiplier effect. New investment is also not forthcoming due to falling profits. The profit falls because while the demand falls, the interest costs assumed earlier have to be paid. The central banks try to control recession by increasing the money supply in the economy and forcing the interest rates down.

Trough

At the worst stage of recession, the business activities hit a temporary bottom. This stage of business cycle is termed as *trough*. At this point, the consumption spending tries to stabilize at a relatively lower level and the investment spending is also minimal. Prices may continue to fall in quite a few of the businesses. In other words, this is the lowest temporary level to which the economic activity falls as a result of recession. The output and employment bottom out at their lowest levels during a given period between any two successive peaks. Profits are low and unemployment looms large. The confidence is the economy and its future is abysmally low. Although due to the efforts of the Central Bank and the banking system, the money is readily available in plenty and that too at low interest rates, there are a few borrowers as pessimism is widespread.

Recovery

With such a dismal state of affairs, some very positive event should occur in the economy, the upswing may takeoff. This stimulus to national income may come from either replacement demand for worn-out equipment, government stimulation of consumption spending either through tax cuts or more spending on public works, lower interest rates, increase in confidence level, or any other random event. Once national income starts growing, the accompanying rise in consumption spending helps sustain the momentum. The multiplier remains at a high rate. As general confidence level goes up, the consumer credit increases because the households are now more willing to borrow funds and the lenders also are more willing to lend money.

The increasing consumer spending will ask for an increased output from the businesses. If the capital stock had depleted during recession immediately, then the accelerator effect takes over. However, if the recession was prolonged and long term, then large amount of idle capacity may exist and the accelerator effect may take some time to get in. Whatever may be the case, increasing consumer spending will attract heavy investment spending and the economy will recover at a fast pace. The increasing business activity will also increase the demand for money. As recovery intensifies, the price levels may also increase.

For an economy that grows over time, the business cycle shows a positive trend where every successive peak and trough is higher than the peak and trough of the previous cycle. The period from a trough to a peak is called an *expansion, recovery,* or *boom*. During an expansion, both output and employment grow. The period from a peak to a trough is called *contraction, recession* or *slump*, and this is the time when output and employment fall.

The business cycle is symmetrical, if the length of an expansion is the same as the length of a contraction. However, all business cycles are not symmetrical. For example, it is possible for the expansion phase to be longer than the contraction phase. When contraction comes, it may be fast and sharp while expansion may be slow and gradual. Moreover, the economy is not nearly as regular as the business cycle in the figure indicates. While there are ups and downs in the economy, they tend to be erratic.

 ## MONEY AND MONEY SUPPLY

Money

Money is anything that is generally accepted as a medium of exchange. Most people take the ability to obtain and use money for granted. People take for granted that they can walk into any store, restaurant, or boutique and buy whatever they want, as long as they have enough currency notes in their pockets. The idea that you can buy things with money is so natural and obvious that it seems absurd to even mention it. Money serves three crucial functions in any economy. These are:

(a) **A medium of exchange:** Money is vital to the working of a market economy. The alternative to a monetary economy is barter economy where people exchange goods and services for other goods and services directly instead of exchanging via the medium of money. A barter system requires a double coincidence of wants for trade to take place. That is, to effect a trade, one person has to find another who has what he wants, and the other person must also want what the first one has.

Some agreed-to medium of exchange or means of payment, eliminates the double-coincidence-of-wants problem. Under a monetary system, money is exchanged for goods or services when people buy things and goods or services are exchanged for money when people sell things. No one ever has to trade goods for other goods directly.

(b) **A store of value:** Money also serves as a store of value, that is, an asset that can be used to transport purchasing power from one time period to another. If you raise potatoes and at the end of the month sell them for more than what you want to spend and consume immediately, you may keep some of your earnings in the form of money until the time you want to spend it.

There are many other stores of value besides money. The surplus earnings can be held by buying such things as antique paintings, gold, or diamonds, which could be sold later when earnings need to be spent. Money has several advantages over these other stores of value. First, it comes in convenient denominations and is easily portable. Second, because money is also a means of payment, it is easily exchanged for goods at all times. These two factors compose the liquidity property of money. The main disadvantage of money as a store of value is that the value of money falls when the prices of goods and services rise. When this happens, it may be better to use those other goods and services as a store of value.

(c) **A unit of account:** Money also serves as a unit of account, a consistent way of quoting prices. All prices are quoted in monetary units. A textbook is quoted as costing Rs. 250, not 30 pens or 20 floppies. A standard unit of account is extremely useful when quoting prices.

Thus **money** may be defined as anything that is generally acceptable as a means of exchange and at the same time can be used as a measure and store of value.

There was a time when the government backed currency notes in circulation by holding a certain amount of gold in its vaults. However, currency notes are no longer backed by any commodity and are exchangeable only for other denomination rupee notes and so on. Still, paper money is accepted as a means of payment and a store of value because the government has taken steps to ensure that its money is accepted. The government declares its paper money to be legal tender and must be accepted in settlement of debts. It does this by fiat and hence the term *fiat money*.

Apart from declaring its currency legal tender, the government also promises the public that it will not print paper money so fast that it loses its value. Expanding the supply of currency so rapidly that it loses much of its value has been a problem throughout history and is known as *currency debasement*. Debasement of the currency has been a special problem of governments that lack the strength to take the politically unpopular step of raising taxes or reducing interest rates on small saving schemes. Printing of money which is to be used for government expenditures of goods and services, can serve as a substitute for tax increases and interest decreases, and weak governments have often relied on the printing press to finance their expenditures.

Money Supply

Money supply is the total stock of money available to a society for use in connection with the economic activity of the nation at a point of time. Money supply comprises of two elements, namely (i) currency with the public and (ii) demand deposits with the public. The term public refers to households, firms, and institutions other than banks and the government. While the public uses money, government and banks are the money producers.

Currency with the public, in a nation, is the sum total of the currency notes in circulation issued by the Central Bank. Say, for example, currency with the public in India is the sum total of the currency notes in circulation issued by the RBI, number of rupee notes and coins in circulation and small coins in circulation. The cash reserves with banks must remain with them and hence have to be deducted from the above sum. The demand deposits with the public are the bank deposits held by the public. Bank deposits are either demand deposits or time deposits. While demand deposits can be withdrawn by the public by drawing cheques on them, time deposits mature only after a fixed period and are money that people hold as a store of value.

Measuring money supply. The money supply can be measured in several ways. However, four concepts of measure of money supply are most common. They are as follows:

  (i) Money supply, $M1$
  This is the narrow measure of money supply.

$$M1 = C + DD + OD$$

  where, C = Currency notes and coins with the public
  DD = Demand deposits with all commercial and co-operative banks
  OD = Other deposits with the Central Bank.

  $M1$ is also known as *transactions money*. As its name suggests, this is the money that can be directly used for transactions, that is, to buy things. Further, $M1$ is a stock measure, that is, it is measured at a point in time. It is the total amount of currency notes and coins outside of banks and the total amount in demand deposits on a specific day. Since the money included in $M1$ can easily be used as a medium of exchange, it is the most liquid measure of money supply.

  (ii) Money supply, $M2$
  This is a broader concept of money supply than $M1$.

$$M2 = M1 + SD$$

  where, SD = Saving deposits with post office savings banks

  The saving deposits with post offices are in between demand deposits with banks and time deposits with banks, with regard to liquidity. They are not chequeable accounts, that is, they cannot be withdrawn, in part or in full, by drawing cheques on them.

  (iii) Money supply, $M3$
  $M3$ is a broad concept of money supply. It includes time deposits with banks in addition to the money supply, $M1$.

$$M3 = M1 + TD$$

  where, TD = Time deposits with all commercial and cooperative banks

  This measure uses time deposits because although time deposits cannot be withdrawn through drawing cheques on them but loans from banks can easily be obtained against such deposits. Further, they can be withdrawn any time by foregoing some interest earned on them. Of late, $M3$ has become a popular measure of money supply.

(iv) Money supply, M4

This measure includes deposits with post office savings organization besides M3. It however excludes contributions made by public to the National Savings Certificates (NSCs).

Whatever may be the measure used, money supply is determined by four factors, namely, bank credit to government, bank credit to private sector, changes in net foreign exchange assets and government's currency liabilities to public.

Because a wide variety of financial instruments bear some resemblance to money, it has been advocated to include almost all of them as part of the money supply. In recent years, for example, credit cards have come to be used extensively in exchange. One of the very broad definitions of money includes the amount of available credit cards as part of the money supply.

There are no rules for deciding what is money and what is not. However, for our purpose here, money will always refer to the transactions money (M1) and the symbol used will be simply M instead of M1. For simplicity, we will say that the money supply is the sum of two general categories, namely, currency in circulation and that in deposits.

The Banking System

Most of the money today is "bank money" of one type or another. Any understanding of money requires some knowledge of the structure of the banking system.

Banks and other financial intermediaries borrow from individuals or firms having excess funds and lend to those who need funds. For example, commercial banks receive funds in various forms, including deposits in chequeable and saving accounts, commercial loans, and so on. Banks and bank like institutions are called financial intermediaries because they mediate or act as a link between people who have funds to lend and those who need to borrow. The main categories of financial intermediaries are commercial banks, developmental finance institutions, non-banking finance companies, savings and loan associations, life insurance companies, and pension funds.

To appreciate how banks create money, consider the origins of the modern system. In the fifteenth and sixteenth centuries, citizens of many lands used gold as money, particularly for large transactions. Because gold was both inconvenient to carry around and susceptible to theft, people began placing their gold with goldsmiths for safekeeping. On receiving the gold, goldsmiths would issue a receipt to the depositors, charging them a small fee for looking after their gold. After a time, these receipts became a form of paper money making it unnecessary to go to the goldsmith to withdraw gold for a transaction.

Goldsmiths functioned as warehouses where people stored gold for safekeeping. The goldsmiths found, however, that people did not come often to withdraw gold. This was largely because the paper receipts that could easily be converted to gold were as good as gold, rather better than gold as they were more portable, safer from theft, and so on. As a result, goldsmiths had a large stock of gold continuously on hand.

Because they had what amounted to extra gold, the goldsmiths gradually realized that they could lend out some of this gold without any fear of running out of gold. Instead of just keeping their gold idle in their vaults, they earned interest on loans. The goldsmiths thus changed from mere depositories for gold into bank like institutions that had the power to create money. This transformation occurred as soon as goldsmiths began making loans. Without adding any more real gold to the system, the goldsmiths increased the amount of money in circulation by creating additional claims to gold, that is, receipts which entitled the bearer to receive a certain quantum of gold on demand. Thus, there were more claims than the quantum of gold.

Goldsmiths-turned-bankers, however, did face certain problems. Once they stared making loans, their outstanding receipts (claims on gold) were greater than the amount. If the owners of gold receipts all presented their receipts and demanded their gold at the same time, the goldsmiths would be in trouble as all the people will not be able to get their gold at once.

Under normal circumstances, people would be happy to hold receipts instead of real gold, and this problem would never arise. If, however, people began to worry about the goldsmiths' financial safety, they might start having doubts about whether their receipts really were as good as gold.

Knowing there were more receipts outstanding than the quantum of gold in the goldsmith's vault, people might start to demand gold for receipts. This situation leads to a paradox. It makes perfect sense to hold paper receipts instead of gold if you know you can always get your gold for the receipt. Under normal circumstances, goldsmiths could feel perfectly safe in loaning out more gold than they actually had in their possession. But once someone (and everyone else) start to doubt the safety of the goldsmiths, then he (and everyone else) would be foolish not to demand his gold from the vault.

A run on the goldsmiths, now a run on a bank, occurs when many people present their claims at the same time. These runs tend to feed on themselves. If a person sees another going to the goldsmith to withdraw gold, the other person may also become nervous and decide to withdraw his gold as well. It is the fear of a run that actually causes the run. Runs on a bank can be triggered by a variety of causes such as rumours that the bank may have made loans to borrowers who cannot repay, wars, failures of other institutions that have borrowed money from the bank, and so on.

Accounting in banks. A glance at the basic accounting principles will be quite helpful in understanding the working of the modern banking system. Just as any other balance sheet, the balance sheet of a bank also consists of assets and liabilities.

Assets are things that a firm owns that have a certain value. For a bank these assets include the bank building, its furniture, its holdings of government securities, cash in its vaults, bonds, stocks and so on. Most important among a bank's assets are its *loans*. A borrower gives the bank an *IOU,* a promise to repay a certain sum of money on or by a certain date. This promise is an asset of the bank because it is worth something. The bank could and sometimes does sell the IOU to another bank for cash. Other bank assets include cash on hand and deposits with the Central Bank.

A firm's liabilities are its debts, or the amount it owes to anyone. A bank's liabilities are the promises to pay or IOUs that it has issued. A bank's most important liabilities are its deposits. Deposits are debts owed to the depositors, because when you deposit money in your account, you are in essence making a loan to the bank.

The basic rule of accounting says that if we add up a firm's assets and then subtract the total amount it owes to all those who have lent it funds, the difference is the firm's net worth. Net worth represents the value of the firm to its stockholders or owners.

Banks are legally required to hold a certain percentage of their deposit liabilities as reserves. The percentage of its deposits that a bank must keep as reserves is known as the *Required Reserve Ratio*. Two types of reserves ratios are required to be maintained by the banks, namely, Cash Reserve Ratio (CRR) and Statutory Liquidity Ratio (SLR).

Money Creation

Like the goldsmiths, today's bankers seek to earn by lending money out at a higher interest rate than they pay to their depositors for using their money. In modern times, the chances of a run on a bank are fairly small and the Central Bank protects the private banks in various ways. Therefore, banks usually give loans up to the point where they can no longer do so because of the reserve requirement restriction.

A bank's required amount of reserves is equal to the required reserve ratio times the total deposits in the bank. The difference between a bank's actual reserves and its required reserves is its excess reserves. That is,

$$\text{Excess Reserves} = \text{Actual Reserves} - \text{Required Reserves}$$

If banks give loans up to the point where they can no longer do so because of the reserve requirement restriction, it means that banks give loans up to the point where their excess reserves are zero.

This is because, when a bank has excess reserves, it has credit available, and it can give loans. Actually, a bank can give loans only if it has excess reserves. When a bank gives a loan, it creates a demand deposit for the borrower. This creation of a demand deposit causes the bank's excess reserves to fall because the extra deposits created by the loan use up some of the excess reserves the bank has on hand.

An increase in bank reserves leads to a greater than one-for-one increase in the money supply. The relationship between the final change in deposits and the change in reserves that caused this change is referred to as the *money multiplier*. It is given by

$$\text{Money multiplier} = \frac{1}{\text{Required reserve ratio}}$$

Functions of the Central Bank

Central Banks are sometimes known as "bankers' banks" because primarily only banks can have accounts with them. In some exceptional cases foreign governments can also have accounts with them. A private citizen cannot go to the nearest branch of the Central Bank and open a chequeable account or apply to borrow money.

Although from a macroeconomic point of view the Central Bank's crucial role is to control the money supply, it also performs several other important functions for banks. These functions include clearing inter bank payments, regulating the banking system, and assisting the banks in a difficult financial position. The Central Bank is also responsible for managing exchange rates and the nation's foreign exchange reserves. In addition, it is often involved in negotiations on international economic issues between nations. The function of clearing inter bank payments allows banks to shift money virtually instantaneously. All they need to do is wire the Central Bank and the funds move at the speed of electricity from one computer account to another.

Besides facilitating the transfer of funds between banks, the Central Bank is responsible for many of the regulations governing banking practices and standards. For example, the Central Bank has the authority to control mergers between banks, and it is responsible for examining banks to ensure that they are financially sound and conform to a host of government accounting regulations. The Central Bank also sets reserve requirements for all financial institutions.

One of the most important responsibilities of the Central Bank is to act as the lender of last resort for the banking system. As our discussion of goldsmiths suggested, banks are subject to possibility of runs on their deposits. Deposit insurance is less likely to create panic. Because depositors know they can always get their money, even if the bank fails, they are less likely to withdraw their deposits. Not all deposits are insured, so the possibility of a panic still remains. However, the Central Bank stands ready to provide funds to a troubled bank that cannot find any other sources of funds.

The Central Bank is an ideal lender for two reasons. First, providing funds to a bank that is in dire straits is risky and not likely to be very profitable. So it is hard to find private lending institutions willing to do this. The Central Bank being a nonprofit institution whose function is to serve the overall welfare of the public would certainly be interested in preventing catastrophic banking panics. Second, the Central Bank has an essentially unlimited supply of funds with which to bail out banks facing the possibility of runs. The reason is that the Central Bank can create reserves at will. A promise by the Central Bank that it will support a bank is very convincing. Unlike any other lender, the Central Bank can never run out of money. Therefore, the explicit or implicit support of the Central Bank should be enough to assure depositors that they are in no danger of losing their funds.

The Central Bank's balance sheet. The assets column of the Central Bank's balance sheet includes gold, loans to banks and government securities. The loans to banks, are an asset of the Central Bank in the same way a private commercial bank's loans are among its assets. The Central Bank sometimes gives loans to commercial banks that are short of reserves. Government Securities, which form the largest of the Central Bank's assets, are obligations of the government such as Treasury Bills (T-bills) and Bonds.

The bulk of the Central Bank's liabilities are currency notes. Like any ordinary commercial bank, the Central Bank also accepts deposits. These deposits are liabilities.

The bulk of the Central Bank's deposits come from commercial banks, as the commercial banks are required to keep a certain share of their own deposits as deposits at the Central Bank. A bank's deposits with the Central Bank are an asset from the bank's point of view, and those same reserves are a liability from the Central Bank's point of view.

The Central Bank also accepts a small volume of deposits from the Treasury. In effect, the Central Bank acts as the bank for the nation's government. When the government needs to pay for something like a new aircraft carrier, it may write out a cheque to the supplier of the carrier drawn on its chequeable account at the Central Bank. Similarly, when the government receives revenues from tax collections, fines or sales of government assets, it may deposit these funds in its account at the Central Bank.

Central Bank and Money Supply

Three tools are available to the Central Bank for controlling the money supply: (a) changing the required reserve ratio; (b) changing the discount rate; and (c) engaging in open market operations.

Required reserve ratio. The simplest way for the Central Bank to alter the supply of money is to change the required reserve ratio. The required reserve ratio establishes a link between the reserves of the commercial banks and the deposits (money) that commercial banks are allowed to create. The reserve requirement effectively determines how much money is available with a bank to lend. Since money supply is equal to the sum of deposits inside banks and the currency in circulation outside banks, reserves provide the leverage that the Central Bank needs to control the money supply.

As stated earlier, reserves that are required to be maintained by the banks are of two types, namely, Cash Reserve Ratio (CRR) and Statutory Liquidity Ratio (SLR). The *Cash Reserve Ratio* is the percentage of total deposits of a bank that it has to keep with the Central Bank in the form of cash. *Statutory Liquidity Ratio*, on the other hand, refers to the portion of the total deposits of a bank that it is required to keep with itself in the form of specified liquid assets, that is, cash plus approved government securities.

Decreases in the required reserve ratio allow the banks to have more deposits with the existing volume of reserves. As banks create more deposits by making loans, the supply of money increases. The reverse is also true. If the Central Bank wants to restrict the supply of money, it can raise the required reserve ratio, in which case banks will find that they have insufficient reserves and must therefore reduce their deposits by calling in some of their loans. The result is a decrease in the money supply.

The Central Bank generally makes less use of the changes in the reserve requirement to control the money supply. In part, this reluctance stems from the fact that since these reserves, specifically the CRR, earns no interest, the higher the reserve requirement, the more the penalty imposed on those banks holding reserves. This affects the performance of the banks. It is also true that changing the reserve requirement ratio is a crude tool. Because of lags in bank's reporting to the Central Bank on their reserve and deposit positions, a change in the requirement today does not affect banks for about two weeks. However, the fact that changing the reserve requirement expands or reduces credit in every bank in the nation, makes it a very powerful tool if at all the Central Bank does use it.

Discount rate.   Banks may borrow from the Central Bank. The interest rate they pay to the Central Bank is known as the *discount rate*. When banks increase their borrowing, the money supply increases. Thus bank borrowing from the Central Bank leads to an increase in the money supply. Banks that borrow from the Central Bank must eventually repay, and when they do, the money supply goes back down by exactly the amount by which it initially increased.

The Central Bank can influence bank borrowing through the discount rate. The higher the discount rate, higher is the cost of borrowing and the less borrowing banks will want to do. If the Central Bank wants to curtail the money supply, for example, it raises the discount rate and discourages banks from borrowing from it, thus restricting the growth of reserves, and ultimately deposits.

In practice, the Central Bank does not often use the discount rate to control the money supply. It does change the discount rate from time to time to keep it in line with other interest rates, but most often the discount rate follows the other rates instead of leading them.

Changing the discount rate to control the supply of money has several problems associated with it. First, although raising the discount rate does discourage borrowing by banks thereby reducing their ability to expand the money supply, it is never clear in advance exactly how much of an effect a change in the discount rate is going to have. If banks are very short of reserves, they may decide to borrow from the Central Bank even if the discount rate is quite high. In other words, the discount rate cannot be used to control the money supply with great precision, because its effects on bank's demand for reserves are uncertain. Second, changes in the discount rate can be largely offset by movements in other interest rates. If the discount rate is set at 6 per cent and the rate paid by T-bills is 5 per cent, banks will not borrow from the Central Bank to purchase T-bills.

Open market operations.   By far the most significant of the Central Bank's tool for controlling the money supply is its open market operations. *Open market operations* refer to the buying and selling of government securities by the Central Bank in the open market.

Consider the case when Central Bank sells some of its holdings of government securities to the general public. Central Bank's holding of government securities will decrease, because the securities it sold will now be owned by someone else. Purchasers of securities pay for these securities by writing cheques drawn on their banks and payable to the Central Bank. Thus the money supply would contract. Similarly, the Central Bank can expand the money supply by buying government securities from people who own them, just the way it reduces the money supply by selling these securities.

Each business day, the open market desk at the Central Bank buys or sells government securities, usually to large security dealers who act as intermediaries between the Central Bank and the private markets.

An open market purchase of securities by the Central Bank results in an increase in reserves and an increase in the supply of money by an amount equal to the money multiplier times the change in reserves. Similarly, an open market sale of securities by the Central Bank results in a decrease in reserves and a decrease in the supply of money by an amount equal to the money multiplier times the change in reserves.

Open market operations are the Central Bank's preferred means of controlling the money supply for several reasons. First, open market operations can be used with some precision. If the Central Bank needs to change the money supply by just a small amount, it can buy or sell a small volume of government securities. If it wants a larger change in the money supply, it can buy or sell a larger amount. Second, open market operations are extremely flexible. If the Central Bank decides to reverse the course, it can easily switch from buying securities to selling them. Finally, open market operations have a fairly predictable effect on the supply of money.

Supply Curve for Money

The foregoing discussions have clearly established that the Central Bank can control the money supply at a given point in time by changing the discount rate, by changing the required reserve ratio, or by engaging in open market operations. In this sense, the supply of money is completely determined by the Central Bank and the money supply curve, as shown in Figure 11.16, is a vertical line.

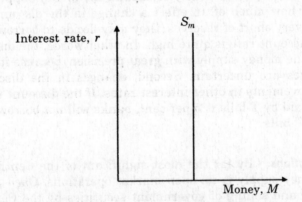

FIGURE 11.16 Money Supply Curve

A vertical money supply curve signifies that the Central Bank sets the money supply independent of the interest rate. It means that the interest rate does not affect the RBI's decision on how much money to supply. In practice the curve may not be perfectly vertical as the Central Bank's money supply behaviour is influenced not only by the state of the economy, but perhaps also by the interest rate.

Demand for Money

The interest rate and the level of national income influence how much money households and firms wish to hold. The demand for money depends on how much of its financial assets the household or the firm wants to hold in the form of money that does not earn interest versus how much it wants to hold in interest-bearing securities, such as bonds. Figure 11.17 depicts the money demand curve. Following may be the motives behind the demand for money.

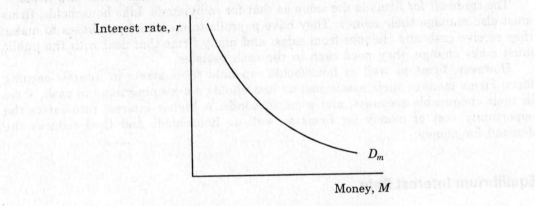

FIGURE 11.17 Money Demand Curve

The transaction motive. The decision to hold money involves a trade-off between the liquidity of money and the interest income offered by other kinds of assets. The main reason for holding money instead of interest-bearing assets is that money is useful for buying things. This is known as the *transaction motive.*

The quantity of money demanded, that is, the amount of money households and firms wish to hold is a function of the interest rate. Because the interest rate is the opportunity cost of holding money balances, increases in the interest rate reduce the quantity of money that firms and households want to hold, and decreases in the interest rate increase the quantity of money that firms and households want to hold.

The precautionary motive. It so happens that households and firms may hold money more than what they require for their current transactions. Uncertainty of future receipts and expenditure causes people to hold money as a precaution. This is known as the *precautionary motive.* Such a type of demand for money may be expected to vary with the level of income. It also varies inversely with the interest rate.

The speculation motive. A number of theories have been offered to explain why the quantity of money households desire to hold may rise when interest rates fall, and fall when interest rates rise. One involves household expectations and the relationship of interest rates to bond values. When market interest rates fall, bond values rise and when market interest rates rise, bond values fall.

Now consider the desire to hold money balances instead of bonds. If market interest rates are higher than normal, they may be expected to come down in the future. If and when interest rates fall, the bonds that were bought when they were high will increase in value. When interest rates are high, the opportunity cost of holding cash balances is high and there is *speculation motive* for holding bonds in lieu of cash, a speculation that interest rates will fall in the future. Similar reasoning applies to an expectation of rising interest rates.

Total demand for money. The total quantity of money demanded in the economy is the sum of the demand for demand deposits and cash, by both households and firms.

The trade-off for firms is the same as that for individuals. Like households, firms must also manage their money. They have payrolls to meet and purchases to make; they receive cash and cheques from sales; and many firms that deal with the public must make change, they need cash in the cash register.

However, firms as well as households can hold their assets in interest-earning form. Firms manage their assets just as households do, keeping some in cash, some in their chequeable accounts, and some in bonds. A higher interest rate raises the opportunity cost of money for firms as well as households and thus reduces the demand for money.

Equilibrium Interest Rate

The point at which the quantity of money demanded equals the quantity of money supplied determines the *equilibrium interest rate* in the economy.

Supply and demand in the money market. The Central Bank controls the money supply through its manipulation of the amount of reserves in the economy. Because we are assuming that the Central Bank's money supply behaviour does not depend on the interest rate, the money supply curve is a vertical line. In other words, we are assuming that the Central Bank uses its three tools (the required reserve ratio, the discount rate, and open market operations) to achieve its fixed target for the money supply.

Figure 11.18 superimposes the vertical money supply curve on the downward-sloping money demand curve. Only at interest rate r^* is the quantity of money in circulation, that is, the money supply equal to the quantity of money demanded.

Borrowing and lending are continuous processes. The treasury sells government securities (bonds) more or less continuously to finance the deficit. When it does, it is borrowing, and must pay interest to attract bond buyers. Buyers of government bonds are, in essence, lending money to the government, just as buyers of corporate bonds are lending money to corporations that wish to finance investment projects.

Consider r_1 in Figure 11.18. At r_1, the quantity of money demanded is D_{m1} and the quantity of money supplied exceeds the quantity of money demanded. This means there is more money in circulation than households and firms want to hold. Thus, at r_1, firms and households will attempt to reduce their money holdings by buying bonds. When there is money in circulation looking for a way to earn interest, that is, when

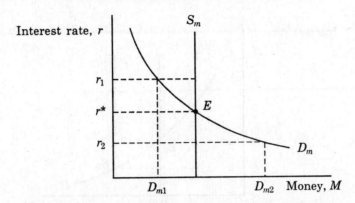

FIGURE 11.18 Supply and Demand in Money Market

demand for bonds is high, those looking to borrow money by selling bonds will find that they can do so at a lower interest rate. If the interest rate is initially high enough to create an excess supply of money, the interest rate will immediately fall, discouraging people from moving out of money and into bonds.

Now consider r_2, where the quantity of money demanded (D_{m2}) exceeds the supply of money currently in circulation. The households and firms do not have enough money on hand to facilitate ordinary transactions. They will try to adjust their holdings by shifting assets out of bonds and into their bank accounts. At the same time, the continuous flow of new bonds being issued must also be absorbed. The government and corporations can sell bonds in an environment where people are adjusting their asset holdings to shift out of bonds only by offering a higher interest rate to the people who buy them. If the interest rate is initially low enough to create an excess demand for money, the interest rate will immediately rise, discouraging people from moving out of bonds and into money.

Money supply and interest rate. The Central Bank can affect the interest rates. It can reduce the interest rate by expanding the money supply (S_m). To expand S_m, the Central Bank can reduce the reserve requirement, cut the discount rate, or buy government securities in the open market. All these practices expand the quantity of reserves in the system. Banks can grant more loans, and the money supply expands the initial money supply curve and shifts it to the right, from S_{m0} to S_{m1}, as depicted in Figure 11.19.

At r_0, there is an excess supply of money. This immediately puts downward pressure on the interest rate as households and firms try to buy bonds with their money to earn that high interest rate. As this happens, the interest rate falls, and it will continue to fall until it reaches the new equilibrium interest rate, r_1. At this point, $S_{m1} = D_m$, and the market is in equilibrium.

If the Central Bank wanted to drive the interest rate up, it would contract the money supply. It could do so by increasing the reserve requirement, by raising the discount rate, or by selling government securities in the open market. Whichever, tool the Central Bank chooses the result would be lower reserves and a lower supply

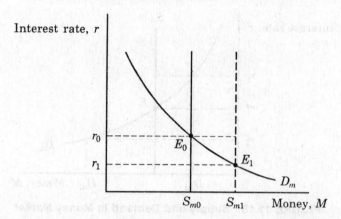

FIGURE 11.19   Increase in Money Supply and Interest Rate

of money. Also, S_{m0} would shift to the left and the equilibrium interest rate would rise.

Thus an increase in the supply of money from S_{m0} to S_{m1} lowers the rate of interest from r_0 to r_1.

Money demand and interest rate.   The equilibrium interest rates can also be affected by shift in money demand. The demand for money depends on both the interest rate and the volume of transactions. Here we use the level of aggregate output (income) as a rough measure of the volume of transactions. The relationship between money demand and aggregate output (income), N is positive, that is, increases in N mean a higher level of real economic activity and vice versa. More is being produced, income is higher and there are more transactions in the economy. Consequently, the demand for money on the part of firms and households in aggregate is higher. Thus, an increase in N shifts the money demand curve to the right.

Figure 11.20 illustrates such a shift. N increases, causing money demand to shift from D_{m0} to D_{m1}. The result is an increase in the equilibrium level of the interest rate

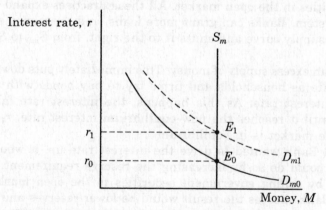

FIGURE 11.20   Increase in Demand and Interest Rate

from r_0 to r_1. Similarly, a decrease in N would shift D_m to the left, and the equilibrium interest rate would fall.

The money demand curve also shifts when the price level changes. If the price level rises, the money demand curve shifts to the right, because people need more money to engage in their day-to-day transactions. With the quantity of money supplied unchanged, however, the interest rate must rise to reduce the quantity of money demanded to the unchanged quantity of money supplied which is a movement along the money demand curve. Thus an increase in the price level is like an increase in N in that both events increase the demand for money. The result is an increase in the equilibrium interest rate.

If the price level falls, the money demand curve shifts to the left, because people need less money for their transactions. However, with the quantity of money supplied unchanged, the interest rate must fall to increase the quantity of money demanded to the unchanged quantity of money supplied. Thus, a decrease in the price level leads to a decrease in the equilibrium interest rate.

FISCAL POLICY

Fiscal Policy is a tool, in the hands of a government, to influence the level of GDP in the short run using taxes and government spending. It is about bringing changes in taxes and spending so as to affect the demand for goods and services, and hence the output in the short run.

We know that the total spending including that of the government is given by

$$\text{Total spending} = C + I + G$$

where,
  C = Autonomous consumption
  I = Investment
  G = Government purchases

Any increase in government purchase increases the total spending and hence shifts the $C + I + G$ line upward, just as increases in investment or autonomous consumption do.

Figure 11.21(a) shows how increases in government spending affect GDP. The increase in government spending from G_0 to G_1 shifts the $C + I + G$ line upward and increases the level of GDP (income) from N_0 to N_1.

The multiplier for government spending is also the same as for changes in investment or autonomous consumption:

$$\text{Multiplier for government spending} = 1/(1 - \text{MPC})$$

An initial increase in government spending raises GDP (income). The increase in income generates further increase in demand as consumers increase their spending. The government programs affect the disposable personal income of the households.

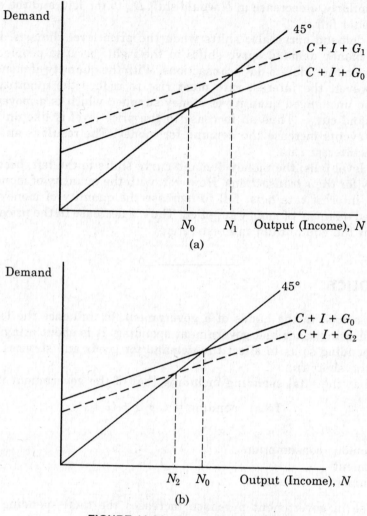

FIGURE 11.21   Fiscal Policy Effects

The consumption spending depends on income after taxes and transfers, or $N - T$, where T are the net taxes. The consumption function with taxes is:

$$C = C_a + b(N - T)$$

Figure 11.21(b) shows how an increase in taxes will decrease the level of GDP. As the level of taxes increases, the demand line will shift downward by b (the increase in taxes) and the equilibrium income will fall from N_0 to N_2.

Since the demand line does not shift by the same amount with taxes as it does with government spending, the formula for the tax multiplier is slightly different. It is given as:

$$\text{Tax multiplier} = -b/(1 - b)$$

The tax multiplier is negative because increases in taxes decrease disposable personal income and lead to a reduction in consumption spending.

The multiplier for government spending is larger than the multiplier for taxes. Thus equal increases in both, government spending and taxes, will increase GDP. The multiplier for equal increases in government spending and taxes is also known as the balanced budget multiplier because equal changes in government spending and taxes will not unbalance the budget.

When a government increases its spending or cuts taxes to stimulate the economy, it will increase the government's budget deficit. The *budget deficit* of a government is the difference between its spending and its tax collections.

Fiscal policy is thus a very important tool of macroeconomic policy. It is also an important instrument to stabilize the economy, that is, to overcome recession and to control inflation. Fiscal policy is a set of guidelines for the government's earning and spending. By suitable changes in these two variables, the fiscal policy aims at regulating the aggregate demand.

The expansionary fiscal policy is used to cure recession. In this policy, the government expenditure is increased and the taxes are reduced. Both these measures increase the money supply and thus raise the aggregate demand in the economy. Contractionary fiscal policy, on the other hand, prescribes for a decrease in the government expenditure and an increase in the tax rates. This would decrease the money supply leading to a fall in the aggregate demand and the general price level so as to control inflation. While the expansionary fiscal policy enlarges the budgetary deficit, the contractionary fiscal policy reduces it. Let us discuss both these fiscal policies in a little detail.

Expansionary Fiscal Policy

Any government policy aimed at stimulating aggregate output (income) is said to be *expansionary*. An expansionary fiscal policy is an increase in government spending (G) or a reduction in net taxes (T) aimed at increasing aggregate output (income) (N).

Government purchases and net taxes are the two tools of a government fiscal policy. The government can stimulate the economy, i.e., it can increase aggregate output (income), either by increasing government purchases or by reducing net taxes. Though the impact of a tax cut is somewhat smaller than the impact of an increase in G, both have a multiplier effect on the equilibrium level of N.

Consider an increase in government purchases. This increase in expenditure causes firms' inventories to be smaller than planned. Unplanned inventory reductions stimulate production, and firms increase output. However, because added output means added income, some of which is subsequently spent, consumption spending (C) also increases. Again, inventories will be smaller than planned and output will rise even further. The final equilibrium level of output is higher by a multiple of the initial increase in government purchases.

As aggregate output increases, an impact is felt in the money market. The increase in income increases the demand for money (D_m). For the moment, assume that the Central Bank holds the quantity of money supplied (S_m) constant. The resulting disequilibrium, with the quantity of money demanded greater than the quantity of money supplied, causes the interest rate (r) to rise.

The increase in interest rate has a side effect. A higher interest rate causes planned investment spending (I) to decline. Because planned investment spending is a component of planned aggregate expenditure ($C + I + G$), the decrease in I works against the increase in G.

This tendency for increase in government spending to cause reductions in private investment spending is called the *crowding-out effect*. Without any expansion in the money supply to accommodate the rise in income and increased money demand, planned investment spending is partially crowded out by the higher interest rate. The extra spending created by the rise in government purchases is offset to some extent by the fall in planned investment spending. Income still rises, but the multiplier effect of the rise in G is lessened because of the higher interest rate's negative effect on planned investment.

This crowding-out effect is illustrated graphically in Figure 11.22. An increase in government purchases from G_0 to G_1 shifts the planned aggregate expenditure curve ($C + I_0 + G_0$) upward. The increase in aggregate output (income) from N_0 to N_1 causes the demand for money to rise, which results in a disequilibrium in the money market. The excess demand for money raises the interest rate from r_0 to r_1 causing planned investment spending to decrease from I_0 to I_1. The fall in I pulls the planned aggregate expenditure curve back down, which lowers the equilibrium level of income to N^*.

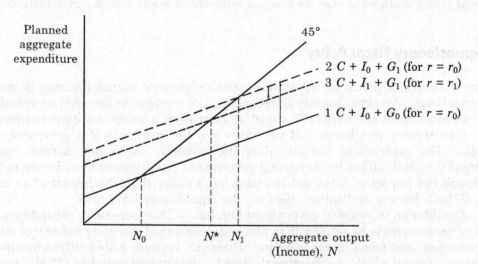

FIGURE 11.22 Crowding-out Effect

An increase in government spending from G_0 to G_1 shifts the planned aggregate expenditure schedule from 1 to 2. The crowding-out effect of the decrease in planned investment, brought about by the increased interest rate, then shifts back the planned aggregate expenditure schedule from 2 to 3.

Effects of an expansionary fiscal policy:

$$G \uparrow \text{ or } T \downarrow \Rightarrow N \uparrow \Rightarrow D_m \uparrow \Rightarrow r \uparrow \Rightarrow I \downarrow$$

Exactly the same reasoning holds for changes in net taxes. The ultimate effect of a tax cut on the equilibrium level of output depends on how the money market reacts. The expansion of aggregate output (income), that a tax cut brings about, will lead to an increase in the interest rate and thus a decrease in planned investment spending. The ultimate increase in aggregate output (income) will therefore be less than it would be if the interest rate did not rise.

Contractionary Fiscal Policy

Any government policy that is aimed at reducing aggregate output (income) is said to be *contractionary*. Where expansionary policy is used to boost the economy, contractionary policy is used to slow down the economy. Considering that one of the four major economic goals is economic growth, why would the government adopt policies designed to reduce aggregate spending. One important reason for it to do so is to control inflation because a decrease in aggregate spending will bring down the rising prices.

A contractionary fiscal policy is a decrease in government spending (G) or an increase in net taxes (T) aimed at decreasing aggregate output (income) (N). The effects of this policy are the opposite of the effects of an expansionary fiscal policy.

A decrease in government purchases or an increase in net taxes leads to a decrease in aggregate output (income), a decrease in the demand for money (D_m), and a decrease in the interest rate (r). The decrease in aggregate output (income) that accompanies a contractionary fiscal policy is less than it would be if we did not take the money market into account because the decrease in interest rate also causes planned investment (I) to increase. This increase in planned investment offsets some of the decrease in planned aggregate expenditure brought about by the decrease in government spending. This also means the multiplier effect is smaller than it would be if we did not take the money market into account. The effects of a decrease in government spending, or an increase in net taxes, can be represented as shown below:

Effects of a contractionary fiscal policy:

$$G \downarrow \text{ or } T \uparrow \Rightarrow N \downarrow \Rightarrow D_m \downarrow \Rightarrow r \downarrow \Rightarrow I \uparrow$$

 MONETARY POLICY

Monetary Policy is a tool that incorporates the actions that the Central Bank takes to influence the level of GDP. The Central Bank can influence the level of output in the short run through open market operations, changes in reserve requirements or changes in the discount rate.

These tools can be used to form a suitable monetary policy in the times of both recession as well as inflation. The aggregate demand can be raised in recession period by adopting an expansionary or easy monetary policy while it can be reduced to control inflation through a contractionary or tight monetary policy.

Monetary policy regulates the money supply in an economy. It is concerned with the cost and availability of credit. The broad objectives of monetary policy are to establish equilibrium at full employment level of output, ensure price stability by controlling inflation and deflation and promote economic growth of an economy.

The easy monetary policy can be used to cure recession by making the Central Bank undertake open market operations and buy securities in the open market from public and banks. This would increase the availability of credit with the banks and currency with public. Secondly, the Central Bank may lower the bank rate at which it offers loans to the commercial banks. The banks may then borrow more from the Central Bank resulting in an increase in availability of credit to investors and businessmen and that too at lower rates of interest. Thirdly, the Central Bank may reduce the required reserve ratio for the commercial banks. This would release the tied up funds of the banks for providing loans. Credit availability to the private sector may also increase if the Central Bank lowers the statutory liquidity ratio. All these measures will lead to an increase in the money supply and will also lower the cost of credit.

The tight monetary policy on the other hand entails the Central Bank to perform open market operations and sell securities in the open market to banks and public. The Central Bank may also step up the bank rate and raise the required reserve ratio. All these measures will suck the credit from the market. The money supply will decrease and the cost of credit will rise. The general price level would decrease and inflation can be controlled using this policy.

Expansionary Monetary Policy

As we have seen, any government policy aimed at stimulating aggregate output (income) is said to be expansionary. An expansionary monetary policy is an increase in the money supply aimed at increasing aggregate output (income) (N). The Central Bank can increase the money supply in the system through the three tools as mentioned in detail before under its functions, namely, by open market purchases, lowering down the required reserves ratio or decreasing the discount rate.

Using an expansionary monetary policy, when the Central Bank decides to increase the supply of money, the increase in the quantity of money supplied pushes down the interest rate. Lower interest rate causes planned investment spending to rise. The increased planned investment spending means higher planned aggregate expenditure, which in turn means increased output as firms react to unplanned decreases in inventories. This increase in output (income) leads to an increase in the demand for money and the money demand curve shifts to the right. This means that the interest rate decreases less than it would have if the demand for money had not increased.

Figure 11.23 shows how an expansionary monetary policy works. In Figure 11.23(a), the supply of money increases from S_{m0} to S_{m1} and interest rates fall from r_0 to r_1. In Figure 11.23(b), investment spending increases from I_0 to I_1 by the increment ΔI. In Figure 11.23(c), the increase in investment spending shifts the total demand line

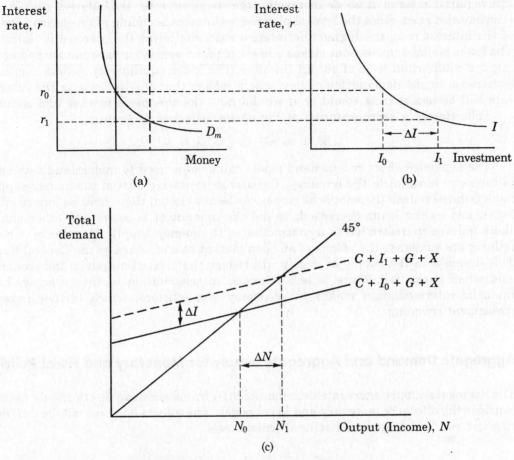

FIGURE 11.23 Monetary Policy Effects

upward by the same incremental amount ΔI. The GDP increases from N_0 to N_1, increasing by the increment ΔN.

The entire sequence of events depicting the effects of an expansionary monetary policy can be summed up as follows:

$$M_s \uparrow \Rightarrow r \downarrow \Rightarrow I \uparrow \Rightarrow N \uparrow$$

Contractionary Monetary Policy

By now we know that a contractionary policy of the government aims at reducing the aggregate output (income) of the economy. A contractionary monetary policy leads to a decrease in the money supply aimed at decreasing the aggregate output (income).

Using the contractionary monetary policy, when the Central Bank decreases the money supply through either open market sale of government securities, increasing the required reserve ratio or increasing the discount rate, the interest rate in the economy also rises. Since the level of planned investment spending is a negative function of the interest rate, the higher the interest rate, the lower the planned investment. The lower planned investment means a lower planned aggregate expenditure and hence a lower equilibrium level of output (income). The lower equilibrium income results in a decrease in the demand for money, which means that the increase in the interest rate will be less than it would be if we did not take the goods market into account.

Following is a representation of the entire sequence of events:

$$M_s \downarrow \Rightarrow r \uparrow \Rightarrow I \downarrow \Rightarrow N \downarrow$$

The expanded short run demand model can also be used to understand why bank failures are harmful to the economy. Because deposits are part of the money supply, bank failures reduce the supply of money. As banks closed, they could no longer grant loans, and as the loans decreased, so did the amount of deposits into other banks. Bank failures therefore led to a contraction of the money supply. The effects of bank failures are similar to the effects of an open market sale of bonds by the Central Bank. This decrease in the supply of money will reduce the level of output in the economy. And when banks fail, there is less financial intermediation in the economy. Less financial intermediation makes the economy less efficient, which further reduces investment spending.

Aggregate Demand and Aggregate Supply for Monetary and Fiscal Policies

The aggregate supply/aggregate demand (AS/AD) framework can be effectively used to consider the effects of monetary and fiscal policy. The effects however will be different in short run and long run. Let us discuss these.

Short run effects. The two fiscal policy variables are government purchases (G) and net taxes (T) while the monetary policy variable is the quantity of money supply (S_m). While an *expansionary* policy aims at stimulating the economy through an increase in government purchases or money supply or a decrease in net taxes, a *contractionary* policy aims at slowing down the economy through a decrease in government purchases or money supply or an increase in net taxes. While an expansionary policy shifts the AD curve to the right, a contractionary policy shifts it to the left.

When considering the effects of a policy change, we must be careful to note where along the short run AS curve the economy is, at the time of the change. If the economy is initially on the flat portion of the AS curve, as shown by point A in Figure 11.24, then an expansionary policy, which shifts the AD curve to the right, results in a small price increase relative to the output increase. The increase in equilibrium output (from N_0 to N_1) is much greater than the increase in equilibrium price level (from P_0 to P_1). This is the case in which an expansionary policy works well. There is an increase in output with little increase in the price level.

If the economy is initially on the steep portion of the AS curve, as shown by point B in Figure 11.25, then an expansionary policy results in a small increase in equilibrium

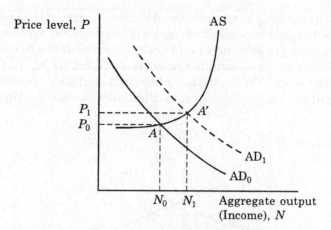

FIGURE 11.24 AS/AD Framework

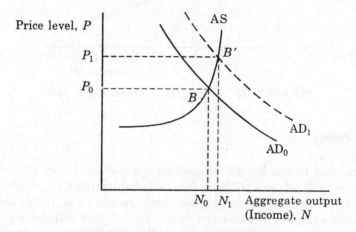

FIGURE 11.25 AS/AD Framework

output (from N_0 to N_1) and a large increase in the equilibrium price level (from P_0 to P_1). In this case, an expansionary policy does not work well. It results in a much higher price level with little increase in output. The multiplier is therefore close to zero. Output is initially close to capacity, and any attempt to increase it further leads mostly to a higher price level.

Thus it is important to know where the economy is before a policy change is put into effect. The economy is producing on the nearly flat part of the AS curve if most firms are producing well below capacity. When this is the case, firms will respond to an increase in demand by increasing output much more than they increase prices. If the economy is producing on the steep part of the AS curve, firms are close to capacity and will respond to an increase in demand by increasing prices much more than they increase output.

Long run effects. In the long run, since the AS curve is vertical, so neither monetary policy nor fiscal policy has any effect on aggregate output in the long run.

In the Figure 11.26, the monetary and fiscal policies shift the AD curve. If the long run AS curve (LAS) is vertical, output always comes back to N_0. In this case, policy affects *only* the price level. The multiplier effect of a change in government spending on aggregate output in the long run is zero. Similarly the tax multiplier is also zero.

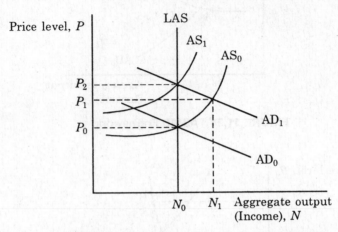

FIGURE 11.26   Aggregate Demand and Supply

Stabilization Policy

The government can use either fiscal policy or monetary policy to alter the level of GDP. If the current level of GDP is below full employment or potential output, the government can use expansionary policies such as tax cuts, increased spending, or increases in money supply to raise the level of GDP and reduce unemployment. If, however, the current level of GDP exceeds full employment or potential output, the rate of inflation will increase. To avoid this, the government can use contractionary policies to reduce the level of GDP back to full employment or potential output.

Both expansionary policies and contractionary policies are examples of stabilization policies. *Stabilization policies* are a set of actions that reduce the level of GDP back to full potential output.

Though this sounds simple but in practice, it is very difficult to stabilize the level of aggregate output. This is because generally there are lags, or delays, in stabilization policy. Lags arise because decision-makers are often slow to recognize and respond to changes in the economy, and monetary/fiscal policies take time to operate.

Lags. Poorly timed policies can magnify economic fluctuations. Suppose that GDP was currently below full employment but would return to full employment on its own within one year and that stabilization policies took a full year to become effective. If policymakers tried to expand the economy today, their actions would not take effect until a year from now. One year from now, the economy would normally, by itself, be back at full employment. But one year from now, if stabilization policies were enacted, the economy would be stimulated unnecessarily, and output would exceed full employment.

There are two broad classes of lags: *inside lags* and *outside lags*. 'Inside lags' are the delays in implementing policy while 'outside lags' refer to the time it takes for the policies to actually work.

Inside lags.   Inside lags occur for two basic reasons. One reason is that it takes time to identify and recognize a problem. For example, the data available to policymakers may be poor and conflicting. While some economic indicators may look fine, others may appear worrisome. It often takes from several months to a year before it is clear that there is a serious problem with the economy. The other reason for inside lags is that once a problem has been diagnosed, it still takes time before any action can be taken.

Outside lags.   Both monetary and fiscal policies are subject to outside lags, the time it takes for policy to be effective. Consider monetary policy. The Central Bank can increase the money supply to rapidly lower the interest rate, but firms must change their investment plans before monetary policy can be effective. Fiscal policy is also subject to outside lags. If taxes are cut, individuals and businesses must change their spending plans to take advantage of cut; it will take some time before any affects of the tax cuts will be felt in the economy. It will also take some time before increase in spending will raise GDP.

Policy Mix

Policy mix refers to the combination of monetary and fiscal policies in use at a given time. Having discussed the fiscal and monetary policies separately, it should be appreciated that fiscal and monetary policy can be used simultaneously. For example, both government purchases (G) and the money supply (S_m) can be increased at the same time. While the increase in government purchases raises both N and r, an increase in money supply raises N but lowers r. Therefore, if the government wanted to increase N without changing r, it could do so by increasing both government purchases and money supply by the appropriate amounts.

A policy mix that consists of a decrease in government spending and an increase in money supply would favour investment spending over government spending. This is because both the increased money supply and the fall in government purchases would cause the interest rate to fall, which would lead to an increase in planned investment. The opposite is true for a mix that consists of an expansionary fiscal policy and a contractionary monetary policy. This mix favours government spending over investment spending. Such a policy will have the effect of increasing government spending and reducing the money supply. Tight money and expanded government spending would drive the interest rate up and planned investment down.

INFLATION

Prices of individual goods and services are determined in many ways. In competitive markets, the interaction of many buyers and many sellers, that is, the operation of supply and demand, determines prices. In imperfectly competitive markets, prices are determined by producers' decisions. Further, in any economy, prices are continuously changing as markets adjust to changing conditions.

Inflation may be defined as a general rise in the prices in a persistent manner. It causes a loss in the purchasing power of a currency. It happens when many prices increase simultaneously. This means that it is not necessary that prices of all the goods and services are rising. It is likely that even during periods of high inflation, some prices may be relatively constant and some may even be falling. But prices of a vast majority of goods and services are increasing simultaneously. We measure inflation by looking at a large number of goods and services and calculating the average increase in their prices during some period of time.

It is useful to distinguish between a one-time increase in the overall price level and an increase in the overall price level that continues over time. Inflation is often used to refer only to increases in the price level that continue over some significant period. Such periods are known as periods of *sustained inflation*.

Price indexes. Inflation is measured by price index numbers. As we know, a price index measures the general level of prices in reference to some base period. The rate of inflation can be calculated for any specific year by subtracting the last year's price index from this year's index, dividing that difference by the last year's index and multiplying by 100 to express it as a percentage.

Here is an example. Suppose that a price index in a nation was 200 in the year 2003 and 210 in the year 2004. Then the inflation rate between 2003 and 2004 was

$$\text{Inflation rate} = (210 - 200)/200 = 0.05 = 5\%$$

That is, the nation experienced a 5% inflation rate.

The most popular price index is the *Consumer Price Index* (CPI). The CPI is computed by using a bundle of goods meant to represent the market basket purchased monthly by the typical consumer. The quantities of goods in the bundle that are used for the weights are based on extensive surveys of consumers. The CPI is widely used by both government and the private sector to measure changes in prices facing consumers. It is given by

CPI in year 'n' = (Cost of basket in year 'n'/Cost of basket on base year) × 100

One major limitation of CPI is that it considers a fixed basket of goods. When prices rise, consumer generally switches from costly to affordable goods. The CPI may then give a distorted idea of the cost of living. In reality, the increase in prices is probably less than the reported indexes tell us. The principal reason for this overstatement is that measuring quality improvements is a difficult proposition.

Another popular price index is *Producer Price Index* (PPI), also called *Wholesale Price Index* (WPI). It is an index of prices that producers receive for products at all stages in the production process, not just the final stage. The index is calculated separately for various stages in the production process. The three main categories are finished goods, intermediate goods, and raw materials.

One advantage of the PPI is that it detects price increases early in the production process. Because its movements sometimes foreshadow future changes in consumer prices, it is considered to be a leading indicator of the future consumer prices.

A quantitative appreciation of inflation is provided by the *Rule of* 70. This rule permits a quick calculation of the number of years it takes the price level to double.

$$\frac{\text{Approximate number of years}}{\text{required to double the price}} = \frac{70}{\text{Percentage annual inflation rate}}$$

Costs of inflation.   The costs of inflation can be taken into two categories. One includes costs associated with fully expected or anticipated inflation while the other includes the costs associated with unexpected or unanticipated inflation.

Anticipated inflation.   There are costs associated even with anticipated inflation. First, there are the actual physical costs of changing prices, which are called *menu costs*. These are the administrative costs associated with simply keeping up. Shopkeepers have to recalculate and repost prices frequently, and this takes time that could be used more efficiently. Restaurant owners, catalogue producers, and any other business that must post prices will have to incur costs to change their prices because of inflation.

Interest rates tend to rise with anticipated inflation. When interest rates are high, the opportunity cost of holding cash outside of banks is high. People will hold less real cash balances when there is inflation. If they hold less cash, they must visit the bank/ATM more frequently because they will run out of cash sooner. Such additional wear and tear necessary to hold less cash is categorized as *shoe-leather cost*.

In practice, our tax system and financial system do not fully adjust even to fully anticipated inflation. Inflation lowers the real after-tax return because the tax system is based on nominal income and not real income. This increase in taxes was not a deliberate action of the legislature, it is solely a creature of inflation.

Many financial markets are also not fully adjusted for inflation. For example, some nations have usury laws or ceilings on interest rates. These ceilings are on nominal rates and not real rates. At times of high inflation, some lenders may require nominal rates above the usury ceilings to provide them with an adequate real return. If they cannot lend at rates above the ceiling, the market may actually disappear.

Unanticipated inflation.   The first cost of unanticipated inflation is arbitrary redistribution of income. Anyone making a nominal contract to sell a product would lose. For example, workers who set nominal wages based on expected inflation would earn a lower real wage. Buyers with nominal contracts, such as firms setting nominal wages, would gain. These are unfair redistributions of income caused by unanticipated inflation. These redistributions eventually impose real costs on the economy.

If a society experiences unanticipated inflation, individuals and institutions will change their behaviour. If unanticipated inflation becomes extreme, individuals spend more of their time trying to profit from inflation rather than working at productive jobs. The economy becomes less efficient when people take actions based on beating inflation.

When unanticipated inflation occurs regularly, the degree of risk associated with investments in the economy increases. Increases in uncertainty may make investors reluctant to invest in capital and to make long-term commitments. Because the level of investment falls, the prospects for long-term economic growth are lessened.

It is also commonly believed that debtors benefit at the expense of creditors during an inflation. For instance, consider a case when A loans Rs. 100 to B to be paid back in a year, and prices increase 10% in the meantime. In this case, A gets back 10% less in real terms than what was loaned to B. While anticipated inflation can be built in the lending-borrowing deal as a mark-up, an unanticipated inflation can hurt creditors. So inflation that is higher than expected benefits debtors and inflation that is lower than expected benefits creditors.

All these costs are compounded as inflation rises. Studies have shown that as inflation rises, costs of both anticipated inflation and unanticipated inflation increase. At high inflation rates, these costs grow rapidly, and at some point, policymakers are forced to engineer a recession to reduce the inflation rate. Although unemployment and recessions are quite costly to society, they sometimes become necessary in the face of high inflation. No matter what the real economic cost of inflation may be, people do not like it. It makes them uneasy and unhappy.

It is important to note that it is not easy to distinguish anticipated inflation from unanticipated inflation. Mostly inflation is a mixture of the two. Moreover, in all nations, institutions can adjust to inflation only partially.

Whether one gains or looses during a period of inflation depends on whether his/her income rises faster or slower than the prices of things purchased. People living on fixed incomes are most often mentioned while discussing the impact of inflation. If the income is fixed and prices rise, the ability to purchase goods and services falls proportionately.

Types of Inflation

Most economies in the world today are suffering from this problem of inflation. The prices may rise either because of an increase in demand or due to an increase in the cost. Accordingly inflation is of two types, namely, demand-pull inflation and cost-push inflation.

Demand-pull inflation. Prices in any market are determined by the equation of demand and supply. The equilibrium price would be disturbed if either of these factors changes in relation to the other. An increase in demand with the supply remaining same or a reduced supply for the same demand level will cause the prices to increase. The economy may attempt to spend beyond its capacity to produce. It may seek some point beyond its production possibility curve. The business sector cannot respond to this excess demand by increasing the real output because all available resources are already fully employed. This excess demand will fuel up the prices of fixed real output causing demand-pull inflation. The essence of such an inflation is 'too much money chasing too few goods'.

Demand-pull inflation refers to a situation where the aggregate demand for goods and services exceeds the available supply of the output and this causes the general rise in price level of the economy. The rise in price of onions some years ago was a typical case of demand-pull inflation. This normally is the case when the pressure of demand is such that it cannot be met by the available supply, which has attained its saturation, and thus cannot be stepped up any further.

The reader may note here that the aggregate demand is the sum of consumer's spending on consumer goods and services, governments spending on consumer goods, and services and investment of the entrepreneurs. Any attempt by a particular consumer sector of an economy to secure an increased share in the output, than that which could have come to it under a stable economy, would lead to inflation.

Thus demand-pull inflation is initiated by an increase in aggregate demand. Figures 11.27(a) and (b) demonstrate the working of demand-pull inflation. Inflation begins with a shift of the aggregate demand schedule from AD_0 to AD_1, which causes the price level to increase from P_0 to P_1. Output also increases from N_0 to N_1. If the economy is operating on the horizontal portion of the AS curve, as in Figure 11.27(a), most of the effect will be an increase in output instead of an increase in the price level. If the economy is operating on the steep portion of the AS curve at the time of the increase in aggregate demand, as in Figure 11.27(b), most of the effect will be an increase in the price level instead of an increase in output.

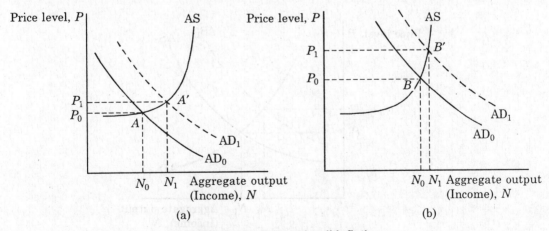

FIGURE 11.27   Demand-pull Inflation

In the long run, the initial increase in the price level will cause the AS curve to shift to the left as input prices (costs) respond to the increase in output prices. If the long run AS (LAS) curve is vertical, as depicted in Figure 11.26, the increase in costs will shift the short run AS curve to the left from AS_0 to AS_1, pushing the price level higher, to P_2. A shift in aggregate demand from AD_0 to AD_1 will result, in the long run, in no increase in output and a price-level increase from P_0 to P_2.

Cost-push inflation. Prices may rise even when there is no increase in aggregate demand. This could hold true if the cost of goods and services increase. Whenever due to any reason, the price of any one or more factors of production increases; the resultant cost of goods and services will rise. The producers pass on this rise in cost to the consumers by increasing the price of their goods and services. Such rise in the general price level is known as *cost-push inflation*. A rise in the price of products due to the increase in diesel prices is the case of cost-push inflation.

This type of inflation arises on the supply side of the market. The rise in general price level is due to the increase in per unit production cost. The per unit production cost is the average cost of a particular level of output. It is found by dividing the total cost of resource inputs by the amount of output produced. Rising per unit production costs squeeze profits and reduce the amount of output that the firms are willing to supply at the existing price levels. As a result, the economy wide supply of goods and services declines. This decline in supply drives up the price level.

Under this scenario, costs are pushing the price level upward as against the earlier case where the demand was pulling it upward. Two most common sources of cost-push inflation are (i) increase in nominal wages and (ii) increase in the prices of non-wage inputs such as raw material and energy.

An increase in costs, also known as a cost shock, shifts the AS curve to the left, as Figure 11.28 shows. If we assume the government does not react to this shift in AS by changing fiscal or monetary policy, the AD curve will not shift. The supply shift will cause the equilibrium price level to rise from P_0 to P_1 and the level of aggregate output to decline from N_0 to N_1.

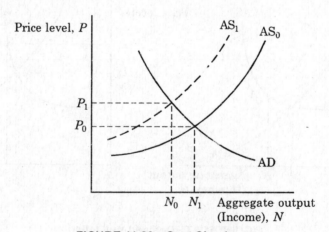

FIGURE 11.28 Cost Shock

The government could counteract the cost shock by engaging in an expansionary policy (an increase in G or S_m, or a decrease in T). This would shift the AD curve to the right, and the new AD curve would intersect the new AS curve at a higher level of output as shown in Figure 11.29. The problem with this policy, however, is that the intersection of the new AS and AD curves would take place at a price even higher than P_1 of Figure 11.28. Cost shocks are thus bad news for policy makers. The only way they can counter the output loss brought about by a cost shock is by having the price level increase even more than it would, without the policy action.

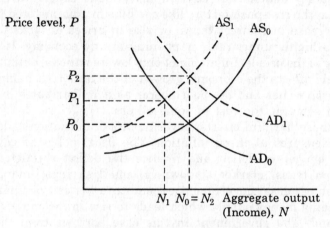

FIGURE 11.29 Cost-push Inflation

When firms are making their price/output decisions, their expectations of future prices may affect their current decisions. If a firm expects that its competitors will raise their prices, in anticipation it may raise its own price. Expectations can lead to an inertia that makes it difficult to stop an inflationary spiral. If prices have been rising and if people's expectations are adaptive i.e., if they form their expectations on the basis of past pricing behaviour, then firms may continue raising prices even if demand is slowing or contracting. In terms of the AS/AD diagram, an increase in inflationary expectations that causes firms to increase their prices shifts the AS curve to the left. The AS curve represents the price/output response of firms. If firms increase their prices because of a change in inflationary expectations, the result is a leftward shift of the AS curve.

An increase in the money supply can lead to an increase in the aggregate price level. An increase in the money supply (S_m) shifts the AD curve to the right and results in a higher price level. The higher price level causes the demand for money to increase. With an unchanged money supply and an increase in the quantity of money demanded, the interest rate will rise, and the result will be a decrease in planned investment spending.

If however, the Central Bank decides to expand the money supply to keep the interest rate constant, the AD curve shifts to the right again. This pushes prices up even further. Higher prices in turn increase the demand for money, which requires a further increase in the money supply and so on. When the economy is operating on the steep part of the AS curve, this effort of Central Bank to keep the interest rate constant could lead to a hyperinflation, a period of very rapid increases in the price level.

Checking inflation. The inflation in developing economies like India is normally a mix of demand-pull and cost-push inflation. When due to the demand-pull inflation, the general price level rises, workers demand a rise in their wages to offset the rising cost of living. This in turn raises the cost of production. The increase in cost of production brings about the cost-push inflation. As a result, the economy witnesses a persistent rise in the general price level under the combined impact of demand-pull factors such as rise in budgetary deficits, increase in investment expenditure or expansion of money supply and the cost-push factors like the hike in administered prices of essential commodities, increase in indirect taxes, or rise in prices of factors of production.

Inflation is a highly undesirable happening in any economy. It badly affects the standard of living of the people. Inflation not only lowers national output and employment but also adversely affects the economic growth of the nation. It hampers social justice by making the rich richer and the poor poorer as it redistributes income and wealth in the favour of some at the cost of some others.

Because of these harmful effects, governments of all nations adopt various fiscal and monetary measures to check inflation. The fiscal policy of government can be used to reduce budgetary deficit and finance the deficit through greater resource mobilization from taxes, market borrowings, small savings, and pruning down of wasteful and non-essential government expenditure instead of financing the budget deficit by expanding money supply which leads to rise in income of people and hence aggregate demand. The government in this case borrows from the Central Bank, which issues new currency.

The monetary policy of the government, which concerns the cost and availability of credit, can also be used to check inflation by squeezing the credit and reducing the aggregate demand. Higher interest rates and lower availability of credit will not only discourage more investment in stock and consumer durables, but also induce more savings as the rates of interest on savings and fixed deposits will also automatically increase. The availability of credit with the banks can be reduced by the RBI through the stepping up of the Cash Reserve Ratio (CRR) and the Statutory Liquidity Ratio (SLR).

Besides the fiscal and monetary policies, the government can also take some other measures to control the rise in prices. It may import the goods in short supply to equate the aggregate demand with the aggregate supply. The supply may also be raised through a fuller utilization of the productive capacity. The reverse of inflation is *deflation* where the general price level falls persistently. A high inflation rate prevailing simultaneously with a high unemployment rate creates *stagflation*.

Inflation and natural rate of unemployment. The long run aggregate supply (LAS) curve is vertical. In the short run, we know that some input prices, which are costs to firms, lag increases in the overall price level. If the price level rises without a full adjustment of costs, firm's profits will be higher and output will increase. In the long run, however, input prices may catch up to output price increases. If input price rises in subsequent periods thus driving up costs, the short run aggregate supply curve will shift to the left and aggregate output will fall.

This situation is illustrated in Figure 11.30. Assume the initial equilibrium is at the intersection of AD_0 and LAS. Now consider a shift of the aggregate demand curve

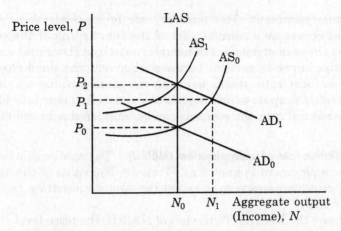

FIGURE 11.30   Aggregate Demand and Supply Curves

from AD_0 to AD_1. If input prices lag changes in the overall price level, aggregate output will rise from N_0 to N_1. This is a movement along the short run AS curve AS_0. In the long run, input prices may catch up. For example, next year's labour contracts may make up for the fact that wage increases did not keep up with the cost of living this year. If input prices catch up in the longer run, the AS curve will shift from AS_0 to AS_1 and drive aggregate output back to N_0. If input prices ultimately rise by exactly the same percentage as output prices, firms will produce the same level of output as they did before the increase in aggregate demand.

This N_0 is sometimes called *potential GDP*. Aggregate output can be pushed above N_0 in the short run. However, when aggregate output exceeds N_0, there is upward pressure on input prices and costs. The unemployment rate is already quite low, firms are beginning to encounter the limits of their plant capacities, and so on. At levels of aggregate output above N_0, costs will rise, the AS curve will shift to the left, and the price level will rise. Thus, potential GDP is the level of aggregate output that can be sustained in the long run without inflation.

The relationship between inflation and unemployment is known as *Phillips Curve* (refer Figure 11.31). Phillips curve is vertical in the long run and corresponds to the

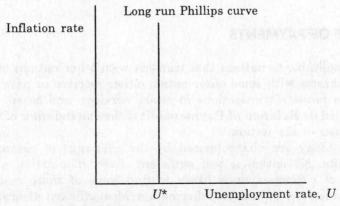

FIGURE 11.31   Long run Phillips Curve

natural rate of unemployment. The *natural rate of unemployment* refers to the unemployment that occurs as a normal part of the functioning of the economy. It is sometimes taken as the sum of frictional unemployment and structural unemployment. The long-run Phillips curve is vertical because whenever the unemployment rate is pushed below the natural rate, wages begin to rise thus pushing up the costs. This leads to a lower level of output, which pushes the unemployment rate back up to the natural rate. At the natural rate, the economy can be considered to be at full employment.

Non-Accelerating inflation rate of unemployment (NAIRU). The relationship between change in inflation and unemployment is known as *PP curve*. The value of the unemployment rate where the PP curve crosses zero is called the *Non-Accelerating Inflation Rate of Unemployment* (NAIRU).

Figure 11.32 shows the NAIRU. To the left of NAIRU, the price level is accelerating, that is, there are positive changes in the inflation rate and to the right of NAIRU, the price level is decelerating indicating negative changes in the inflation rate. Only when the unemployment rate is equal to the NAIRU that the price level is changing at a constant rate, that is, there is no change in the inflation rate.

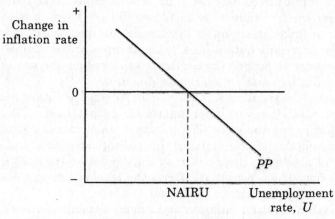

FIGURE 11.32 NAIRU

 BALANCE OF PAYMENTS

This term is applicable to nations that transact with other nations of the world. Any nation that transacts with some other nation either receives or pays a consideration. The record of a nation's transactions in goods, services, and assets with the rest of the world is called its **Balance of Payments.** It is thus an indicator of the international economic position of the nation.

Economies today are characterized by the exchange of resources among the constituent units. No nation is self sufficient. Even if a nation possesses all the resources that it consumes, it is likely to find some of those resources in better quality and at a lower cost in some other nation. Most efficient utilization of resources would thus be possible only when the goods, services, and capital are procured from the nations where they are available at lower cost and sold to the nations where they have a demand or demand at a higher price. And whenever there is exchange of commodities, balance of payments becomes a significant factor to consider.

The consideration that the nation receives is in the currency of the foreign nation. All currencies other than the domestic currency of a given nation are referred to as the *foreign exchange*. As an example, say, for India, all currencies other than the *Rupee* comprise the foreign exchange. A nation earns foreign exchange when it sells products, services, or assets to another nation. It spends foreign exchange when its citizens, be it individuals or firms, buy things whose prices are quoted in other currencies. Thus the balance of payments is also the record of a nation's sources (supply) and uses (demand) of foreign exchange.

The balance of payments can be either on current account or on capital account. While the current account deals with payment for currently produced goods and services, the capital account deals with the payments of debts and claims. The current account of balance of payments has a direct effect on the level of income of a nation. The capital account, on the other hand, does not effect the level of income directly and influences the volume of assets that a nation holds. The balance of payments in any economy must always balance, that is, all the receipts taken together must be equal to all the payments together. A detailed description of the two accounts is as follows:

The current account.   The current account comprises of the nation's trade in goods. This category includes exports and imports of goods. While the exports earn foreign exchange for the nation and are a **credit** item on the current account, the imports use up foreign exchange and are a **debit** item.

Services are another important constituents of the current account. Most nations buy services from and sell services to other nations. They are then either using up foreign exchange or earning it. The difference between a nation's exports of goods and services and its imports of goods and services is its *balance of trade*. If exports of goods and services are less than imports of goods and services, a nation is said to have a *trade deficit*. A *trade surplus*, on the other hand, occurs when the exports of goods and services of a nation are more than their imports.

The third item in the current account concerns the *investment income*. The citizens of a nation hold foreign assets (stocks, bonds, and real assets like buildings and factories). Dividends, interest, rent, and profits paid to such asset holders are a source of foreign exchange. Conversely, when foreigners earn dividends, interest and profits on assets held in the nation, foreign exchange is used up.

The fourth item is *net transfer payments*. Transfer payments from a nation to foreigners are another use of foreign exchange. Some of these transfer payments are from private citizens and some are from the government. The term 'Net' refers to the difference between payments from the nation to foreigners and payments from foreigners to the nation.

If we add net exports of goods, net export of services, net investment income, and net transfer payments, we get the *balance on current account*. The balance on current account shows how much a nation has spent on foreign goods, services, investment income payments and transfers relative to how much it has earned from other nations.

When the balance is negative, a nation has spent more on foreign goods and services, investment income payments and transfers than it has earned through the sales of its goods and services to the rest of the world, investment income received and transfers. If a nation has spent more on foreign goods, services, investment income payments, and transfers than it has earned, its net wealth position vis-a-vis the rest of the world must decrease.

The capital account. For each transaction recorded in the current account, an offsetting transaction is recorded in the capital account. Consider the purchase of a Japanese car by an Indian citizen. Say that the yen/rupee exchange rate is 0.40, and the yen price of the car is 2.5 million yen, which is Rs. 1,00,000. The Indian citizen takes Rs. 1,00,000, exchange it for 2.5 million yen, and then buys the car. In this case, Indian imports increase by Rs. 1,00,000 in the current account and foreign assets in India increase by Rs. 1,00,000 in the capital account. The net wealth position of India vis-a-vis the rest of the world decreases by Rs. 1,00,000. The key point here to realize is that an increase in a nation's imports results in an increase in foreign assets in the nation. The nation must pay for the imports, and whatever it pays with, is an increase in foreign assets in the nation. Conversely, an increase in a nation's exports results in an increase in the nation's assets abroad, because foreigners must pay for such exports.

A nation's assets abroad are divided into private holdings and government holdings. Similarly, foreign assets in a nation are divided into foreign private and foreign government assets. The sum of these is the *balance on capital account*. If there were no errors of measurement in the data collection, the balance on capital account would equal the negative of the balance on current account, since for each transaction in the current account there is an offsetting transaction in the capital account. Another way of looking at the balance on capital account is that it is the change in the net wealth position of the nation vis-a-vis the rest of the world. If the balance on capital account is positive, this means that the change in foreign assets in the nation is greater than the change in the nation's assets abroad, which is a decrease in the net wealth position of the nation.

If a nation has positive net wealth position vis-a-vis the rest of the world, it can be said to be a creditor nation. Conversely, if it has negative net wealth position, it is a debtor nation.

For a nation's economy to be sound, its balance of payments should be in equilibrium. This happens when after excluding the accommodating items there is neither deficit nor surplus in the balance of payments. Accommodating items are the short-term capital movements in the capital account such as borrowings from the IMF/Central Banks of other nations, drawing from SDR and change in the foreign exchange reserves with the Central Bank. Although all nations strive to keep their balance of payments in equilibrium, mismatch between a nation's exports and imports generally cause disequilibrium. The equilibrium can be restored through trade policy measures, deflation, devaluation of national currency and exchange control by the government.

EXCHANGE RATES

Exchange rate, in its most simple connotation, is the rate at which one currency can be exchanged for another. What started as a fixed rate system, finally gave way to floating or market-determined exchange rates in the early seventies. While governments in most nations still intervene to ensure that exchange rate movements are orderly, the exchange rates today are, by and large determined by the unregulated forces of supply and demand. Exchange rates play a crucial role in determining the performance of any economy. They determine the price of imported goods relative to domestic goods and can have significant effects on the level of imports, exports and movement of capital between nations.

Exchange rates under a floating rate system are determined by the supply and demand for the concerned currencies. This can be explained with the help of transactions between any two nations, say United States of America and India. The same logic can then be generalized to a world with many trading partners.

Households, firms and governments exchange rupees for dollars and dollars for rupees every day. The demand for rupees comes from those who have dollars with them but want to exchange them for rupees for some expenditure that has to be paid for in rupees. Some such situations are that of US importers who purchase Indian goods and services, US citizens travelling in India who want to ride the train, stay in a hotel or eat at a restaurant, US firms building a plant in India or US citizens buying an Indian stock or bond.

Similarly, the holders of the rupees who need dollars to pay for their consumption will supply rupees in the foreign exchange market. Situations as enumerated above for the US households, firms and government, if applied to their Indian counterparts will exemplify such cases.

The supply of a currency on the foreign exchange market should not be confused with the corresponding money supply, which is the sum of all the money currently in circulation. For India, for example, the demand for and supply of dollars on the foreign exchange markets determine exchange rates while the demand for rupee and the total rupee supply determine the interest rate.

Figure 11.33 shows the demand curve for dollars in the foreign exchange market. When the price of dollars i.e., the exchange rate is lower, it takes fewer rupees to buy

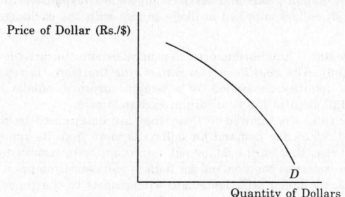

FIGURE 11.33   Demand for Dollars

US goods and services and so forth. Lower net prices should increase the demand for US products and encourage investment and travel in United States. If prices in India do not change, an increase in the quantity of US goods and services demanded by Indians will increase the quantity of dollars demanded. The demand-for-dollars curve in the foreign exchange market thus has a negative slope.

When the price of dollar falls, US goods and services appear less expensive to Indian buyers. If the US prices are constant, Indian buyers will buy more of US goods and services, and the quantity of dollars demanded will rise.

Figure 11.34 shows a supply curve for dollars in the foreign exchange market. At a higher exchange rate, each dollar buys more rupees, making the price of Indian goods and services lower to the Americans. The Americans will buy more of Indian goods when the price of dollar is high (the value of the rupee is low). An increase in US demand for Indian goods and services is likely to increase the quantity of dollars supplied. The curve representing the supply of dollars in the foreign exchange market thus has a positive slope.

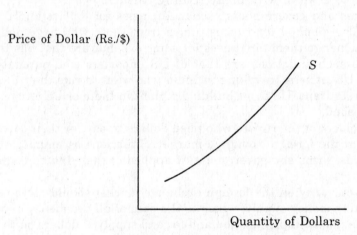

FIGURE 11.34 Supply of Dollars

When the price of dollar rises, an Indian can obtain more rupees for each dollar. This means that the Indian goods and services appear less expensive to US buyers. Thus, the quantity of dollars supplied is likely to rise with the exchange rate.

Equilibrium exchange rate. Equilibrium price in general denotes the price level at which demand equals supply. The *equilibrium exchange rate* therefore, is reached at the point at which the quantity demanded (of a foreign currency) equals its quantity supplied. Figure 11.35 depicts the equilibrium exchange rate.

When exchange rates are allowed to float, they are determined by the forces of supply and demand. When the demand for dollars is more than its supply then the price of dollars will rise, that is, the dollar will appreciate with respect to the rupee. Similarly, supply in excess of the demand for dollars will cause the price of dollar to fall. In other words, the dollar will depreciate with respect to the rupee.

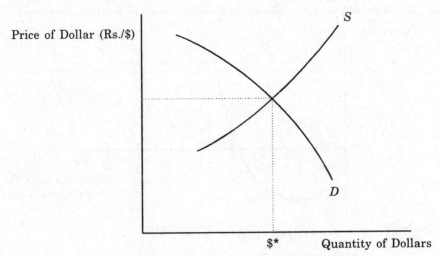

Price of Dollar (Rs./$)

$*   Quantity of Dollars

FIGURE 11.35   Equilibrium Exchange Rate

Though there are several factors that determine the exchange rates, the main among these are the 'purchasing power parity' and the 'relative interest rates'.

Effects of exchange rates on the economy.   The exchange rate is an important factor for any economy, to an extent that it is also called the economic barometer of a nation, just as GDP. It gives the comparative economic position of a nation with respect to another. The level of imports and exports depends on exchange rates as well as on income and other factors. Any change in the exchange rates changes the levels of imports and exports of the nation. Changes in exports and imports can in turn affect the level of real GDP and the price level.

A depreciation of a nation's currency can serve as a stimulus to the economy. When a nation's currency depreciates, its import prices rise and its export prices in foreign currencies fall. When the local currency is cheap, local products are more competitive than the products produced in the rest of the world, and foreign-made goods look expensive to the nation's citizens. If foreign buyers increase their spending on local goods, and domestic buyers substitute local goods for imports, aggregate expenditure on domestic output will rise, inventories will fall, and real GDP will increase.

However, the effect of currency depreciation on the balance of trade is ambiguous in the sense that it is not unidirectional. It is observed that when a currency starts depreciating, the balance of trade is likely to worsen for the first few quarters, after which the balance of trade may improve. As shown in Figure 11.36, since the curve resembles the letter J, the effect of exchange rate on a nation's balance of trade is also called the *J-curve effect*.

Initially, a depreciation of a nation's currency may worsen its balance of trade. The negative effect on the price of imports may initially dominate the positive effects of an increase in exports and a decrease in imports. The balance of trade is equal to

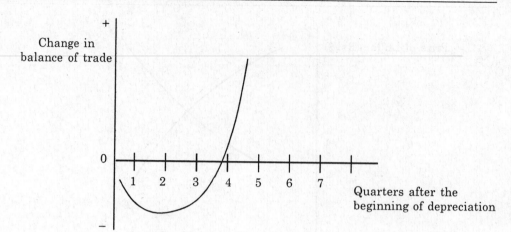

FIGURE 11.36 J-Curve Effect

exports revenue minus imports costs, including exports and imports of services. That is,

$$\text{Balance of Trade} = P_e \times Q_e - P_i \times Q_i$$

where,

P_e = Price of exports
Q_e = Quantity of exports
P_i = Price of imports and
Q_e = Quantity of imports

Currency depreciation affects the items on the right side of this equation as follows. The quantity of exports increases and the quantity of imports decreases. Both have a positive effect on the balance of trade, lowering the trade deficit or raising the trade surplus. The price of exports in local currency is not likely to change very much, at least not initially, while the price of imports increases. An increase in the price of imports in the local currency thus has a negative effect on the balance of trade.

The net effect of currency depreciation on the balance of trade could go either way. Depreciation stimulates exports and cuts back imports, but it also increases the price of imports in foreign currency. It seems that the negative effect dominates initially. The impact of depreciation on the price of imports is generally felt quickly, while it takes time for exports and imports quantities to respond to price changes. In the short run, the value of imports increases more than the value of exports and hence the balance of trade worsens. The initial effect is likely to be negative, but after exports and imports have had time to respond, the net effect turns positive. The more elastic the demand for exports and imports is, the larger the eventual improvement in the balance of trade.

The depreciation of a nation's currency tends to increase its price level. This so happens because of two reasons. First, when a nation's currency is less expensive, its products are more competitive on world markets, so exports rise. In addition, domestic buyers tend to substitute domestic products for the now-more-expensive imports. This means that the planned aggregate expenditure on domestically produced goods and services rises, and the aggregate demand curve shifts to the right. The result is a higher price level, higher output, or both. If the economy is close to capacity, the result is likely to be higher prices. Second, depreciation makes imported inputs more expensive. If costs increase, the aggregate supply curve shifts to the left. If aggregate demand remains unchanged, the result is an increase in the price level.

Monetary policy with flexible exchange rates.

The knowledge of exchange rates can also help us in understanding what happens when monetary policy is used first to stimulate and then to contract the economy.

Consider a situation where an economy is below full employment and the Central Bank decides to expand the money supply. The Central Bank expands the volume of reserves in the system, perhaps through open market purchases of government securities. This results in a decrease in the interest rate. The lower interest rate stimulates planned investment spending and consumption spending.

This added spending causes inventories to be lower than planned and the aggregate output (income) to rise, but there are two additional effects. One, the lower interest rate has an impact on the foreign exchange market. A lower interest rate means a lower demand for domestic securities by foreigners, so the demand for the local currency drops. Two, the domestic investment managers will be more likely to buy foreign securities, which are now paying relatively higher interest rates and hence the supply of local currency rises. Both events push down the value of the local currency.

To invest abroad, they will need to sell the local currency and buy foreign currency of the nation where they intend to invest. This will affect the exchange rate, the rate at which one currency trades for another currency. As investors sell their local currency to buy foreign currency, the exchange rate, which is the value of the local currency from the perspective of the domestic investor, will fall. A fall in the exchange rate or a decrease in the value of a currency is called *depreciation*. Thus lower interest rates will cause the local currency to depreciate, which means that it declines in value.

The lower value of the local currency makes the local goods cheaper to foreigners. Foreign residents will want to buy more of local goods as they become less expensive to foreign residents. So the nation will export more to the foreign nations.

However, lower value of the local currency will make it more expensive for the nation's residents to buy foreign goods. So as the exchange rate falls, imports become more expensive and the nation's residents tend to import fewer goods.

Thus as the exchange rate falls, local goods become cheaper and foreign goods become more expensive. The nation will export more goods and import fewer goods. Because exports increase and imports decrease, net exports will increase. The increase in net exports increases the demand for the nation's goods and increases GDP in the short run.

A cheaper local currency is a good thing if the goal of the monetary expansion is to stimulate the economy, because a cheaper local currency means more exports and fewer imports. If consumers substitute local goods for imports, both the added exports and the decrease in imports mean more spending on local products, so the multiplier actually increases.

Now suppose inflation is a problem and the Central Bank wants to slow it down with tight money. Here again, floating exchange rates help. Tight monetary policy works through a higher interest rate. If the Central Bank raises interest rates, investors from around the world will want to invest in the nation. As they buy the local currency, the exchange rate will increase, and the local currency will increase in value. An increase in the value of a currency is called *appreciation*. The appreciation of the local currency will make Indian goods more expensive to foreigners and imports cheaper for the residents of the nation.

An increase in interest rates will cause the exports to decrease and imports to increase, thereby decreasing the net exports. The decrease in net exports will decrease the demand for local goods and lead to a fall in output in the short run.

To summarize, an increase in interest rates will reduce both investment spending and net exports. A decrease in interest will increase investment spending and net exports. Monetary policy is even more powerful in an open economy then in a closed economy.

Fiscal policy with flexible exchange rates.   The openness of the economy and flexible exchange rates do not always work to the advantage of policy makers. Consider a policy of cutting taxes to stimulate the economy. Spending by households rises, but not all this added spending is on domestic products. Some of it may leak out of the domestic economy, reducing the multiplier.

As income rises, so does the demand for money. This means the amount of money people desire to hold for transactions and not the demand for local currency in the foreign exchange market. Unless the Central Bank is fully accommodating, the interest rate will rise. A higher interest rate tends to attract foreign demand for domestic securities. This tends to drive the price of the local currency up, which further blunts the effectiveness of the tax cut. If the value of the local currency rises, exports are less competitive in world markets, and the quantity of exports will decline. Similarly, a strong local currency makes imported goods look cheaper, and domestic citizens spend more on foreign goods and less on domestic goods, again reducing the multiplier.

Apart from this, without a fully accommodating Central Bank, three factors work to reduce the multiplier, namely, a higher interest rate from the increase in money demand may crowd out private investment and consumption, some of the increase in income from the expansion will be spent on imports and a higher interest rate may cause the local currency to appreciate, discouraging exports and further encouraging imports.

 GLOBALIZATION AND INDIAN BUSINESS

Globalization has completely transformed the way Indian businesses used to operate. At a time when the world is doing away with the economic borders, nations especially the developing ones like India have to encompass wide ranging reforms in their industrial, trade, fiscal, and monetary policies. In such a vibrant business environment, leave apart sustainable development, the mere survival of the businesses in these nations will depend on how globally competitive can they become. They will witness some far-reaching changes and will have to overcome the limitations posed by the past regulatory environment. Quality and efficiency will become the buzzwords.

Globalization may be defined as the process of integration of the world into one huge market. This calls for the removal of all the political, geographical, and trade barriers among nations. Companies go global due to several reasons. Rapid shrinking of time and distance across the globe, domestic markets no longer remaining adequate and rich or the foreign markets becoming large enough to justify foreign investment are some of the prominent factors for the companies to seek global markets. Globalization is however a double-edged sword. It can be both, beneficial and harmful to an economy. Multinational corporations should therefore be allowed to enter with a note of caution.

The people managing the businesses now have an overwhelming responsibility on their shoulders. Not only they have to be successful, they also have to be effective. A greater knowledge of international business and a deeper appreciation of total quality management is imperative for survival. Managerial ethics also deserve a greater concern. In order to be globally competitive, the Indian businesses should be able to formulate certain strategies to overcome the challenges posed by the globalization and convert them into opportunities. Some such strategies are as follows:

(i) Behavioural strategy. In such a stiff global competition, the productivity of knowledge and knowledge workers will not be the only competitive factor but also the decisive one that would determine the survival and sustainable growth of any organization.

The era of liberalization and globalization requires continuous updation of knowledge and honing of skills of the human resource. Human capital is to be assessed as the most important strategic resource. Today's complex environment demands managers with interdisciplinary brilliance. To groom managers to be fit to survive is essential. The challenges from the external environment in developing economies are such that only conventional wisdom cannot suffice.

Human resource strategy requires doing to be integrated with planning. Management structures should be such that they magnify the roots of a person. Predictability of behaviour and action is required. There should be no redundancy in workmen skills or in the total learning available with the managers. Empowerment is must. The organization should go beyond strategic planning to strategic thinking as a continuum to succeed.

Globalization brings in rapidly changing markets and tougher competition. More companies now realize that they must transform their functioning. The challenge is to unlearn the old ways of working and much more than to learn new ways. Strategic innovation is stymied due to resistance to change, which basically is due to inertia of success, uncertainty about what to change into, uncertainty surrounding new strategic positions, and the challenges of implementation.

Companies should recognize potential inconsistencies in their change programs, understand that empowerment has its limits, establish working conditions that encourage an employee's internal commitment, and realize that morale and empowerment are but the penultimate criteria. The ultimate goal is, and should always be, performance.

Determining what change would be useful for the organization and making people realize the need for that change is extremely critical. Implementation of change is likely to be much more easier and effective if the people are prepared for the change by involving them in the change process.

Change in organizations has been recognized as the most important prerequisite not only for growth but for survival as well. Only those companies will be successful today that can initiate a change in technology, marketing or organization and manage to lead in changes over competitors.

Organizations in order to survive find the existing tools and skills ineffective in finding solutions to problems that lead to crisis. Such crisis can be managed by enhancing managerial effectiveness. In order to do so, the organizations should ensure proper interaction between area of influence and the area of concern. They must design training programs for improving managerial effectiveness, which could help in making organizational roles effective. A manager should be clear about what the outputs are and should possess the ability to change his style to meet situational demand.

Efforts should be made to develop a comprehensive version for managerial strategies. Managers should be motivated to become proactive. Skills for understanding individual and interpersonal process for effective team building should be developed and managers should be helped to appreciate leadership role for organization building. Besides this, problem-solving orientation should be leveraged with decision-making skills.

(ii) Operations strategy.   With the trade borders doing away, the Indian products will have to compete and perform well with those of the developed nations. Low prices cannot be a substitute for quality in the global market. Producing such quality goods and maintaining the quality necessitates world class manufacturing (WCM). Principles of world class manufacturing are based on successful Japanese management practices that have brought impressive quality and productivity to the shop floor such as 5S, TQM, TQC, JIT, Kaizen, and Kanban. Of these, 5S has become the most popular as it emphasizes a people oriented and a practice oriented approach. It is based on the belief that every individual can improve his workplace leading to better environment and total quality.

Successful implementation of WCM requires participation of all people, commitment of top management, leadership and periodic visit of the CEO, support of all and self-sustenance. WCM ensures a better workplace, easier operations, discipline, greater efficiency and effectiveness, better resource utilization, lesser breakdowns, greater team spirit and cooperation, lower costs, and higher productivity besides high quality.

Managing technology is an essential imperative for gaining maximum productivity from available resources with minimum time, especially for the developing economies. Technology is widely recognized as a strategic resource and a competitive weapon for development. It is an important parameter for corporate growth and performance and its acquisition requires special skills, knowledge and experience.

Technology management apart from being a vehicle to bring science and engineering knowledge to solution of problems, should also be a source of providing competitive advantage through sustained learning. Technology management in developing nations basically involves scanning and absorption of new technology, adaptation and application of new technology to suit local conditions and the eventual use of indigenously developed technology to create products that compete successfully in the global markets.

Most of the companies that are in the process of accelerating their growth, suffer from the lack of proper technology management. They should identify their present needs and future prospects, concentrate on acquisition and utilization of technologies which have already been well established in the developed economies and then enhance their own capability for innovation through effective absorption of advanced technologies from abroad. The technology management should embrace guidelines to cover a wide ranging complex set of related areas keeping in mind the capital scarcity which acts as a major hindrance in converting usable ideas into viable products.

Organizations should plan a gradual transition to technological independence through absorption and upgradation of proven technology. They should strive for research autonomy and excellence by maintaining their existing businesses and at the same time preparing for future businesses.

(iii) Marketing strategy. In an increasingly competitive world, marking global presence is possible not by out manoeuvering competition but by satisfying the customer. The companies must study their customers, who ultimately provide the drive, energy and the quest for an unparalleled quality, service, and reliability. There is a need to recognize the fact that a satisfied customer is their biggest asset and that he/she is a free advertisement with value addition. At the same time a dissatisfied customer is even more damaging to the company's business and image. Companies must be committed to 'along with the customer' path. Training the customer to dance to the customer's tune is crucial to survival. The fact that 'I must feel proud of my work and our customer must reflect it' should be the primary aim of every employee of an organization.

Developments in technology have brought in concepts like internet marketing, TV home shopping, remote shopping etc. which have made it possible to transform the retail environment away from customer loyalty and towards customer intimacy, away from mass marketing and towards micro-marketing.

(iv) Investment strategy. One of the major areas that will be concerning global businesses is investment decisions. Foreign investment decisions are beset with a variety of problems that are not encountered by domestic firms. Despite this, there is an upward trend of making investments abroad because of comparative cost advantage, tax benefits, and spreading of risks.

The data pertaining to incremental foreign investment outlays, operating costs, and benefits exclusive to the project should be carefully assimilated. Both costs and benefits are to be measured on cash flow basis and not on the basis of accounting profits.

Like domestic decisions, foreign capital budgeting decisions are taken on the basis of the NPV criterion as it is consistent with the objective of maximization of shareholder's wealth. Companies will generally be faced with the problem of choosing between continuing to export their product and installing a manufacturing facility abroad at the destination for exports.

Due consideration should be given to factors such as exchange control risks, timing and magnitude of taxes on income from foreign investments, restriction on repatriation of income, political risk, economic risk and the like while evaluating the cash flows. It is equally important for evaluating the investments to determine correctly the weighted average cost of capital giving due care to the availability of overseas funds.

(v) Governance strategy. The economic and business scene has changed drastically over the last few years. Trade barriers have been lifted, the world is becoming a smaller market, bottom lines are taking precedence and quality is the buzzword to survive and maintain sustainable development in this competitive environment.

The businesses now have access to opportunities worldwide. At the same time they are also faced with threats of their own survival with the incoming global players. And only the fittest survive. Resources are becoming scarce and attention is therefore being given to the development of greater skills. There is a growing realization that good corporate governance which hinges primarily on complete transparency, integrity and accountability of the management to all the stakeholders, is a must not only to gain credibility and trust, but also as a part of strategic management for survival, consolidation, and growth. Globalization and the presence of foreign institutional investors have, increased investor awareness and competitive market forces, and induced a demand for simplification, greater accountability, and transparency of operations.

The system of corporate governance would need to reflect the economic and social culture of India. Companies should design a code of ethics and statement of business practices and not only publish them internally and externally, but also set a role model by living up to these in practice. The basic influence on the governance system would be that of investors, institutions and demand of fund providers who would expect high standards of financial reporting and disclosure and adequate concern for the right of the shareholders.

Companies should evolve a code of best practice, which will primarily be concerned with the role of directors, especially the balance between the executive and non-executive directors and also the independence of the chairman and the CEO or managing director.

The basic objective of corporate governance relates to the effectiveness of the management and accountability of the board of directors. Its success is based on complete transparency and an arms length relationship between owners and managers. A desirable standard of corporate governance should maximize corporate value that would ultimately mean enhancement of shareholder's wealth.

(vi) Risk management strategy. With businesses crossing boundaries, the Indian companies are faced with complexities in international finance and cross currency exposures. This gives rise to various types of risks. The companies should be able to comprehend all the risk associated with their business instead of managing only the easily identifiable and quantifiable ones. Also there should be no gap in understanding the limitations of the tools used to manage their risks. In order to manage risk, the managers must understand the firm's strategic exposure, align risk management with corporate strategy, and learn when it is worth reducing risk.

The risk management paradigm should rest on the premises that the key to creating corporate value is making good investments, which involves generating enough cash internally to fund those investments. Cash flows can often be disrupted by movements in external factors such as exchange rates, commodity prices, interest rates, and tax structure thus potentially compromising a company's ability to invest. Thus, the risk management paradigm should have a single overarching goal of ensuring that a company cash available to make value-enhancing investments.

Although businesses can manage risk in a variety of ways like using insurance, letters of credit, joint venture, derivatives etc. but the top management should consider broader business strategies and management expertise while defining risk management policies.

(vii) Corporate strategy. The business entities facing global competition need to shift towards a more specific and sharper strategic focus based on realizing their core competencies that would give them a definite competitive advantage in the world market. To capture a disproportionate share of profits from future markets, a company must build the competencies that will make a disproportionate contribution to future customer value based on its people and their ability to innovate. The winning organizations continuously introduce new products and at the same time do not hesitate to retire their old products rather than let their competitors do it for them.

Efforts should be made to understand the relationship between resources, capability and a thorough knowledge of the mechanisms through which competitive advantage can be sustained over time. Managers can leverage their organization's skills and resources for enhanced competitiveness. The core competencies are the central subjects of corporate strategy. Only such strategies provide improved return on capital, lowered risk, greater flexibility, and better responsiveness to customer needs at lower costs.

QUESTIONS

1. What does Macroeconomics deal in?

2. What are the different constituent groups in an economy and how do payments flow among them?

3. Explain the concept of Gross Domestic Product (GDP). Present your views on the usefulness of the concept as an economic measure of the well being of any nation.

4. The expenditure approach and the income approach to calculate GDP lead to the same value for GDP because every expenditure by a buyer is at the same time an income for the seller. Comment.

5. What is equilibrium GDP and how can it be calculated?

6. How does the aggregate expenditure theory relate an economy's equilibrium real GDP to the total spending?

7. Define unemployment and write a descriptive note on various types of unemployment. How does unemployment affect the society?

8. Highlight the origins of the banking system as we know of now.

9. What is money supply? How can it be measured?

10. How does the government use fiscal policy as a tool to influence the level of output (income) in an economy?

11. "Monetary policy is a mechanism to regulate the money supply in an economy". Elucidate the statement.

12. What is inflation? Discuss the different types of inflation.

13. Write short notes on the following:

    (a) Keynesian cross
    (b) NAIRU
    (c) Consumption function
    (d) Measures of money supply
    (e) Balance of payments
    (f) Exchange rates

14. "The balance of payment is an indicator of the international economic position of a country". Discuss the validity of the statement.

15. State which of the following statements are true or false.

    (a) Macroeconomics is a study of aggregates.
    (b) Inflation is the general rise in the prices of essential commodities, in a persistent manner.
    (c) Inflation in developing countries is generally cost-push inflation.
    (d) Frictional unemployment occurs due to technological progress.
    (e) All bank deposits are time deposits but all time deposits are not bank deposits.
    (f) Fiscal policy can be used to regulate the aggregate demand.
    (g) Income line represents the aggregate demand curve of an economy.
    (h) Consumption function relates an economy's consumption to the level of income.

CASE STUDIES

Case 11.1 Advertising Saga

Walking through the jam packed, colourful and lively streets of Mumbai two management students, Ankita and Ruchika were noticing the various billboards and hoardings put up throughout the city. While observing the different advertisements coming in their way they randomly entered into a conversation related to the advertising industry, which was like this:

Ankita: Admen are no fun these days. Most of them are dull as ditchwater, talk of strategy and branding, and give you a constant whine about stingy clients and poor margins. A few weeks with them and you will need a stiff drink to rid yourself of that gloomy feeling. If they are right, then mass media advertising—those glorious 30-second commercials and full-page colour ads—is dying a slow death, as advertisers turn to events, public relations (PR), direct marketing (DM) or other such boring things.

Ruchika: Don't let that fool you. Advertising never had it so good. Back in 1992 when Manmohan Singh set the economy free, the hip and happening advertising industry was a puny Rs 1,150 crore billings business. But by 2003, long after the moaning had begun on the 'relevance' of advertising, billings stood at over Rs. 11,000 crores. So even if those fat margins have been falling, it's happening on a base that has grown by 10 times.

Ankita: OK I agree with what you say but this is not the good news on advertising. The good news is that what is driving the now double-digit growth is simply good old advertising. The kind that makes you want to curl up and simper at the person sitting next to you. The kind that gives you that feeling of being part of the great Indian middle-class dream.

Ruchika: Definitely yes, just switch on your television set for examples. The 'Wherever You Go Our Network Follows,' campaign helped add over 2 million subscribers to the Hutch network. Hyundai, Hitachi, Asian Paints, LG, Nokia, ICICI Bank and Fevicol are all part of the increasing list of brands that have good creative advertising beaming at you.

Ankita: This is not the edgy 'Cannes-style' advertising that the agency business got caught up with in the 1990s. It is a 'plug into the Indian consumer' and 'MTV plus Channel V' kind of mass advertising. It has turned around the fortunes of agencies such as O&M, McCann, Leo Burnett and Lowe among others.

Ruchika: Honours like becoming jury at Cannes come not from winning awards but from churning out clutter-breaking, mass-market advertising that is rejuvenating brands across product categories. Sure that's not new. Scores of creative directors have done it earlier. What is new is that they are doing it with a consistency and on a scale that Indian advertising has never seen before. It is a bit like what Ektaa Kapoor did to soapscreativity with scale. Coca-Cola got a second lease of life in India thanks to Joshi's 'Thanda Matlab Coca-Cola' campaign.

Ankita: Most of this may seem intuitive; isn't an agency supposed to churn out great creativity and build brands? Well, yes, but they lost their way somewhere in between.

Ruchika: So why are agencies talking themselves down? The ad industry is in a perpetual state that things were better earlier. At about 10–12 per cent this year, growth rate is one-fourth of what it was in the early nineties. Sure costs have gone up, but not more than the rate of inflation. Besides, the biggest component of cost in the agency business is people. That remains one of the lowest in the world, making India a fairly competitive market for advertising services.

Ankita: Then how the industry lost the plot?

Ruchika: The story would have been different if India had opened up its economy earlier, as China did in the 1970s. Then advertising in India would have got its first big push 20 years before it did. But it was only post 1992 that India liberalized. As a competitive market emerged in soaps, shampoos, fridges and computers, so did the media options to reach more people. Soon international agencies moved in. But unlike the US or Europe, the Indian ad business did not evolve gradually. It has grown at a frantic pace for over 12 years. This has, probably, caused confusion and structural problems. But the industry has emerged none the worse for it. When the market opened, both Indian and foreign FMCG and durable goods companies—big advertisers then—upped ad spends. You then had an industry cruising at 22 per cent operating margins, taking home 5–10 per cent in net profits.

The economy saw its first big downturn only in 1997. As advertisers came under margin pressure, they attacked advertising costs. And when artwork or ad film firms started offering direct discounts to advertisers, they just cut the agency out. This became the norm. But all debates got buried by 1998-99, as there was a surge in growth. Every year a new category—telecom, cars and then dotcoms—came looking for advertising, keeping growth rates at a steady 10–17 per cent.

Ankita: So this is the renaissance of the advertising industry?

Ruchika: This creative resurgence is for real. The future of advertising in India, at least for the next five years, is about good old mass media-led, creatively sound advertising. The evidence is in the numbers, which prove more conclusively than ever that India is a mass market with rising purchasing power. Mass markets are best-reached using mass media advertising, which gets the best results with great creativity.

Elementary, isn't it? Yet marketers have not even scratched the surface when it comes to tapping into this purchasing power. It shows in our Ad spend to GDP ratio which has consistently remained as low as 0.35 as compared to 1.39 for USA, 1.52 for Brazil and even 0.58 for China in the year 2004. And this too is growing at a modest rate of 12 per cent. So, by any standards, we are hugely under-advertised. India will thus remain a mass market that requires mass media answers. Unlike mature Western markets, areas like telecom, automobiles, durables, retail or entertainment are still booming in India. This renaissance is definitely to stay for a longer time and will take the advertising industry to newer heights.

What phenomenon is being talked about in the case above? Is advertising industry showing cyclical trends? Discuss the various stages of the business cycle for the industry and predict the future prospects.

(*Source:* Business World, August 23, 2004)

Case 11.2   Rising Inflation

For now, liquidity in the money market seems to be at a comfortable level, going by the repos subscription numbers. But, given the rising domestic headline inflation rate and the looming possibility of an increase in global interest rates, there will be some strain on the abundance of funds, especially foreign inflows.

Market players have started casting their doubts on foreign fund flows. They are of the view that if the no firm policy signals emerge, foreign investors might take a re-look at their investment plans for India. Further, with the signs of rising interest rates globally, especially in the US, the case for foreign fund outflows is quite justified. The global bond yields there have started looking up for quite some time back.

On the domestic front, inflation is posing a problem. The inflation rate stood higher at 5.02 per cent compared with 4.67 per cent the previous week. This has affirmed the market fears that rising inflation rates will spur the case for higher interest rates sooner or later. Therefore, liquidity even if abundant currently, has ceased to be a trigger for the bond market for a possible rally in prices.

There seems to be no near-term problem for liquidity. This was due to the absence of major outflows from the banking system, apart from the treasury-bill auctions under the government's borrowing program and market stabilization scheme this week. The auctions will amount to an outflow of Rs. 4,000 crore. Also, there will be inflows to the tune of Rs. 1,592 crore from coupon redemptions and gilt maturities.

Call money rates are expected to rule lower as there is enough supply of and tepid demand for funds. About Rs. 60,000–65,000 crore is currently locked with the Reserve Bank of India (RBI) as outstanding under the seven-day repos. While this amount will come back into the banking system in parts, as and when the seven-day repos mature, lack of any outflows from the system will ensure abundant liquidity in the call money market. Moreover, due to absence of major outflows during the preceding weeks, there seems to be not much demand. The call money rates recently touched a high of 6.5 per cent due to intraday liquidity mismatches. This was due to misjudgment of banks in their liquidity management (for putting money under repos and keeping aside funds to meet the auction outgo of around Rs. 10,000 crore).

There are four auctions of treasury bills forthcoming. There will be two 91-day t-bill issues and two 364-day t-bill ones. One set of a 91-day t-bill issue and 364-day t-bill issue will be auctioned for Rs. 500 crore and Rs. 1,000 crore receptively as part of the government's borrowing program. Another set will be auctioned for a total of Rs. 2,500 crore under the market stabilization scheme.

It is expected that the cut-off interest rates on these bills will meet the markets' hopes. Going by the previous cut-off rates, this week's rates are to be around the current market rates. With the outlook on short-term interest rates being bullish, trading interest in the t-bill market is likely to be brisk. At times of uncertainty, these instruments help in making quick profits without overloading the portfolio with high-coupon, long-term bonds.

How does inflation affect money supply in an economy? Discuss the use of repos and t-bills by the Reserve Bank of India in regulating the flow of money. What is the significance of the market stabilization scheme of the RBI?

(*Source:* Business Standard, June 07, 2004)

Glossary

Accounting Costs: The costs that are recorded in the books of accounts and are used for accounting, auditing and financial control.

Active Forecasts: Estimates of future situation considering the likely future actions of the firm.

Actual Costs: Costs that are actually incurred in acquiring or producing goods or services.

Administered Pricing: The pricing method, used generally for essential commodities, where the government ensures that such commodities are made available to the citizens at a reasonable price.

Aggregate Demand: The expenditure that the households and the firms are undertaking on consumption and investment.

Aggregate Domestic Savings: The sum total of the savings made by all the three components of an economy, i.e. the households, firms and government.

Aggregate Supply: The total money value of goods and services produced in an economy.

Autonomous Consumption: Such consumption, which exists regardless of the level of income.

Average Cost: Total cost divided by the quantity produced.

Average Physical Product: Average Physical Product of a factor of production is the total physical product of that factor divided by the quantity of that factor while all the remaining factors are held constant.

Average Propensity to Consume: Consumption per unit of income.

Average Propensity to Save: Savings per unit of income.

Average Revenue: Total revenue divided by the quantity sold.

Balance of Payments: An account for all receipts and payments occurring out of the exchange of goods, services and capital between a country and the rest of the world.

267

Balance of Trade: The difference between a nation's exports of goods and services, and its imports of goods and services.

Break Even Income: The point where the households consume their entire income and the consumption equals savings.

Budget Line: A line representing all combinations of two products that can be purchased for a given amount of money.

Business Cycle: The phenomenon of recurring ups and downs in the levels of economic activity extending over a period of time.

Cartel: A formal and overt agreement in a group of firms, in an oligopoly market, for setting up the price and output levels.

Cash Reserve Ratio: The percentage of total deposits of a bank that it has to keep with the Central Bank in the form of cash.

Collusion: A covert and informal agreement between members of a group of firms, in an oligopoly market, for deciding their price-output levels.

Collusion Model: This model recognizes that the oligopoly firms are definitely dependent on each other in their price-output decision-making. They thus enter into some sort of informal agreement for the price and output levels.

Complementary Goods: Goods, which are used along with some other goods.

Constant Returns to Scale: If the output increases in the same proportion to the increase in inputs, it is a case of constant returns to scale.

Consumer Equilibrium: A consumer is in equilibrium when he has maximized his utility subject to his income/budget.

Consumers Complete Enumeration Survey: A method for forecasting demand, which is based on a complete survey of all the consumers for the commodity under question.

Consumers Sample Survey: A miniature form of the complete enumeration method, where instead of surveying all the consumers of a commodity, only a few representatives are surveyed.

Consumption: The act of satisfying one's wants.

Consumption Function: The mathematical relationship between the amount of consumption and the level of income.

Consumption Schedule: A set of data depicting the relationship between consumption and income.

Cost-push Inflation: General rise in prices due to an increase in the cost of goods and services as a result of an increase in the prices of the factors of production.

Cournot's Model: This model assumes that the rival firms in an oligopoly market do not react to a change in the price of a firm. Each firm takes its price-output decision independent of those of its competitors.

Cross Elasticity of Demand: A measure of responsiveness of demand for one product to the changes in the price of another.

Crowding-out effect: The tendency of increase in government spending to cause reductions in private investment spending.

Cubic Function: A function where the power of the independent variable is three.

Decreasing Returns to Scale: A case where the output's increase is less than the increase in all the inputs.

Deflation: The reverse of inflation wherein the price level falls persistently.

Demand: The quantity of a good or service desired by a customer, duly supported by the ability and willingness to purchase, with reference to a particular set of variables on which it depends.

Demand Forecasting: Ascertaining the expected level of demand in the period under consideration.

Demand Function: The relationship of demand with the determinants that influence it.

Demand-pull Inflation: A situation where the aggregate demand for goods and services exceeds the available supply of output, and causing a general rise in price level of the economy.

Depreciation: The measure of a decrease in values of capital assets on account of their wearing out over the period of use.

Derivative: The mathematical concept of finding out the change in one variable due to a very small change in some related variable.

Differential Pricing: A pricing method where the product is priced in such a manner that the same product is available at different prices under different circumstances.

Discount Rate: The interest rate that the banks pay to the Central Bank when they borrow money from the Central Bank.

Diseconomies of Scale: The phenomenon where the long-run average cost increases with the increase in plant size.

Disposable Personal Income: The amount of income that the households can spend or save.

Economic Costs: The costs that help in managerial decision-making for achieving the economic objectives of a firm.

Economics: The science of choice when faced with unlimited ends and scarce resources having alternative uses.

Economies of Scale: Economies of scale are said to exist when the long-run average cost decreases with the increase in plant size.

Economy: The conditions under which goods are produced in a country and the manner in which the people are gainfully employed.

Elasticity: The percentage change in a dependent variable resulting from one per cent change in an independent variable.

Elasticity of Demand: The ratio of percentage change in demand to the percentage change in one of the determinants of demand.

Employment: The condition where large number of able-bodied persons of working age who are willing to work can get work at current wage levels.

Endogenous Variables: Variables that can be controlled by the firm, i.e. those that are internal to the firm.

End Use Method: A method focusing on forecasting the demand for intermediary goods.

Entry Barriers: Certain structural features of a market that enable the existing companies to raise the prices of their products persistently above the costs without attracting new entrants.

Equilibrium: A state of balance. It is an ideal situation when forces acting on an object in opposite direction are exactly equal.

Equilibrium GDP: The output level whose production will create a total spending just sufficient to purchase that output. It is the level of GDP where the total quantity of goods produced equals the total quantity of goods purchased.

Exchange Rate: The rate at which one currency can be exchanged for another.

Exogenous Variables: Variables which are beyond the control of the firm.

Expansion Path: The locus of all possible least cost combinations of input for a production function.

Expected Rate of Net Profit: The net profit in percentage terms that one expects to earn out of the business.

Expert Opinion Survey: This technique for forecasting demand seeks the views of experts on the likely level of demand in future.

Explicit Costs: Out-of-pocket costs for which a cash payment is made.

Final Goods: The goods and services that are purchased by the consumer for final use and not for any further processing, manufacturing, or resale.

First Degree Price Discrimination: A pricing scheme that makes each consumer pay the maximum amount that he is willing to pay.

Fiscal Policy: A tool, in the hands of a government, to influence the level of GDP in the short run using taxes and government spending. It is about bringing changes in taxes and spending so as to affect the demand for goods and services, and hence the output in the short run.

Fixed Costs: The costs that remain constant with respect to the output. They might exist even if no output is produced.

Forecasting: An estimation of the future situation.

Foreign Exchange: All currencies other than the domestic currency of a given nation.

Frictional Unemployment: Unemployment occurring when due to technological progress and structural changes, some persons presently fully employed are likely to lose jobs.

Full Cost Pricing: A pricing practice in which the product is priced by adding the desired margin to the full cost of the product.

Full Employment: A situation wherein all those who are willing and able to work at the prevailing wage rate are in fact employed for the work in which they are trained. This even allows for a 3–4% of frictional and seasonal unemployment.

Function: A mathematical relationship between two variables wherein one of the variables depends on the other.

Giffen Goods: Inferior goods, consumed mostly by poor consumers as essential commodities, whose demand increases with the increase in their price and vice versa.

Globalization: The process of integration of the world into one huge market.

Going Rate Pricing: Pricing, which is guided by the going rate of that product in the market.

Government Purchases: The purchases of newly produced goods and services by central, state, and local governments. These include any goods that the government purchases plus the wages and salaries of all government employees.

Gross Domestic Product: The money value of all final goods and services produced in domestic territory of a country during an accounting year.

Gross National Product: The total market value of all final goods and services produced by the nation in a year.

Gross Private Domestic Investment: Total investment in capital by the private sector.

Historical Costs: The past cost that is actually incurred at the time of acquisition of an asset.

Implicit Costs: Costs that don't involve a cash outlay. They are also known as Book Costs.

Income: Amount of money which wealth yields.

Income Elasticity of Demand: A measure of percentage change in the demand for a commodity due to one per cent change in the consumer's income, *ceteris paribus*.

Increasing Returns to Scale: A case where the output increases more than the increase in all inputs.

Indifference Curve: The locus of points, each representing a different combination of two goods, which provide the same level of utility to the consumer.

Inflation: A general rise in the prices in a persistent manner.

Intermediate Goods: Such goods and services that are purchased by an intermediary for further processing, manufacturing, or resale.

Investment: The addition made to the total stock of capital.

Investment Schedule: A relationship, which shows the amounts that businesses plan to invest at each possible level of output (income).

Isocost: The locus of all those combinations of input which have the same cost, i.e. which can be purchased for a given expenditure level. The isocosts are also known as Budget Lines.

Isoquant: The locus of all those combination of inputs, which when combined efficiently, produce the same quantity of output.

Law of Demand: Other things remaining same, i.e. *ceteris paribus*, the demand for goods increases as its price decreases and vice versa.

Law of Diminishing Marginal Rate of Substitution: The quantity of a commodity that a consumer is willing to sacrifice for an additional unit of another keeps on decreasing as he continues substituting one commodity for another.

Law of Diminishing Marginal Utility: As a consumer increases the consumption of a product, the utility gained from successive units goes on decreasing.

Law of Diminishing Returns: As the quantity of a variable input increases, while all other factors of production are held constant, the resulting output increases, but at a diminishing rate beyond a certain point.

Law of Equimarginal Utility: A consumer maximizes his total utility by distributing his entire income optimally among the various commodities consumed by him. This is done in such a manner that the marginal utility derived per unit of expenditure, i.e. per rupee, is same for all commodities.

Least Cost Combination of Inputs: An input combination, which costs minimum out of a given choice of alternative input combinations producing the same output. It is also called *Optimal Combination of Inputs*.

Linear Function: A function in which the power of independent variable is one.

Linear Programming: An analytical technique for finding out optimal solutions to managerial problems characterized by constraints.

Logarithmic Function: A function where the dependent variable is a logarithmic value of the independent variable.

Long-run: The situation having all the factors as variable.

Long-run Cost: The cost which varies with output when all the factor inputs change.

Long-run Cost-output Relationship: The behaviour of cost to the changes in output when even the plant size is varying i.e. all the factors inputs are variable.

Loss Leadership Pricing: When the products are priced low not to maintain their own demand but to take care of the demand of some other products of the firm.

Macroeconomics: The branch of economics, which studies the aggregate behaviour of an economic system.

Managerial Economics: The discipline that deals with the application of the economic concepts, theories and methodologies to the practical problems of business/firms in order to formulate rational managerial decisions for solving those problems.

Marginal Cost: The cost of producing one additional unit of the commodity.

Marginal Cost Pricing: When it is not possible for the firm to price the product comfortably, firms who have been operating for quite some time and have already covered up their fixed costs sell their product at a lower price, which just covers the variable or the marginal cost.

Marginal Efficiency of Capital: The discounting rate that equates the present value of the cash flows generated by an investment project to the present value of cash outflows, i.e. the cost of that investment project.

Marginal Physical Product: Marginal Physical Product of a factor of production is the change in total physical product obtained due to use of one additional unit of that factor of production, holding all other inputs constant.

Marginal Propensity to Consume: The change in consumption due to a unit change in the income level.

Marginal Propensity to Save: The change in savings resulting from an additional unit of income is known as the marginal propensity to save.

Marginal Rate of Substitution: The rate at which one commodity can be substituted for another, if the utility is to remain unchanged.

Marginal Rate of Technical Substitution: The amount of one input factor that must be substituted for one unit of another input factor in order to maintain a constant output.

Marginal Revenue: The change in total revenue due to the sale of one additional unit of the output.

Microeconomics: The branch of economics that deals with small individual units of an economy.

Monetary Policy: A tool that incorporates the actions that the Central Bank takes to influence the level of GDP. The Central Bank can influence the level of output in the short run through open market operations, changes in reserve requirements or changes in the discount rate.

Money: Anything that is generally acceptable as a means of exchange and at the same time can be used as a measure and store of value.

Money Multiplier: The relationship between the final change in deposits and the changes in reserves that caused this change.

Money Supply: The total stock of money available to a society for use in connection with the economic activity of the country at a point of time.

Monopolistic Competition: A market structure characterized by a large number of buyers, a large number of sellers, product differentiated only due to branding and no entry and exit barriers.

Monopoly: A market structure having a single seller, a large number of buyers, product having no close substitute, i.e. highly differentiated and high entry and exit barriers.

National Income: The aggregate factor income which arises from the current production of goods and services by a nation's economy.

Natural Rate of Unemployment: The unemployment that occurs as a normal part of the functioning of the economy.

Net Exports: Total exports minus total imports.

Net Factor Payments to the Rest of the World: The payments of factor income to, minus the receipts of factor income from, the rest of the world.

Net Value Added: The contribution of each producing unit to the current flow of goods and services.

Non-accelerating Inflation Rate of Unemployment: The value of the unemployment rate where the PP Curve crosses zero.

Objective Function: The equation that expresses the goal of the linear programming problem.

Oligopoly Market: A market structure characterized by a large number of buyers, only a few sellers, product that can be homogeneous or heterogeneous and entry and exit barriers.

Open Market Operations: The buying and selling of government securities by the Central Bank in the open market.

Opportunity Cost: The notional cost of sacrificing the alternatives. In other words, it is the value of a resource in its best alternative use.

Output Elasticity: The percentage change in the output associated with one per cent change in all the inputs.

Passive Forecasts: Estimation of the value of dependent variable, while taking into account no action of the firm, affecting the independent variables.

Peak: The stage of business cycle that signifies the temporary maximum of the expansionary period.

Perfect Competition Market: A market structure characterized by a large number of buyers, a large number of sellers, a homogeneous product and an absence of entry and exit barriers.

Personal Consumption Expenditures: These are expenditures by consumers on goods and services.

Personal Income: The sum of all incomes actually received by all the households during a given year.

Personal Saving: The amount of disposable personal income left after total personal spending.

Personal Saving Rate: The percentage of disposable personal income saved.

Phillips Curve: The relationship between inflation and unemployment.

Policy Mix: The combination of monetary and fiscal policies in use at a given time.

Price: Value when expressed in terms of money.

Price Discrimination: A pricing phenomenon wherein the same product is sold by a firm in different markets at different prices at the same time.

Price Elasticity of Demand: The measure of the responsiveness of demand for a product to the changes in the price of the product, keeping all the other variables constant.

Principle for Least Cost Combinations of Inputs: An optimal combination of any two inputs, say labour and capital, requires that the ratio of their marginal physical products be equal to the ratio of their prices.

Production: Any economic activity directed towards the satisfaction of human wants. It is also defined as a process of converting an input into a more valuable output.

Production Function: The technological relationship between the output and its inputs.

Profit Maximization: The generation of largest absolute amount of profits over the time period being analyzed.

Promotional Elasticity of Demand: The measure of responsiveness of demand for a commodity to the changes in the outlay on advertisement and other promotional efforts.

Quadratic Function: A function with the power of independent variable of two.

Relevant Cost: The cost that actually affects a given business decision and should therefore be considered in the decision process.

Replacement Cost: The current cost of purchasing an asset now.

Required Reserve Ratio: The percentage of its deposits that a bank must keep as reserves.

Return to a Factor: The relationship between output and variation in one input while keeping the other factor inputs constant. This relationship is also known as productivity of a factor of production.

Returns to Scale: The relationship between output and variations of all the inputs taken together.

Sales Force Opinion Survey: This method forecasts demand by asking the employees of the company who are a part of the sales and marketing team to predict the future levels of demand.

Savings: The excess of income over expenditure.

Saving Schedule: The relationship between saving and income.

Seasonal Unemployment: Unemployment existing when a particular productive activity is seasonal in nature; the persons employed in it become unemployed during the slack season.

Second Degree Price Discrimination: A form of price discrimination, which is based on the volume of consumer purchase.

Short-run: The period during which one or more inputs of a firm are fixed. In other words, it is the period where at least one factor of production is constant.

Short-run Cost: The cost that varies with output when fixed plant and equipment remain the same.

Short-run Cost-output Relationship: The behaviour of cost with varying output in the short-run, i.e. for a particular plant size.

Simultaneous Equations Method: Forecasting of demand using multiple simultaneous equations. This is a complex statistical method of forecasting where a complete model is developed explaining the behaviour of all the economic variables.

Slack Variables: The variables that are added to the linear programming problem's constraint inequalities so as to make up for the difference in order to make them equalities.

Stabilization Policies: A set of actions to reduce the level of GDP back to full potential output.

Stagflation: A situation of a high inflation rate prevailing simultaneously with a high unemployment rate.

Statutory Liquidity Ratio: The portion of the total deposits of a bank that it is required to keep with itself in the form of specified liquid assets, that is, cash plus approved government securities.

Subsidies: Payments made by the government for which it receives no goods or services in return.

Substitute Goods: Goods that are used in place of some other goods.

Switching Costs: Costs to the consumers for changing from purchasing one product to purchasing another.

Third Degree Price Discrimination: A pricing mechanism where pricing is based on the characteristics of buyers.

Total Cost: The sum total of the costs incurred on producing all the units of a commodity.

Total Physical Product: Total physical product of a factor of production is defined as the total production obtained by employing different quantum of that factor input, keeping all the other factors constant. It denotes the total output from a production system.

Total Revenue: The sum total of the revenue received on selling all the units of the commodity.

Trade Association Pricing: A pricing practice where the pricing decision for a product is taken by an association and the member firms only follow the central decision.

Trade Deficit: It occurs when a nation buys more goods from abroad than it sells.

Trade Surplus: It occurs when exports exceed imports.

Trend Projection Method: Method of forecasting demand wherein the historical data is collected and fitted into some type of a trend, i.e. repetitive behaviour pattern. This trend is then extrapolated into the future to get the demand in the forecast period.

Trough: The worst stage of recession where the business activities assume a temporary bottom in the business cycle.

Underemployment: Underemployment is said to exist when persons are only partially employed or are employed in inferior jobs though they can do better ones.

Unemployment: The situation where large number of able-bodied persons of working age who are willing to work at current wage levels cannot find such work.

Unemployment Rate: The ratio of the number of people unemployed to the total number of people in the labour force.

Utility: The want satisfying quality of goods.

Value: The goods/services that we can have in exchange for goods.

Variable Costs: The costs that vary with the changes in output.

Wealth: Anything that has value.

References

Ackley, G., *Macroeconomic Theory*, Macmillan, New York, 1962.

Allen, R.G.D., *Macroeconomic Theory*, St. Martin's Press, New York, 1967.

Allen, R.G.D., *Mathematical Analysis for Economists*, Macmillan, London, 1938.

Baumol, W.J., *Economic Theory and Operations Analysis*, Prentice-Hall of India, New Delhi, 1972.

Branson, W.H., *Macroeconomic Theory and Policy*, Universal Book Store, New Delhi, 1996.

CA Study Material of Economics, ICFAI, New Delhi, 2001.

Charnes, A., and Cooper W.W., *Management Models and Industrial Applications of Linear Programming*, John Wiley, New York, 1961.

Chiang, A.C., *Fundamental Methods of Mathematical Economics*, McGraw Hill, New York, 1984.

Crum, W.L. and Schumpeter J.A., *Rudimentary Mathematics for Economists*, McGraw Hill, New York, 1946.

Dean, J., *Managerial Economics*, Prentice-Hall of India, New Delhi, 1976.

Dorfman, R., Samuelson P.A., and Solow R.M., *Linear Programming and Economic Analysis*, McGraw Hill, New York, 1958.

Duesenberry, J.S., *Business Cycles and Economic Growth*, McGraw Hill, New York, 1958.

Gass, S., *Linear Programming Methods and Applications*, McGraw Hill, New York, 1964.

Gould, J.P., and Ferguson C.E., *Microeconomic Theory*, Richard Irwin, Homewood, 1980.

Graham, P., *Managerial Economics*, Addison Wesley, Massachusetts, 1980.

Hague, D.C., *Managerial Economics—Analysis for Business Decisions*, Longmans, London, 1969.

Hansen, A.H., *Monetary Theory and Fiscal Policy*, McGraw Hill, New York, 1949.

Harris, D.J., *Mathematics for Business, Management and Economics*, John Wiley, New York, 1985.

Henderson, J.M., and Quandt R.E., *Microeconomic Theory*, McGraw Hill, New York, 1971.

Hirshleifer, J., *Price Theory and Applications*, Prentice-Hall, New Jersey, 1980.

Johnston, J., *Econometric Methods*, McGraw Hill, New York.

Klein, L.R., *The Economics of Supply and Demand*, John Hopkins, Baltimore, 1983.

Lancaster, K.J., *Consumer Demand*, Columbia University Press, New York, 1971.

Leontief, W., *Input-Output Economics*, Oxford University Press, New York, 1985.

Lyons, I.L., and Zymelman M., *Economic Analysis of the Firm*, Pitman Publishing, New York, 1966.

Marshall, A., *Principles of Economics*, Macmillan, London, 1922.

Musgrave, R.A., *The Theory of Public Finance*, McGraw Hill, New York, 1959.

Patinkin, D., *Money, Interest and Prices*, Harper and Row, New York, 1965.

Robinson, J., *The Economics of Imperfect Competition*, Macmillan, London, 1933.

Samuelson, Paul A. and Nordhaus, William D., *Economics*, Tata McGraw Hill, 1998.

Schultz, H., *Theory and Measurement of Demand*, University of Chicago Press, Chicago, 1964.

Shubik, M., *Strategy and Market Structure*, John Wiley, New York, 1959.

Spencer, M.H., and Siegelman L., *Managerial Economics*, Richard Irwin, Homewood, 1964.

Stigler, G.J., *The Theory of Price*, Macmillan, New York, 1966.

Varien, H., *Intermediate Microeconomics*, Norton, New York, 1993.

Wagner, H.M., *Principles of Operations Research*, Prentice Hall of India, New Delhi, 1973.

Walsch, V.C., *Introduction to Contemporary Microeconomics*, McGraw Hill, New York, 1970.

Wold, H., *Demand Analysis*, John Wiley, New York.

Zudak, L.S., *Managerial Economics*, Harper and Row, New York, 1980.

Index